T0174908

It's All Analytics!

The Foundations of AI, Big Data, and
Data Science Landscape for Professionals
in Healthcare, Business, and Government

It's All Analytics!

The Foundations of AI, Big Data, and Data Science Landscape for Professionals in Healthcare, Business, and Government

Scott Burk, Ph.D.

Gary D. Miner, Ph.D.

CRC Press
Taylor & Francis Group
Boca Raton London New York

CRC Press is an imprint of the
Taylor & Francis Group, an **informa** business
A PRODUCTIVITY PRESS BOOK

First edition published 2020
by CRC Press
6000 Broken Sound Parkway NW, Suite 300, Boca Raton, FL 33487-2742

and by CRC Press
2 Park Square, Milton Park, Abingdon, Oxon, OX14 4RN

© 2021 Taylor & Francis Group, LLC
CRC Press is an imprint of Taylor & Francis Group, LLC

Reasonable efforts have been made to publish reliable data and information, but the author and publisher cannot assume responsibility for the validity of all materials or the consequences of their use. The authors and publishers have attempted to trace the copyright holders of all material reproduced in this publication and apologize to copyright holders if permission to publish in this form has not been obtained. If any copyright material has not been acknowledged please write and let us know so we may rectify in any future reprint.

Except as permitted under U.S. Copyright Law, no part of this book may be reprinted, reproduced, transmitted, or utilized in any form by any electronic, mechanical, or other means, now known or hereafter invented, including photocopying, microfilming, and recording, or in any information storage or retrieval system, without written permission from the publishers.

For permission to photocopy or use material electronically from this work, access www.copyright.com or contact the Copyright Clearance Center, Inc. (CCC), 222 Rosewood Drive, Danvers, MA 01923, 978-750-8400. For works that are not available on CCC please contact mpkbookspermissions@tandf.co.uk

Trademark notice: Product or corporate names may be trademarks or registered trademarks, and are used only for identification and explanation without intent to infringe.

ISBN: 978-0-367-35968-3 (hbk)
ISBN: 978-0-367-49379-0 (pbk)
ISBN: 978-0-429-34398-8 (ebk)

Typeset in ITC Garamond STD
by Deanta Global Publishing Services, Chennai, India

Contents

Foreword Number One

The applications of computational methods in machine learning and artificial intelligence are rapidly changing the world that we work and live in. Many traditional industries and professions are being fundamentally reimagined as AI industries. It is becoming imperative for those at every level in companies and organizations (not to mention the general public) to understand both "what will AI do FOR me?" and "what will AI do TO me?".

The rapid acceleration in the development and deployment of these technologies is creating an increasing gap in understanding. Many who need to know don't even know what they don't know. This, coupled with hyperbolic news releases on some new AI application-of-the-moment, leaves the nontechnical observer with no easy solution to bridging this gap.

Fortunately, Scott Burk and Gary Miner have astutely recognized this gap in understanding and offer a starting point for bridging this gap in *It's All Analytics!* This volume provides a "20,000 foot overview" of these technologies and serves as an easily-grasped read for beginning the journey to deeper understanding or broadening one's knowledge base. While it is geared towards those with little or no understanding of AI and machine learning, it is a valuable resource for those working in these areas who may have a siloed view of the fields.

The authors are uniquely qualified to deliver this overview as they are both not only industry practitioners of these technologies, but also educators skilled at making these topics accessible to the neophyte. They have obviously paid great attention to readability and organized the material in a way that provides a memorable framework for pinning the reader's newly gathered knowledge. Additionally, the book is richly referenced with additional resources for taking a deeper dive into specific subject matter.

I'd like to be among the first to congratulate the authors on this timely, engaging, useful, and highly informative read.

John W. Cromwell, M.D., FACS, FASCRS
Associate Chief Medical Officer | Director of Surgical Quality and Safety
University of Iowa Hospitals & Clinics
Director, Division of Gastrointestinal, Minimally Invasive, and Bariatric Surgery
Clinical Associate Professor
University of Iowa Carver College of Medicine
Faculty, Interdisciplinary Graduate Program in Informatics
University of Iowa Graduate College
Iowa City, Iowa

Foreword Number Two

Written with focus on the underlying concept of the entire series of books

This book seeks to reduce the "sea of terms" in Data Science to a systematic terminology to describe general aspects of AI and Data Science. This system of terms will permit multiple stakeholders in an organization to speak the same "language" across the enterprise. This common language will permit close integration between analytics and those functions in the organization that precede analytics (e.g. database design and management) and those deployment functions that follow it (e.g. marketing campaigns).

This book is not a complete expression of the subject, yet it is comprehensive in terms of the scope of each part without being comprehensive in detail. This book is not designed to show the learner how to build an analytical model with a given tool. Rather, it shows learners how to organize their thinking about the plethora of terms and concepts in Data Science to provide sufficient insight to permit practitioners to do it properly later on. Many books are available to show precise sequences of steps with a given tool for building analytical models

This book is Part I of a three-part series, each one of which will be covered in a separate book. Part II will describe: (1) the design and management of the database functions necessary to support analytics properly; (2) The structure of the analytics process (e.g. the CRISP-DM analytics process model), and; (3) The general structure of a modeling application (e.g. the major steps in building a predictive analytics model). Part III will present a survey of analytics applications in business and industry. Neither of these books should be considered as a stand-alone resource in the overall process of applying analytics in an organization. All 3 parts should be combined to compose the design of any analytics application in an organization.

Development of models without the proper deployment system may relegate the models to the "shelf", because they can't be deployed efficiently in the organization.

Each book (and indeed each chapter) is written to be independent of information in previous chapters, as far as possible. This degree of independence is facilitated by repeat of relevant terms and principles introduced in previous chapters, which are required to understand the information in the current chapter. As such, these chapters are learning "objects", which are more or less self-contained. These learning objects must be combined together to form a seamless solution during execution.

Both this book and the entire series present a "layered" approach to learning the practice of Data Science. Each layer is designed to be as functionally independent as possible, yet easily related to previous layers and subsequent layers. This layered learning approach follows the Layered Learning Practice Model (LLPM) shown to be very effective in training learners to provide specific clinical or patient services in the practice of Oncology.

Robert Nisbet, Ph.D.
Goleta, California

Foreword Number Three

Almost 30 years ago I began using the term "Information Democracy" to describe a world where everyone has timely, relevant, and actionable insights to carry out the tasks associated with their role – and align them with the overarching strategy of the organization.

Since that time, we've made some progress, but not nearly as much as we would have hoped. In fact, based on our most recent research, a majority of organizations report that less than half of their users have such access.

Further to this point, only 43% indicate that they consistently use data in their decision-making process. And, only a third of organizations claim high or extremely high data literacy.

Further clouding things is the constant barrage of technologies, techniques, and buzzwords that bombard us each day – including artificial intelligence, data science, machine learning, IoT, edge computing, etc.

The only way that we can make real progress is through education about the importance and value of business intelligence and analytics, increasing data literacy and establishing a solid understanding of all relevant approaches.

To that end, Drs. Burk and Miner have created what is an excellent addition to the growing body of work available on the subject. In contrast to the many volumes on the subject, their approach has made many of these topics readily accessible to the novice or manager seeking a basic understanding as well as to the data science professional seeking a well-organized reference.

The future of an information democracy is highly dependent upon knowledgeable management and skilled users. Accordingly, as organizations strive to increase their data literacy, and leverage data science, this book should be required reading.

Howard Dresner
Chief Research Officer
Dresner Advisory Services
www.dresneradvisory.com

Preface

The Basis for This Book and the Series

The authors have been collaborating on the ideas in this book for years. We met while working together in the software and technology sector. Each of us has backgrounds in statistics, machine learning, analytics, healthcare, and business. We noticed that while the products and solutions in the artificial intelligence (AI), data science and analytics space offered tremendous value, there was a great deal of misunderstanding of the terminology in and around this space. Furthermore, we noticed a lot of "reinvention" of methods that existed for years, meaning that in this "reinvention" many of the same concepts acquired "new names," thus adding to the confusion, especially when attempting to communicate among different disciplines.

This book will dive into many different domains: AI, machine learning, visual business intelligence (BI), analytics, and more. For brevity, when we are not explicitly writing about a particular domain (AI, data science), we choose to use the term "analytics" as a broad and general term for the overarching domain. In the end, you shall see, *It's All Analytics!* We have witnessed companies of all sizes and in multiple industries gain tremendous value from applying analytic methods and technologies. We know there are companies of all shapes and sizes that are beginning their journey. We know many others that have deep roots, but in an applied area and cannot see the "big picture" and know of technologies outside their immediate application area. We know there are those that struggle with a constantly changing sea of terms and technology. We know some are scared of what they don't know, what they are not doing, what they should be doing. Everyone is moving at a million miles an hour and companies are worried they might lose their advantage in a competitive market and need to do something quickly with analytics or expand with some nascent technology. *However, it is time to take a step back: to survey the landscape and synthesize it.* With a pause, we can view the analytics domain holistically.

Even after years of conversations and numerous emails, it was difficult for us to arrive at a title. First, how do you cover a sea of changing terminology, what is hot what is not – even if it is the same thing? Second, we wanted a wide applicability to a variety of industries. Some are at differing levels of maturity and adoption. Thus, the name for this book is a combination of three of the most commonly used domains and the application space where these methods have the most opportunity to advance society.

Additionally, we determined that our ambitions were beyond the scope of a single book. Therefore we are breaking our goals into three books. ***The first***, which you are reading, is a book with a goal of synthesizing disciplines across many educational disciplines and practiced fields at an executive or professional level. ***The second book*** will present design considerations for your analytics architecture across the continuum of your company's program goals – organization, data architecture, analytics architecture. ***The third book*** will provide examples of applications across a very broad variety of business and policy goals.

Professionals Need This Book

Why do you need this book? No other book has a comprehensive view of the landscape. Yes, you can get a lot of information from the Internet, but it is not curated or validated. Is it someone's blog post who is trying to promote themselves as an expert? Anyone can write a blog and there are many analytics websites which are platforms for marketecture (promotion of product or service over capability).

Gartner is an independent analysis firm that reports on the technology sector. They phrased one need for this book in several comments on their website, including the need for members of an organization to speak the same language. Kasey Panetta (Panetta 2019) stated this clearly: "[Our need is to]… champion data literacy and teach data as a second language to enable data-driven business." She continued by stating,

> Imagine an organization where the marketing department speaks French, the product designers speak German, the analytics team speaks Spanish and no one speaks a second language… That's

essentially how a data-driven business functions when there is no data literacy.

She points out that this year (2020), half of all organizations will lack data literacy skills that are needed to achieve business value.

And Valerie Logan, Senior Director Analyst, Gartner, points out another important fact (see Panetta 2019), that the

> prevalence of data and analytics capabilities, including artificial intelligence, requires creators and consumers to "speak data" as a common language…. Data and analytics leaders must champion workforce data literacy as an enabler of digital business and treat information as a second language.

We will help you speak the language in this book. In fact, we will cover the dialects of AI, machine learning, analytics, data science, and statistics and show you what they have in common and what separates them.

What This Book Is and Is Not; Who Should Not Be Reading This Book

This is not an academic book. We don't talk about hyper-parameters, the Stone-Weierstrass theorem or stochastic processes. It is not a scholarly pursuit; it does not include the same rigor as an academic endeavor. However, we will provide many references as well as "Resources for the Avid Learner" throughout the chapters. This book should serve as an introductory reference book and is meant to get you thinking about the broader scope of disciplines beyond what is available in the hype cycle.

It is not meant to be a daily practitioner's step-by-step practice guide. However, it may be very useful to expose a practitioner to a wider view and provide ideas of alternative methods to their problem set. As any carpenter, artist or do-it-yourselfer knows, the right tool makes all the difference in the world.

Therefore, knowing what kinds of problems typically are solved by statistical inference versus machine learning is very helpful.

It does not discuss low-level, nuts-and-bolts recipes for producing machine learning algorithms, applying algorithms, or determining which statistical test should be used for a particular set of data. It does not talk about specific commercial software vendors, although there is a brief mention of open source platforms for illustration.

It is not complete. It would be far too big a task to write, or for that matter read, a complete compendium of over a hundred years of thought and advancement in a wide field. Our goal is to provide a book that helps make sense of this wide field, where there is uniqueness, where there is overlap, and where there is opportunity.

This is not a book on a specific area; it is not an AI book, a statistics book, or a BI book. It is a compilation of disciplines and technologies and contrasts across those disciplines. It is not a recipe book for how to write code or where to find an open source library for a specific machine learning algorithm. It does not tell you when to apply a specific statistical test of inference or the dos and don'ts of creating a BI dashboard. **It is meant to be a synthesis book (a 101 or survey course on data-driven methods if you will)**. It encompasses an evolution and rebirth of fields and technologies and demonstrates how they are interrelated and how they are independently and inter-reliably useful. It sets you up for success in a career in analytics by seeing the big picture. In addition, the series will provide a larger view of analytics across the industry, how to design and operate an enterprise for success in analytics.

This book is not a history book. We do provide some historical elements to provide some interesting detail and context, but these are not intended to be comprehensive in nature. There are some good books on the history of statistics, mathematics, and AI as well as other fields. Note: most of these are written for an academic audience or an audience that desires a deep historical perspective.

How This Book Is Organized

This book contains 12 chapters. This first chapter sets the stage and outlines more specific needs and purposes of the book. Chapter 2 provides business justifications and design recommendations for creating a successful analytics program within your organization. It also explains the hype cycle, what you should pay attention to and what to avoid. Chapter 3 describes the heart and soul of data, processes as well as other fundamentals – models, algorithms, and a standard process for analytics projects. In Chapter 4 we look at "analytics" – far and wide from methodology to application. The rest of the book dives more deeply in the foundations of analytics – BI, machine learning, AI, data science, big data, statistics, and more.

One of our key objectives is to make this book as valuable to the reader as possible. One way we want to provide that value is to make it a resource that can serve as a reference where the reader can pick it up and read a freestanding chapter on its own without having to pick up at the beginning. To make this amenable, we will repeat ourselves; this was a conscious choice that we hope will not be too much of an inconvenience, but a benefit when you revisit us here.

It should be noted that we attempt to offer some consistency where it makes sense. As an example, in Chapters 1 to 3, after the preamble we begin with a section called "The Hip, the Hype, the Fears, the Intrigue, and the Reality." Our goal with this section is to present the reader with what they might find in "the hip," social media, blogs, user channels… or the "hype" from marketers, sellers, excitement journalists in press releases… and then the reality as we see it. We are attempting to help you distinguish the signal from the noise; we cover this concept in Chapter 3.

We also attempt to outline the objectives for the chapter up front in the "Key Words," "Preamble" and "Introduction" sections so that you know what to expect from the chapter. This is intended to support the goal of being a reference book down the line. Chapters conclude with postscripts, references, and "Resources for the Avid Learner" sections.

We want this book to be a pleasure to read as well as to provide valuable information. While this is not a "hands-on" or methods book, we do want you to mentally practice the concepts presented here. We offer many examples and thought exercises in gray boxes to stimulate your reading and improve attention. The book should flow without reading every gray box, but these gray boxes should make for reading that is more enjoyable.

In summary, we have noticed a changing sea of terminology. We know that much of this is generated by companies, technologists and consultants. We recognize software and technology have improved greatly over time, but much has just been relabeled. Without changing names of techniques, it is difficult to sound innovative and fresh. Marketers, product managers and consultants are pushed to be more innovative, to differentiate, and to forge new horizons. We understand. However, we want to help professionals in the field understand some of the underlying foundations, some of the relationships and some ways to think about the subject. Leaders and practitioners are confused about what is relevant and what is not. Fear of missing out (FOMO) is causing panic and mis-investment. We hope to clarify some of these misunderstandings in this book series.

Your Authors,
Scott Burk, Ph.D. Temple, Texas
Gary D. Miner, Ph.D., Tulsa, Oklahoma and Rome, Georgia

Reference

Panetta, Kasey. February 6, 2019. "A data and analytics leader's guide to data literacy," Gartner, www.gartner.com/smarterwithgartner/a-data-and-analytics-leaders-guide-to-data-literacy/.

Endorsements

Almost every company in the world now understands the critical importance of collecting, processing, analyzing, and acting upon data. The largest hurdles impeding companies in this process aren't caused by technical limitations or a lack of trained specialists, but by the people who need to understand how it affects them, what can be done, and how to implement and manage it within their organization, but don't. In this book, Burk and Miner help to solve that problem in language that is straightforward, sensible, and based on their considerable experience. If actionable analytics is a key need for your organization, and you want to minimize the struggle and confusion required to implement it, you should read this book.

Dylan Zwick
Former Director of Data Science, Overstock.com

Burk and Miner have created a map to guide anxious and overwhelmed executives through the rapidly changing and often unwieldy landscape of data and analytics techniques and technologies. Their survey cuts through the hype and hyperbole and enables data practitioners and non-practitioners to clearly communicate how to understand, optimize, and ultimately transform their business processes through analytics. Highly recommended.

Josh Wills
Former Director of Data Engineering, Slack

It's All Analytics! deserves a prominent place on executives' bookshelves. Burk and Miner have undertaken a noteworthy challenge in their synthesis of data science, machine learning, data mining, artificial intelligence, and statistics, presented at a level both useful and provocative to business leaders. The chapter on statistics particularly fills a gap in current discourse about the latest fashions in AI and Machine Learning.

Loren Williams
Former Chief Data Scientist, Big Four

The rise of artificial intelligence brings us excitement and hope, but also causes some anxiety and even fear. The internet is flooded with a sea of terminology and concepts. For anyone who is interested in learning more about AI, numerous online courses, articles, blogs are at finger tips. However, not all information has been curated, thus resulting in a tremendous amount of confusion and a great deal of misunderstanding.

I am thrilled that Scott and Gary compact several decades of history of AI, data science, analytics, an incredible amount of terminology, concepts, and a comprehensive view of the current landscape, all into this one book. With their years of experience across a broad spectrum of industry, the book offers many practical examples and thought exercises, and explains complex concepts in simple language.

Business executives will benefit from this book with in-depth understanding of the technical concept and capability, as well as organizational planning and strategy; people leaders will get help to build a strong team with the right talents, tooling, and capability; technical professionals will broaden their view of the data science world and have a clearer expectation of career path.

I have found this book extremely comprehensive and practical, and it offers an objective and informed view. What makes it even more valuable is that it is a synthesis book and serves as a reference that can be used for many years to come.

If you have an ambition to sail in the sea of AI, this is the compass that you must carry in your pocket.

Xingchu Liu, Ph.D.
President of BlackLocus,
The Home Depot Innovation Lab

It's All Analytics!, by Scott Burk and Gary Miner.

There is a lot to like about this book. A whole lot.

The first thing I liked was that it was interesting. It doesn't read like a cold, boring academic treatise. Instead it reads almost like a mystery novel – where one page invites the next. This plain spoken approach opens the doors of analytics to anyone who is interested.

And that is good. Because in the world to come, analytics is THE key to success and survival.

Explaining analytics to the everyperson is not a simple or easy thing to do. For many years analytics has been wrapped up in confusing algorithms, spurious terms, and specious formulae. Yesterday you had to have a Ph.D. in order to gain a foothold into the wondrous realm of analytics. But in tomorrow's world analytics are going to become so pervasive that analytics will become as common as soda pop or ice cream.

In order to be able to swim with the sharks of tomorrow you have to have the basics of analytics.

And the book *It's All Analytics!* explains concepts and practices in easy-to-understand terms.

This book is for anyone who wishes to be conversant in the language of tomorrow.

Bill Inmon
Recognized by many as the father of the data warehouse
Denver, Colorado

Authors

Scott Burk has been solving complex business and health care problems for 25 years through science, statistics, machine learning, and business acumen. Burk started his career, well actually in analytics, as an analytic chemist after graduating with a double major in biology and chemistry from Texas State University. He continued his education, going to school at night taking advanced courses in science and math at the University of Texas at Dallas (UTD). He then started programming at the toxicology lab where he was working and thus started taking computer science (CS) and business courses until he graduated with a Master's in Business with a concentration in finance soon after from UTD.

Texas Instruments (TI) hired him as a financial systems analyst in Semiconductor Group, but due to TI's needs and Burk's love of computers, he soon became a systems analyst for corporate TI. He worked there for three years and started itching to get back to school (even though he continued to take courses at night [Operations Research and CS] through TI's generous educational program). TI granted him an educational leave of absence and he went to Baylor University to teach in the business school and get a Ph.D. in statistics. He joined Baylor as a non-tenure-track professor teaching quantitative business analysis (today = business analytics).

After graduating, Burk went back to TI as a decision support manager for the consumer arm of TI (today = consulting data scientist), where he engaged in many functional areas – marketing and sales, finance, engineering, logistics, customer relations, the call center, and more. It was a dream job, but unfortunately, TI exited that business.

Burk joined Scott and White, a large integrated healthcare delivery system in Texas as a consulting statistician. He moved into an executive role as Associate Executive Director, Information Systems leading Data Warehousing, Business Intelligence and Quality Organizations working with clinics, hospitals and the health plan. At the same time, he received a faculty appointment and taught informatics with Texas A&M University. He left but later came back to Baylor, Scott and White (BSW) as Chief Statistician for BSW Healthplan.

Burk continued his education, getting an advanced management certification from Southern Methodist University (SMU) and Master's Degree (MS) in data mining (machine learning) from Central Connecticut State University. Burk is a firm believer in lifelong learning.

He also worked as Chief Statistician at Overstock, re-engineering the way they tested and evaluated marketing campaigns and other programs (analytics, statistics). He launched its "total customer value" program. He was a lead pricing scientist (analytics, optimization) for a B2B pricing optimization company (Zilliant) for a number of years. He thoroughly enjoyed working with a richly diverse, well-educated group that affected the way he looks at multidisciplinary methods of solving problems.

He was a Risk Manager for eBay/Paypal, identifying fraud and other risks on the platform and payment system. He has been working the last few years supporting software development, marketing and sales, specifically data infrastructure, data science, and analytics platforms for Dell and now TIBCO. He supports his desire to learn and keep current by writing and teaching in the Masters of Data Science Program at the City University of New York.

Gary Miner received his B.S. from Hamline University, St. Paul, MN with biology, chemistry, and education majors; his M.S. in Zoology & Population Genetics from the University of Wyoming; and his Ph.D. in Biochemical Genetics from the University of Kansas as the recipient of a NASA Pre-Doctoral Fellowship. During the doctoral study years, he also studied mammalian genetics at The Jackson Laboratory, Bar Harbor, ME, under a College Training Program on an NIH award; and another College Training Program at the Bermuda Biological Station, St. George's West, Bermuda in a marine developmental embryology course, on an NSF award; and a third college training program held at the University of California, San Diego at the Molecular Techniques in Developmental Biology Institute, again on an NSF award.

Following that he studied as a post-doctoral student at the University of Minnesota in Behavioral Genetics, where, along with research in schizophrenia and Alzheimer's disease (AD), he learned "how to write books" from assisting in editing two book manuscripts of his mentor, Irving Gottesman, Ph.D. (Dr. Gottesman returned the favor 41 years later by writing two tutorials for the book *Practical Text Mining*). After academic research and teaching positions, Miner did another two-year NIH post-doctoral in psychiatric epidemiology and biostatistics at the University of Iowa, where he became thoroughly immersed in studying affective disorders and Alzheimer's disease. Altogether, he spent over 30 years researching and writing papers and books on the genetics of Alzheimer's disease (Miner, G.D., Richter, R, Blass, J.P., Valentine, J.L, and Winters-Miner, Linda. *Familial Alzheimer's Disease: Molecular Genetics and Clinical Perspectives.* Dekker: New York, 1989; and Miner, G.D., Winters-Miner, Linda, Blass, J.P., Richter, R, and Valentine, J.L. *Caring for Alzheimer's Patients: A Guide for Family & Healthcare Providers.* Plenum Press Insight Books: New York, 1989).

Over the years he has held positions, including professor and chairman of a department, at various universities including the University of Kansas, the University of Minnesota, Northwest Nazarene University, Eastern Nazarene University, Southern Nazarene University, Oral Roberts University Medical School, where he was Associate Professor of Pharmacology and Director of the Alzheimer Disease & Geriatric Disorders Research Laboratories and even for a period of time in the 1990s was a visiting clinical professor of psychology for geriatrics at the Fuller Graduate School of Psychology & Fuller Theological Seminary in Pasadena, CA.

In 1985 he and his wife, Dr. Linda Winters-Miner (author of several tutorials in this book) founded The Familial Alzheimer's Disease Research Foundation (aka "The Alzheimer's Foundation"), which became a leading force in organizing both local and international scientific meetings and thus bringing together all the leaders in the field of genetics of AD from several countries, which then lead to the writing of the first scientific book on the genetics of Alzheimer's disease; this book included papers by over 100 scientists coming out of the First International Symposium on the Genetics of Alzheimer's Disease held in Tulsa, OK in October 1987. During part of this time, he was also an affiliate research scientist with the Oklahoma Medical Research Foundation located in Oklahoma City with the University of Oklahoma School of Medicine.

Miner was influential in bringing all of the world's leading scientists working on genetics of AD together at just the right time when various laboratories from Harvard to Duke University and the University of California-San Diego, to the University of Heidelberg, in Germany, and universities in Belgium, France, England and Perth, Australia were beginning to find "genes" which they thought were related to Alzheimer's disease.

During the 1990s Dr. Miner was appointed to the Oklahoma Governor's Task Force on Alzheimer's Disease, and also was Associate Editor for Alzheimer's Disease for *The Journal of Geriatric Psychiatry & Neurology*, which he still serves on to this day. By 1995 most of these dominantly inherited genes for AD had been discovered, and the one that Miner had been working on since the mid-1980s with the University of Washington in Seattle was the last of these initial 5 to be identified, this gene on Chromosome 1 of the human genome. At that time, having met the goal of finding out some of the genetics of AD, Miner decided to do something different, to find an area of the business world, and since he had been analyzing data for over 30 years, working for StatSoft, Inc. as a senior statistician and data mining consultant, which seemed a perfect "semi-retirement" career. Interestingly (as his wife had predicted), he discovered that the "business world" was much more fun than the "academic world," and at a KDD-Data Mining meeting in 1999 in San Francisco, he decided that he would specialize in "data mining." Incidentally, he first met Bob Nisbet there, who told him, "You just have to meet this bright young rising star John Elder!," and within minutes Bob found John and introduced me to him, as he was also at this meeting (Dr. John Elder had just formed ELDER RESEARCH, INC, and he and I think just two other people were running this "start up operation" in data mining research and consulting; today ELDER RESEARCH INC in Charlottesville, Virginia, has close to 100 employees and is a top Data Mining/Data Analytics consulting firm that has developed solutions for many agencies of our US government along with numerous commercial companies, and also runs training sessions around the world – see John's bio at: https://www.elderresearch.com/company/our-team/john-f-elder-iv-phd).

As Miner delved into this new "data mining" field and looked at statistics textbooks in general, he saw the need for "practical statistical books" and started writing chapters and organizing various outlines for different books. Miner, Nisbet and Elder kept running into each other at KDD meetings, and eventually at a breakfast meeting in Seattle in August of 2005 they decided they needed to write a book on data mining, and right there reorganized Miner's outline, which eventually became the book *Handbook of Statistical Analysis and Data Mining Applications*, 2009, published by Elsevier. And then, in 2012, he was the lead author on a second book from Elsevier/Academic Press, *Practical Text Mining*. And then a third in this "series" in 2015: *Practical Predictive Analytics* and *Decisioning Systems for Medicine*. All thanks are due to Dr. Irving Gottesman, Miner's "mentor in book writing," who planted the seed back in 1970 while Miner was doing a post-doctoral with him at the University of Minnesota.

His latest books were released in 2018, the second edition of the 2009 book *Handbook of Statistical Analysis* and *Data Mining Applications* (www. amazon.com/Handbook-Statistical-Analysis-Mining-Applications/dp/012416 6326/); and a 2019 book written more for the layperson and decision-maker, titled *Healthcare's Out Sick – Predicting A Cure – Solutions That Work!!!* and published by Routledge / Taylor and Francis Group – "A Productivity Press Book" (www.amazon.com/HEALTHCAREs-OUT-SICK-PREDICTING-IN NOVATIONS/dp/1138581097).

Miner is currently working on the second and third books in a series with Scott Burk, Ph.D., and also teaches courses periodically in "Predictive Analytics and Healthcare Analytics" for the University of California-Irvine. Additionally, recently Elsevier asked Gary and his group of authors of their 2015 book: *Practical Predictive Analytics For Medicine*, to write a 2nd edition which he and his large group of authors will be working on this during 2020 for hopefully a 2021 release, as it is now very timely.

Chapter 1

You Need This Book

Keywords: Bias, Media, Hype, Landscape, AI (Artificial Intelligence), ML (Machine Learning), Analytics, Big Data

Preamble

The authors have heard that we need to be data-driven for **more than 20 years**. We hear **the same thing today**! What happened!! Have we ignored the message?? Have we done it wrong? Probably the latter... Thus this book. Why do you need this book? No other book has a comprehensive view of the landscape. Yes, you can get a lot of information from the Internet, but it is not curated or validated. Is it someone's blog post who is trying to promote themselves as an expert? Anyone can write a blog and there are many analytics websites which are platforms for marketecture, which means form without substance.

This book is Part 1 *of a three-part series*. This series will attempt to set the record straight and make it easy for the practitioner or the executive decision-maker to understand what they really need in their setting. In Chapter 1 we look at why you need an unbiased understanding of the subject in order to make the right decisions – how and when you need to be data-driven.

The Hip, the Hype, the Fears, the Intrigue, and the Reality:

Hype, Fear, and Intrigue No 1:

The worrying question today for many is whether democracy can survive artificial intelligence (AI). The reality is that disruptive technologies like AI cannot be put back in the box. AI is becoming a mainstream technology that will need to be effectively integrated into 21st-century decision-making across all institutions – especially government. In the wake of this digital revolution, some functions of government will necessarily be eliminated.

(Araya, *Forbes*, 2019)

Reality

As long as elected officials are in office, they will not cede control to AI or anything else but themselves. Anyway, most AI is augmentation of human intelligence, not replacement of it. As far as we can see, the democratic governments of the West will not be replaced anytime soon. It is interesting that the same article mentions impacts to China and we find these predictions much more likely. With AI, China could definitely entrench its authority into a digital technocracy. Unlike the West, in which there is a major push in pulling back the covers of AI and adopting policies such as GDPR (General Data Protection Regulation), communist countries could use AI to strengthen their hand and control over the masses.

Hype, Fear, and Intrigue No 2:

As Jonathan Zittrain commented in a panel discussion sponsored by Harvard Medical School, Precision Medicine June 2019:

I think of machine learning (artificial intelligence) kind of like asbestos… It turns out that it's all over the place, even though at no point did you explicitly install it, and it has possibly some latent bad effects that you might regret later, after it's already too hard to get it all out.

Reality

How easy it is to turn such comments into an article purporting that AI and machine learning (ML) are the new cancer-causing agents that will make millions sick and law firms rich. However, you really need to take all the comments and the related contexts of these comments into consideration. Many of the statements made were accurate and we will review and analyze these in later sections. However, the reader has seen remarks like the ones mentioned above turned into a gloom and doom sensational article. We do not think this was Professor Zittrain's intent; many of the comments he made were accurate and we will review and analyze these in later sections as well as a related article by Casey Ross.

Hype, Fear, and Intrigue No 3:

Headline – "Will robots take your job? Humans ignore the coming AI (Artificial Intelligence) revolution at their peril" (NBCNEWS.COM, November 2018). Robots are taking over industrial manufacturing and they will soon take over food production and restaurant kitchens. In just a few years they will take over trucking, ride services, the financial industry, accounting, healthcare, and citizen services. Humans will be able to pursue their desires and do whatever they wish without needing to work.

Reality

The AI revolution started back in the 1950s, but you would never guess that based on the headlines today. It is sensationalized like it is brand-new, nascent technology. Even special programming languages like Lisp were adopted to support AI research in the late 1950s. Over the years since then, AI has been resurrected a few times: for example, Texas Instruments created a special computer called the TI Explorer specifically to do very fast (for the time) computing and was used in for AI scheduling of the Hubble Space Telescope even in the 1970s and 1980s and continuing forward (Miller, 1989; and Johnston and Miller, 1992). It is true that this new era of AI this time in the 2nd and 3rd decades of the 21st century is more substantial than ever, but robots will not displace humans. We see AI and other technologies enhancing human existence. It will have positive impacts on everything from personal transportation to augmented citizen services and government (see Mehr, 2017). We must be careful; it benefits most people to have a basic understanding of what AI is, what it is not and how it will impact them. *Every technological revolution has displaced workers but also created new opportunities.* Those workers that were willing to learn new technology and adapt succeeded and those that did not were left to wither.

PREVALENCE OF ANALYTICS, AI AND DATA SCIENCE IN EVERYDAY LIFE

Example of the HYPE about AI and ML– we see it almost EVERY DAY now in the news and social media; here is an example pulled from "One moment in time" on a day in early July 2019:

AI and ML dominate the news including LinkedIn – 7/6/19 (Saturday) pulled from LinkedIn – They do a daily notification on their "DAILY RUNDOWN" newsfeed. The following is just an example, but indicative of how prevalent this subject is in professional news cycles. There are 5 headlines and 4 of the 5 are related to the topics in this book. (www. linkedin.com/pulse/breakthrough-hiv-research-tech-takes-beatles-mo re-top-rundown-us-/)

Scientists claim they have cured nine mice of HIV for the first time in history, according to a new study (Dash, PK; Kaminski, R; Gendelman et al., 2019). The researchers from Temple University and the University of Nebraska Medical Center used a combination of CRISPR gene-editing technology and an antiretroviral therapy called LASER ART to kill the virus. One of the doctors who coauthored the report called it a "major breakthrough." About 1.1 million people in the U.S. live with HIV (Turner, 2019), which is a virus that attacks the body's immune system and if left untreated, can turn into AIDS.

Breaking down the Beatles: Paul McCartney and John Lennon wrote some of the most famous songs in history, yet for the songs where they are listed as coauthors; it is not clear who wrote what. With the help of a machine, a team of researchers from Harvard and Canada's Dalhousie University developed a system where they were able to correctly differentiate Lennon's tracks from McCartney's with 76% accuracy. They then applied this model to eight songs or fragments of songs whose authorship is a bit murky.

Fewer American teens are getting jobs. Over the past nearly two decades, teenage labor force participation has dropped significantly – 15.9% between 2000 and 2018, according to research compiled by the Brookings Institute (Glickman, Brown, and Song, 2019). Fewer teens (16- to 19-year-olds) are seeking summer employment, and they're also becoming less likely to double up on school and work during the academic year. "The intensity of high school may have increased in ways that have helped crowd out non-school activities," per Brookings.

No Amazon? No problem for Long Island City. The Queens neighborhood, according to real estate data acquired by Vox (Molla, 2019), leased more commercial property in the first half of 2019 than it has in any year since such data started to be recorded. Last November, Amazon tapped Long Island City to be the location of its second headquarters (HQ2). And although protests forced the e-commerce giant to scrub its plans, the activity still "functioned as a giant advertisement" (Molla, 2019) for the New York neighborhood.

AI is poised to play a bigger role in healthcare, from speeding up drug development to helping to diagnose disease. But to do so, it needs data (and lots of it). According to the World Health Organization (Wall, 2019), AI can currently only access 20% of global medical data. And while making more available could spur innovation and help overcome resource shortages, it also requires trust – that patient data "won't be used for commercial reasons without their consent or to discriminate against people," WHO chief scientist Soumya Swaminathan tells the BBC (Wall, M., 2019).

And you see it all over the Internet. Credible analyst firms and premier management consulting firms are supporting the new wave, a tsunami into AI, data science and analytics. According to a Forrester Research report from 2017 published in *Forbes* (see Press, 2016). "AI-driven enterprises will steal 1.2 trillion from competitors by 2020." That is a pretty bold claim, but they are not the only research firm making these kinds of predictions. In a 2018 report titled *Notes from the AI frontier: modeling the impact of AI on the world economy* (see Bughin et al., 2018), McKinsey and Co. analyzed 400 use cases in 19 different industries to understand the broad use and significant economic potential of deploying advanced deep learning AI techniques. It found that companies with faster AI adoption and absorption (Front Runners) are creating big economic gains.

Professionals Need This Book

Introduction

Gartner is an independent analysis firm that reports on the technology sector. They phrased one need for this book in several comments on their website including the need for members of an organization *to speak the same language*. Kasey Panetta (Panetta, 2019) stated this clearly: "[Our Need is to]… champion data literacy and teach data as a second language to enable data-driven business." She continued by stating:

> Imagine an organization where the marketing department speaks French, the product designers speak German, the analytics team speaks Spanish and no one speaks a second language… That's essentially how a data-driven business functions when there is no data literacy.

She points out that this year (2020) half of all organizations will lack data literacy skills that are needed to achieve business value.

And Valerie Logan, Senior Director Analyst, Gartner, points out another important fact (see Panetta, 2019), that the

> … prevalence of data and analytics capabilities, including AI, requires creators and consumers to "speak data" as a common language… Data and analytics leaders must champion workforce data literacy as an enabler of digital business and treat information as a second language.

We will help you speak the language in this book. In fact, we will cover the dialects of AI, ML, analytics, data science, statistics and show you what they have in common and what separates them. First, let's look at some incentives for this needed education.

Technology Keeps Raging, but We Need More Than Technology to Be Successful

Technology is raging and has been for several years and data is the new oil. Much of the growth in the last few years could be loosely described as "creating value from data." This is our mantra for this book – ***creating value***

from data! Value could mean increasing sales revenue, reducing avoidable costs, improving patient satisfaction, targeting high-value customers and prospects, creating policy for the broadest social good and much, much more.

The rise and speed of technology innovation have created a lot of stir in the media, the press, universities, businesses, and government. Some of the information is accurate and useful. Some of this information is inaccurate and confusing. Some of it is beyond the reach of the average professional or student because it is either too narrowly focused or too technical without the necessary background. *This book is about simplifying the subject for an interested reader in a non-threating, non-technical, broad viewpoint.* We consider the information presented in this text as what we would cover if we were to teach a "Creating Value from Data 101" course at a university, what some would call a "survey course."

We have spent hundreds of billions of dollars collecting data, but most of it sits in silos. Silos of data never analyzed, never touched again. Not only a sunk cost to acquire but also the cost to maintain, backup or archive – the cost is tremendous. Everyone has talked about monetizing this data, but few are very successful. We have been talking about using it for decades (Green, 2016), but we have barely scratched the surface. To be clear, it is not technology that is hampering the progress. *It is lack of vision, human capital, and execution.* The purpose of this book is to help with increasing the knowledge, enabling execution and *squeezing dollars from data* by informing professionals about *creating value from data.*

We will cover many of the analytical areas at a topical level. It is difficult to keep up with all the advancements in these areas. Society and industry have been collecting data for years and years. We have been increasing our collection exponentially. We actually analyze very little of what we collect, but there are big efforts to change that. We explore these advancements for the professional that desires to understand the big picture of analytics, data science, AI and related fields.

There is a HUGE overlap in the areas where value is created from data. This is not by accident as we will explain. But, for now take a look at the dizzying list of overlapping subject areas:

- Business Intelligence (BI)
- Visual BI, Analytics
- Visual Analytics
- Business Analytics

- Data Analytics
- Predictive Analytics
- Prescriptive Analytics
- Advanced Analytics
- Text Analytics
- Graph Analytics
- Social Analytics
- Network Analytics
- Modern Analytics
- Directed Acyclic Graph (DAG) Analytics
- Statistics
- Optimization
- Data Mining
- Data Modeling
- ML
- Big Data
- Data Science
- Decision Science
- (Enterprise or Business) Decision Management
- Business Process Management
- Data Engineering
- AI
- Computational Intelligence
- Auto ML
- Management Science
- Linear and Mathematical Programming
- Deep Learning, Informatics
- Decision Science
- Many others

We think there is a need for simplification, for "One Global Term" that applies to each of these. We believe *analytics* is the appropriate umbrella term that captures the spirit of all these methods; thus in this book, we will oftentimes use the word *analytics* when we are not focusing on a specific form.

These are some of the most *in vogue* technologies; but additionally, you still have many college subject areas such as accounting, economics, engineering fields, finance, operations research, industrial engineering and related science disciplines that stand on their own and use data to create value. In fact, many of these majors are starting to apply these new Analytics methods. We will not cover these traditional degree areas, as we do not consider them a part of the hype cycle. These disciplines may incorporate some of these new analytic methods but have many of their own methods to solve quantitative problems and are free-standing subjects.

Professionals are also impacted by displacement of jobs to automated technologies – factory automation, cashier-less/no check-out stores, self-driving cars, busses, trains and trucks, automated telemedicine and radiology, smart warehouses, intelligent agents and robots. These are just a few ways AI will disrupt the global workforce. McKinsey (Manyika et al., 2017) reports that as many as 400 and 800 million jobs could be displaced by automation by 2030 worldwide.

Even the AI and analytics industry is predicted to "eat its own," meaning that machines will replace AI programmers and we will have self-aware systems like Skynet in *Terminator*. These highly intelligent machines will replace the smartest data scientists and programmers. Computer software generating computer code has been a reality for many years. These are CASE (Computer Aided Software Engineering) technologies (Wikipedia, 2019b), but yet the need for developers, computer scientists, and applied mathematicians has never been higher. We do not see the machines taking over all the jobs for many years to come, but it does make for interesting reading and has for decades. Do not get us wrong, AI has enhanced our lives greatly and will continue to do so, but this has been going on for years, and given the observed data on automation throughout the years, humans have found a way to stay relevant. We cover more about topics of automation in later chapters, for example, AutoML in Chapter 6.

These developments have been and will continue to dominate a large part of the business news cycle.

ARE YOU FEARFUL?

Do you fear that you are keeping pace with technology on this front? Do you have a general understanding of this space? Are you currently using some of these technologies, but are naïve in some of the others? Is your enterprise engaged in some of these technologies and you want to know more? Are you contemplating a career change and want to grasp a basic understanding of these burgeoning fields? Then keep reading.

Data and Analytics Explosion

The volume of data collected is growing exponentially with no end in sight. According to a study by IDC (International Data Corporation), an analyst reported (Reinsel et al., 2017):

1) IDC predicts that the Global Datasphere will grow from 33 Zettabytes in 2018 to 175 Zettabytes by 2025 (a Zettabyte is 1,000,000,000,000,000,000,000 bytes, 1 billion terabytes. If one person downloaded this amount of data at 25 megabytes per second (average speed in the United States today) it would take 1.8 billion years to download it. If everyone on the planet joined in 24 hours a day it would still take 81 days. See Figure 1.1 (Adapted from Reinsel et al., 2017, Data Age 2025; Seagate, 2020)
2) The compounded annual growth rate (CAGR) of 61% (and this estimate increased by 9% from 2017 to 2018)
3) November 2018 there were 5 billion consumers that interacted with data, but by 2025 it will be 6 billion or 75% of the world's population
   In 2025 there will be 150 billion devices creating data in real time. Many will be edge devices on the manufacturing floor, or sensors in smart cities (Figure 1.1).

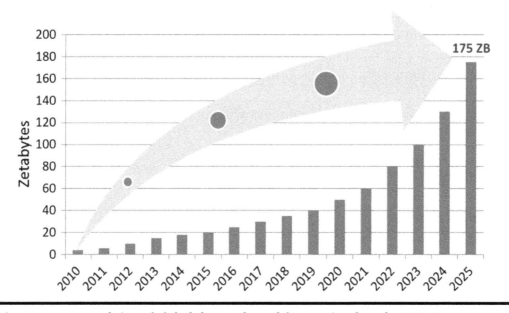

Figure 1.1   Annual size of global data (Adapted from Reinsel et al. 2017, Data Age 2025; The Digitization of the World [IDC Nov 2018]).

IOT AND DATA STATISTICS ARE STAGGERING

Some similar statistics to the IDC report are presented by a product man-ager at a hardware company, Cisco (see Stack, February 2018) on data, Who Is Using Data and How:

IoT and data statistics are staggering, to the point of appearing fantastical:

- ■ *5 quintillion bytes of data produced every day (that's 2.5 fol-lowed by 18 zeros)*
- ■ *By the year 2020, the IoT will comprise more than **30 billion con-nected devices.***
- ■ *These devices include smart home and smart car devices, medical devices from routine patient monitoring like blood pressure and heart rate monitoring to implanted medical devices like pacemak-ers, defibrillators (see the section on Next Generation Medical Devices – Human Enhancement for what may be coming). Agriculture 3.0, includes self-driving tractors, field sensors, satellite data and much more. And of course, automated factories and warehouses are full of sensors and data.*
- ■ *It would take a lifetime to manually analyze the data produced by a single sensor on a manufacturing assembly line*

No wonder studies reveal that:
- ■ *Only **26%** of companies surveyed reported that their IoT initiatives have been successful*

No wonder the Harvard Business Review (Davenport, April 2017) found that:

- ■ ***Less than half*** *of structured data is actively used in decision making*
- ■ ***Less than 1%*** *of unstructured data is analyzed or used at all*

Collecting data is a cost and a liability. First, it takes money to create the connectors into the source data. This could be creating pathways or pipes into databases or data lakes through the extract, transform and load (ETL) process. More commonly now is the creation of application protocol interfaces (APIs) that bring data from the web (services), cloud, software as a service (SaaS) and other data connections – more about this in Chapter 9 on data.

Second, in addition to the cost of creating and supporting the connections, you have the costs of the pipes themselves, fiber, networks, and wireless devices. You have the cost of storage. These costs are not just buying or renting the infrastructure, but the labor associated with keeping everything running, fail-over redundancy and back-up recovery plans. This runs into the billions of dollars in the United States. You could say that this is the cost of running a business. But, not really, as most of this data sits idle. We collect far more than we ever analyze. It is like all the boxes of memorabilia, clothes, and knickknacks in your attic that you keep because you might want it or need it someday. But you never take it out. And, as it ages, it loses value.

More importantly, you have the liability. Heard of any data breaches lately? Companies are often not aware of the information that sits in legacy databases. Moreover, there is legal liability from (former) employees on email systems and related databases that are never purged and thus discoverable in lawsuits and other legal proceedings.

According to *Forbes* (Meehan, 2016) it is estimated that as much as 90% of big data is never analyzed. In fact, it is so large that Gartner has coined a term called "Dark Data." Dark Data describes the information assets organizations collect, process and store, during regular business activities, but generally fail to use for other purposes (for example, analytics, business relationships and direct monetizing). Most organizations fail to use this data, but it could and should be used. Data is a strategic asset.

We have a problem. We have all this data being collected at a great expense, but we are not gaining value from it. That is where the disciplines in this book can help. This book is about taking data that took money to collect, provision and store and turning into actionable insights that drive value by decreasing costs, driving revenue and improving quality. In addition, the value of data decreases with time, so data sitting in silos decrease in value every day.

Now we look at the potential in collecting all that data. Estimates differ, but according to *Forbes* (January 2017) the market for business analytics will be US$203 billion in 2020 and is growing at a 12% CAGR. Contrast this with Computing Technology Industry Association (CompTIA) estimating that the global information technology industry would grow at a rate of 4% in 2019 (CompTIA, 2019), much slower than the analytics market. And data monetization, which is the process of using data to generate revenue, will become a major source of income for this 17× increase in data being collected from 2015 to 2025; and these estimates are constantly being raised so the growth is a rising exponential function. In summary, there will be increasing demand for people that know how to turn data into insights or how data can impact their enterprise or community.

We estimate that virtually every worker in the United States will be impacted by these developments in the next 5 to 10 years. These impacts may be direct, meaning you will be responsible to employ one or more of these methods into your work function. Alternatively, they may be quasi-direct, in that your work process will be a consumer and thus you will need to be trained commensurately. Or, your job will be displaced by these methods.

Our intent in this book is to provide a bird's eye view of the disciplines involved in this revolution, their application and why you should have a basic understanding of them.

IBM is projecting that demand for data scientists will soar by 28% (Columbus, 2017). Based on this article, jobs requiring ML skills are paying an average of US$114,000. If we change the term to "data analyst," we see that in the United States the average salary is US$64,814 per year, but ranges from US$18,000 to US$139,000 depending on what company one is working for (Indeed, updated August 9, 2019). If we change the title to "healthcare data analyst," we see that the average salary is US$61,194, with a range from US$46,000 to US$82,000 (Payscale, 2019; updated August 12, 2019).

But the need for "healthcare data analytics" jobs is going to increase rapidly in the months and years ahead with the supply of qualified people being less than needed, so these salaries should increase.

However, the person that wants to become a data scientist has to apply themselves. In the past we have seen that many people want to learn data science, but yet not too many of these people actually become data scientists. This is probably because learning data science is difficult, as it's a combination of many hard skills (like learning to program in Python and SQL), soft skills (like business skills or communication skills) and "in-between" skills like learning how to use (mostly automated) AI and ML software to get the final predictions and decisions. But before getting these predictions and decisions, about 80% of the data scientist's time is spent on data acquisition and data cleaning (Mester, 2019; Miner et al., 2015; Nisbet, Miner, and Yale, 2018).

A Bright Side of the Revolution

This explosive growth is good news for professionals currently employed in these data related areas, and also for those considering careers in data science. There will be jobs at all levels from the very technical levels of AI and data science, to business analysts and "citizen data scientists" (more about that later), to project managers, subject matter experts, and related professionals. It will also impact everyone on the strategic and operational side of the enterprise: chief executives, chief medical officers, elected officials, and policy directors.

The professional areas covered in this book are not only growing, but also some of the most satisfying according to job surveys. A Harvard Business Review entitled, "Data Scientist: The Sexiest Job of the 21st Century" (Davenport and Patil, 2012) was a watershed article for a fairly newly defined field (while newly defined, it was certainly not new in practice for the most part). It is one of the best descriptions of what a data scientist does, what backgrounds they typically have and their career aspirations and the projected career opportunities. However, at the same time there is an unclear mixing and comingling of terms that include analytics, advanced analytics, big data, quants, analysts, statisticians, programmers, and computer scientists. One of our objectives in this book is to help the common reader parse through articles like this and have an appreciation for the overlap as well as the separation.

WHO KNEW STATISTICS WAS SEXY?

Hal Varian, the chief economist at Google, put it this way: "I keep saying the sexy job in the next ten years will be statisticians. People think I'm joking, but who would've guessed that computer engineers would've been the sexy job of the 1990s?"

What do the polls say on Data Science, AI, and Analytics related jobs? While AI and analytics related jobs are too granular to make a lot of polls, we looked at Glassdoor and U.S. News & World Report and see from these sources that data scientists, statisticians, and other related professionals are ranked as follows:

1) **Data scientists.** Glassdoor (www.glassdoor.com/), a very popular site, placed data scientist as the #1 job for 4 years in a row in their 50 Best Jobs in America Report. For the 2019 report the Job Score was 4.7/5, Job Satisfaction rating was 4.3/5 and a median base salary of US$108K. **Data engineer** was ranked #8 in the 2019 report.

2) **Statisticians.** U.S. News ranked statisticians as #1 in Best Business Jobs, #2 in Best Jobs and #2 in Best STEM (Science, Technology, Engineering, and Math) jobs (https://money.usnews.com/careers/best-jobs/statistician, accessed 7/6/2019).

3) **Mathematicians.** U.S. News ranked mathematicians as #2 in Best Business Jobs, #17 in Best Jobs and #9 in Best STEM jobs (https://money.usnews.com/careers/best-jobs/mathematician, accessed 7/6/2019).

4) **Operations research analysts.** U.S. News ranked operations research analyst as #7 in Best Business Jobs, #34 in Best Jobs and #15 in Best STEM jobs (https://money.usnews.com/careers/best-jobs/mathematician, accessed 7/6/2019).

5) **Software developers.** U.S. News ranked software developer as #1 in Best Jobs, #1 in Best STEM Jobs and #1 in Best Technology jobs

6) **Computer programmers.** U.S. News ranked computer programmer as #10 in Best Technology Jobs

NOTE: STEM (Science, Technology, Engineering, and Math) best jobs include but are not limited to the following:

■ Statistician
■ Software developer
■ Physician assistant
■ Dentist
■ Cartographer
■ Actuary
■ Civil engineer
■ Psychologist

Furthermore, not only is job satisfaction very bright for these careers, but the overall outlook exceedingly sunny and thus we predict that demand will outstrip the supply. McKinsey (2011) estimated there would be a shortage of talent necessary for organizations to take advantage of big data:

> By 2018, the United States alone could face a shortage of 140,000 to 190,000 people with deep analytical skills as well as 1.5 million managers and analysts with the know-how to use the analysis of big data to make effective decisions.

We do not know at this time how accurate this forecast was, but we do know that big data related careers are in demand more than ever. And, it is very important to know that McKinsey puts an emphasis on managers and analysts with the know-how to use the analysis of big data to make effective decisions. This is very important as many think it will be the hard-core data practitioners that will be affected by these changes. But, in reality, all professionals will ultimately be affected. All work processes, patient, customer and citizen engagements, and interactions will change. It will be extremely pervasive and professionals wanting to stay relevant will need a basic understanding of AI, data science and analytics.

A Google search of "analytics jobs" returned 867 million results on 7/7/19. Indeed.com, a popular website for job hunters, returned 158K jobs on the same day for an "analytics" query (United States). Glassdoor.com returned 455K results for the same query. SimplyHired.com returned 116K and Monster.com returned 69K. Needless to say, there are many analytics jobs available. However if you look at job postings for hospital administrator, sales executive/representative, customer service manager, human resource manager, fleet manager, marketing coordinator, and restaurant manager, you will see many of them have some reference to analytics in the job description as desired qualifications and if they don't they likely will in the near future. These are jobs that are well removed from the highly technical demands of AI engineers or career data scientists, but professionals seeking these jobs need some basic knowledge of the subjects. So, you don't have to be a quantitative thinker to benefit from these burgeoning fields. In fact, Thomas Davenport, who is credited with popularizing the term "analytics," states that important qualifications for the field are hybrid skill sets including communicator and trusted advisor.

And, since employers are having a hard time filling the roles, they are becoming very flexible with employee schedules, locations, and pay. For example, companies turn to satellite offices to strengthen their bid for talent. For those looking to hire data science and analytics talent, it's no secret that the location of your data science team can help or hinder your hiring results. Burtch Works (2019) reported they had seen many companies opening satellite offices in multiple urban areas to increase their role's marketability.

Because of this explosive growth and need for software platforms, consultants and professionals in all areas of data science, there is a lot of media coverage of all forms. There are many magazine articles, white papers, blogs, webinars, YouTube videos, websites, social media posts and media of all forms that are ripe with sensationalism and misinformation (some of this is referred to as *marketecture*). We present examples of these throughout the book in our **Hype, Fear, and Intrigue vs Reality** introductory sections of each chapter. It is one of the main themes of the book to separate fact from fiction and educate the reader on the various ways the business, healthcare and government sectors can benefit from using data to transform decision and execution processes.

Where Is Someone to Turn for Information?

It is very common to turn to online sources of information, and this takes a variety of forms. We dive into some of these and discuss the strengths and weaknesses of them. Print media, websites and blogs, education and training programs and corporate programs are some typical sources of information for both seasoned pros and newcomers to gather information.

Books, magazines, and newspapers are sometimes useful sources of information. Unfortunately, magazines and newspapers have to push sensational headlines and titles that are often biased, and motivated more by selling issues than reporting objective facts. We will look at many of them in this book. Books are much more objective. However, there are dozens of books on coding, programming, applying techniques and methods, to problems via very specific subjects like logistic regression or convolutional networks, then there are on the broader issues related to analytics and data science. We saw a real need to present these topics at a more foundational level and thus we are attempting to fill this need by writing this book.

Websites and blogs contain some useful information, but these sources are often skewed either intentionally or unintentionally. Often, the authors on these sites have a vested interest in promoting particular software, platforms or techniques and therefore their content pushes this perspective. Or, they are trained in a narrow space and promote that knowledge as the best option when it may not be the optimal discipline for the problem at hand.

There are a growing number of technical training options available that include full-time, part-time, on-campus degree programs, online degree programs, boot camps, Massively Open Online Courses (MOOCs), workshops and online tutorials and forums. But, most of all these are very technical or geared to a particular field like statistics or data science. And, if you decide to pursue detailed education or a change in career, how do you determine which program or field is best suited to your interests and skills? Most of the courses offered by the major platforms (Coursera, University Adult Extensions, etc.) are "analytics focused."

Internal promotion of analytics programs and corporate training has proven there is a need, but also a ***gap in success***. Not from a technical perspective, but we think the "gap in success" is in the big picture, an understanding of the overarching landscape. This is evidenced in an article note (Press, *Forbes,* January 2017) that confirms the initiation of these programs, but a poor success rate:

> More than 85% of respondents report that their firms have started programs to create data-driven cultures, *but only 37% report success thus far…* Technology is not the problem. The culprits include management understanding, organizational alignment and general organizational resistance. "If only people were as malleable as data," say the authors of the NVP report.

It is not that technology is hampering success. It is people's understanding and acceptance of these technologies. **This is exactly why you need this book**. We provide a framework – what are the most important data-driven technologies and more importantly, what are the most important practiced methods and fields to solve problems. And we offer this in a non-mathematical, non-technical manner.

WHY READ THIS BOOK? SOME REASONABLE QUESTIONS

***A reasonable question*: "We have software companies come into our workplace and they provide technology presentations; why not use the information they present?"**

Software companies have a unique view of this sector that is biased by the products they sell. It is therefore a limited view of the space to the areas to the cover with their solutions. For example, if it is a Visual BI company they will often present their products as solutions to problems that are not the best fit. This is not a criticism of these companies. It is understandable. They know their solutions well and they may solve many of the problems. However, is it the optimal way to solve the problem? Microsoft Excel can solve thousands and thousands of problems. But is it the most effective and efficient tool for many of these problems?

This book is presented at a higher level. We will not be speaking to any specific software, discipline, application or industry. Instead, we will present an introduction to the broad sector much as you would receive in an introductory 101 college class. Not a methods or application presentation. Not a full history course. But a survey course; a course treating briefly the chief topics of a broad field of knowledge.

A REASONABLE QUESTION: "WE HAVE SOLUTION CONSULTANTS THAT COME IN AND NEGOTIATE SERVICES; WHY NOT GET THIS INFORMATION FROM THEM?"

Professional service companies typically partner with a few vendors, apply a few technologies and are biased based on these agreements and tools. That is not to say that at times they don't attempt to be open-minded, it is just a constraint of time and most of these professionals are "in the weeds," meaning by the nature of their job they have to understand the deep detail of technologies they are employing very well and at a very detailed level. This often prevents them from seeing the landscape because of the nature of their work. Again, we address this at a higher level. We are not attached to any particular school or methodology.

A REASONABLE QUESTION: "AREN'T THERE A LOT OF BOOKS ON AI, DATA SCIENCE, AND ANALYTICS?"

Yes, there are. But most of these are about using tools for open source platforms like Python, R, Java, Scala and many others. Some are available for commercial software platforms. Some are application specific like e-commerce analytics, healthcare quality and performance, claim fraud prevention, trade policy analysis, customer loyalty/retention, AI for Internet retail. These are very specific. There are methodology and history texts on statistics, operations research, mathematical programming, and others. Other books are written for particular subjects within mathematics and engineering. You can find classical or Bayesian statistics books, operations research, decision science and most of the topics we cover, but these books cover the subject in a very detailed manner. Again, we are offering a survey or topical view of the entire analytics and data science landscape so we cover many of the topics that are in-between and above what is covered by these texts, especially the process and organizational importance within successful programs.

A REASONABLE QUESTION: "AREN'T THERE GOOD DEGREE PROGRAMS FOR AI, DATA SCIENCE, AND ANALYTICS?"

Yes, there are and we recommend them. There are on campus programs which offer the benefit of getting to know your professors and fellow students more intimately. The bonds are stronger, you get a deeper collegial experience and the personal nature of these programs allows you to engage in the emotional and softer side of an in-person engagement where you can better read tone and emotion. However, these programs require some overhead. The commute time back and forth to campus. You cannot capture some information as quickly, such as screen capture of lectures, as you can with an online program, unless the university technology allows for it, but typically not. All programs are time constrained in that they offer a small set of courses and those taught on-campus are likely to be even more constrained since these courses are more expensive for a university to cover.

Online programs are great in that you can access some of the best universities in the world from your home. You have very little overhead in that you do not have to commute, leave your home or even get dressed! (Unless your program requires you to have your web cam turned on, which some do.) From our experience, the relationships between professor and student, as well as student to student, are much weaker in these courses. One proof point is that group projects work fairly well in on-campus situations and we have seen some fail online, even though one would think the opposite.

And of course, these programs take a significant time investment, approximately four years for undergraduate degrees and two years for graduate programs. As with most things in life it depends on your objectives and constraints (decision science and optimization are upcoming topics that may help you make decisions). The authors have previously and continue to teach in degree granting institutions, and have done so both on-campus and online (Your coauthor, Gary Miner, prefers the online situation for most teaching situations, and finds that individual students communicate both with other students and with the professor via both the "Course Communication Message Boards" and even direct email to the professor, with the format and "class culture" that Gary shepherds).

A REASONABLE QUESTION: "AREN'T THERE GOOD BOOT CAMPS FOR AI, DATA SCIENCE, AND ANALYTICS?"

Yes, but as alluded to earlier, these are highly specific and technical. Most are specific to learning some basics of data science, but most of the time is learning a specific open-source or freemium (a combination of the words "free" and "premium" used to describe a business model that offers both free and premium services) coding language or languages like R, Python, Scala, SQL, Cloud-based ML, and commercial trial software.

They offer nuts and bolts of ML problem types and algorithms used to solve different problems, and much time is devoted to programming. They do not cover process and organizational elements or subjects from a holistic view.

These programs are worthwhile if you need to learn specific skills or get up to speed very quickly. They focus on directions. Some are very good, some are poor and most are expensive so choose wisely.

The costs of these boot camps are highly variable, but can be very expensive for in-person full-time immersive camps with one provider charging US$4,000 for a 1-week course and another charging up to US$17,600 for a 12-week class.

Let us contrast boot camps and degree programs.

BOOT CAMPS

- Initially focused primarily on programming, but they eventually extended into other fields that have a programming component like "Data Science"
- Educational Prerequisites: vary widely (anywhere from basic knowledge of math and programming to completion of Ph.D.-level studies)
- Admission Process: resume, interviews, admission tests
- Instruction: Intensive, in-person courses, taught by practicing data scientists
- Duration: Typically, between 6 weeks and 3 months
- Cost: Usually higher cost than self-study courses, but generally lower cost than tradition MS degree programs (free to US$21,000)
- Attendance: Often requires dedicated full-time, in-person attendance; students must reside within close geographical proximity to the site of instruction
- Outcome: Portfolio of projects, enhanced network; Many boot camps also offer job search assistance
- Examples: Insight Data Science, Metis Data Science Boot camp, Zipfian Academy, Data Incubator, General Assembly, NYC Data Science Academy, Level boot camp

DEGREE PROGRAMS

- Educational Prerequisites: vary widely (anywhere from basic knowledge of math and programming to completion of undergraduate or graduate studies in applied math and/or computer science)

- Admission Process: application, official transcripts from previously attended colleges and universities, reference letters, statement of purpose/letter of intent, resume/curriculum vitae, challenge/entrance exam, interviews, Graduate Record Examination (GRE) or other academic test scores
- Instruction: Research degrees: often taught by full-time university faculty; Professional degrees: frequently taught by part-time university-level instructors who are also practicing data scientists
- Duration: Typically, between 9 and 20 months
- Cost: US$20,000 to US$70,000
- Attendance: Full-time and part-time options available; in-person attendance generally required, but there are an increasing number of online options available (i.e., students increasingly do not need to live within close physical proximity to the university/college)
- Outcome: Portfolio of projects, enhanced professional network; degree
- Examples: UC Berkeley School of Information's (I School) Master of Information and Data Science (MIDS), Northwestern SPS Master's in Data Science (Online), Northwestern University Master of Science in Analytics, University of Illinois at Urbana-Champaign, Master of Computer Science in Data Science (MCS-DS), NYU Master of Science in Data Science, University of Washington Master of Science in Data Science, City University New York (CUNY) School of Professional Studies, Master of Science in Data Science (previously MS in Data Analytics)

A REASONABLE QUESTION: "AREN'T THERE WEB PROGRAMS LIKE COURSERA, EDX, UDEMY, UDACITY AND OTHER MOOCS FOR AI, DATA SCIENCE, AND ANALYTICS?"

These courses are less expensive than boot camps and degree programs. At the same time, they are not normally recognized or rewarded in industry. Completion of material and testing of competency are sometimes not validated by carriers of these programs and therefore professional organizations and employers do not give them as much credit as the other educational options previously presented. They can be time based so essentially staying on a screen for a required time is all that is necessary for completion and no tutorials having to be completed.

However, quality levels of the programs differ and some do offer testing for module or course competency and some offer capstone projects that are reviewed by instructors. One of the authors did take a Big Data MOOC and found it beneficial, but he was not looking for it to increase the odds of landing a job or a career enhancement, but instead it was for self-education of a specific topic where he wanted to gain a better understanding. In-person boot camps and degree programs offer networking and collegial interaction with other students where MOOCs typically do not. So, the main advantage of a MOOC is the price point when a student wants a specific area of study to focus on.

A REASONABLE QUESTION: "CAN'T I JUST DO AN INTERNET SEARCH FOR THIS MATERIAL INSTEAD OF GETTING A BOOK?"

You can do a search for many of the terms in this book, however *you will not find the framework* for analytics and beyond on the Internet. You will not find the contrasts, the distinguishing features nor our unique perspective that has been developed with a combined experience of over fifty years applying the trade. And, "you don't know what you don't know." **The Internet is great for two things.** The first is looking up something specific to your interest. An example is "what is a convolution network?" Another is getting someone's expertise on a narrow subject such as reading a blog or listening to a podcast. The authors will recommend some suggestions on where to find this material on the Internet. But, this is supplementary material and meant as an aside, not the core framework we are presenting here.

Additionally, there is a lot of *misinformation* spread on the Internet. Unfortunately, something can be incorrect, but is referenced as true over and over again, and thus grows into a mutated beast like out of a horror film. One of the authors' favorites was that it took 22,000 crunches to burn a pound of fat. It was supposedly reported in *Men's Health* in 2012. And while we have tried very hard to find the original citation, you can find hundreds of articles and blogs on the Internet that cite it as fact. And the *Men's Health* website even cites itself (Ballantyne, 2012) in a May 1, 2012 article. We have looked for a credible source and have been unable to find one. What are the assumptions? Is this above basal metabolism? If it was above basal metabolism then it would make it more believable, as if you could do 20 crunches per minute, nonstop it would take you over eighteen hours!!! But most people would burn several hundred calories in eighteen hours just by sitting in a chair. So where is the truth here?

And, the Internet is not the only place for misinformation. One of the author's favorite stories that spread even in the scientific community is that spinach is a good source of iron. We believed this until recently (Scott had even suggested eating more spinach to his wife to improve her iron count), because it has been reported, and we also remembered that this is what made Popeye strong! But, if you look at a can of spinach it does not contain very much iron. The problem? The misconception was spun over and over, reported again and again. The real problem began with a 19th-century researcher who misplaced a decimal in its calculation of iron content. This has cycled back and forth. From what we can surmise now, cooked spinach is a good source of iron, but raw spinach is not. We will let you do your own research on this subject (Dove, 2019; and Tang, 2018).

But, feel comfortable that we have done considerable research on the material in the following chapters of this book.

In this book you will not get a narrow focus; instead **you will get a reference that can be used for years**. You will also get an objective view. Almost everything the Internet provides contains some sort of bias. Someone trying to sell something or get a click from someone. We are objective enough to know that we are biased, but not commercially biased. We are not trying to sell you anything, other than this book! We are biased by our limitations of time and exposure and affinity to like certain things, but that is much more objective than you will find from a search reading a blog or listening to a podcast.

This book used correctly will accelerate and expand your knowledge of a very rich field. Rather than approaching the subject from a narrow or haphazard view you can approach it holistically.

A REASONABLE QUESTION: "WITH THE ADVENT OF NEW AI TECHNOLOGIES, CAN'T WE IGNORE ALL THESE OTHER METHODS??"

We will need the contributions of a variety of disciplines for many decades. It is not a new phenomenon that when new (or reinvented) technologies come into vogue that the experts and pundits call for the death of existing technology. One brash example is made in the forward of *Computational Intelligence in Business Analytics* (2014), a quote by Michelle Chamber, pages ix-xi:

> This era of computational intelligence is about to make all of the accomplishments by the baby boomers obsolete.

What a bold and incorrect statement. For one, most of the contributions covered in the book were developed by baby boomers (Fuzzy Sets, Artificial Neural Networks, Genetic Algorithms, Neuro-Fuzzy Systems). These are not new; they are rediscovered due to computational power and savvy practitioners. Recently, there has been pushback against black-box models which lack transparency. Most AI methods are not readily transparent. This pushback is two-fold. First the financial collapse of 2008 is largely due to the lack of transparency of the model's financial firms were using. Secondly, there is a social pushback is occurring against these black box models. An example of this is General Data Protection Regulation (GDPR) that started in the United Kingdom, but is being adopted in various forms across the globe.

Furthermore, the "death of statistics" has been predicted for several years. Statistics is not going away; it has one of the longest histories and will be around for decades. However, there are shortcomings in statistics, just as there are with every method in this book. Our goal is to shine a light on the advantages as well as the shortcomings of these various methods. And to illustrate where which tool is right for the job.

The Problem, Too Many Self-Interests: The Need for an Objective View

The authors have been collaborating on the ideas in this book for years. We met while working together in the software and technology sector. Each of us has a background in statistics, ML, analytics, healthcare and more. We noticed that while the products and solutions in the AI, Data Science, and Analytics space offered tremendous value, there was a great deal of misunderstanding of the terminology in and around this space. Furthermore, we noticed a lot of "reinvention" of methods that existed for years, meaning that in this "reinvention" many of the same concepts, processes and techniques acquired new names, thus adding to confusion, especially when attempting to communicate among different disciplines.

We will dig deep into these fields. But, a couple of quick examples to illustrate our point:

1. AI has been around for over 60 years. It began at a workshop at Dartmouth College called the Dartmouth AI Conference of 1956 (Dartmouth, 2019; Wikipedia, 2019a). Lisp was created as a special computer language to do AI in the 1950s (The 2nd author of this book, Gary Miner, used LISP during his graduate and post-doctoral work). AI had a major resurrection in the 1980s and companies built specialized Lisp machines and the first so-called "expert systems." We will discuss this in greater detail in the chapter on AI (Chapter 7). But, if you were to read the popular press or trade journals you would think that AI is a new technology that is revolutionizing the world. It may revolutionize the world, but that has more to do with recent acceptance and advancements in computing power and algorithms. The foundations of AI are not new, but emphasizing the word "AI" sells.

2. We will see that Data Mining and ML are very closely aligned in a dedicated chapter. However, the term Data Mining is rarely used anymore. It fell out of vogue, why? Simply put, money.

Marketing and sales are about generating new revenue and it is not sexy to sell existing technology with the "old, known name." Technologists also think that they need to put their mark on extensions and revisions of existing technology. But often these "new marks or revisions" are 90% existing technology and thus it gets branded with a new name. No wonder things are confusing. AI is a little different in that the basic term has not changed, *but the meaning has changed* quite a bit. In the end, we must reinvent and remarket to sell technology. We must reinvent and remarket to extend our careers. We understand the drivers for reinvention, but it is confusing. Especially to people just getting started. Is there really a difference between data science and statistics? Is there really anything substantially different that a "data scientist" and a "statistician" do in their jobs?

For brevity, when we are not explicitly writing about a particular domain (AI, data science, ML, etc.), but ***we choose to use the term "analytics" as a broad and general term for the overarching domain.*** We have witnessed companies of all sizes and industries gain tremendous value from applying analytic methods and technologies. We know there are companies of all shapes and sizes that are beginning their journey. We know many others that have deep roots, but in an applied area and cannot see the "big picture" and know of technologies outside their immediate use. We know there are those that struggle with a constantly changing sea of terms and technology. We know some are scared for what they don't know, what they are not doing, what they should be doing. Everyone is moving at a million miles an hour and companies are worried they might lose their advantage in a competitive market and need something quickly, either with analytics or to expand with some other nascent technology. *However, it is time to take a step back.* To survey the landscape and synthesize it.

With pause, we can view the analytics domain holistically.

FOUR PERSONAS OR AVATARS THAT WILL BENEFIT FROM THIS BOOK

Sandy Templeton just got another email from her boss, Ron Liu. Ron is the CEO of a large hospital system and Sandy is the COO reporting to him. Ron is well connected with other large health systems and is a voracious reader of strategy and business journals like the *Harvard Business Review.* He has been pushing Sandy for the last several years to get on board with tech trends. First, it was analytics. Now it is more data science and AI. Sandy knows their system is under pressure from market and technological forces. And Ron not only feels behind his peers, he is now getting a lot of pressure from the board to adopt advances in analytics, data science, and AI. Sandy is worried for her job, moreover her entire career. She is not keeping up with the trends. She kept hearing about analytics, recently it was data science and now everything she hears is AI. She has implemented some corporate dashboards and everyone loves them, but she is feeling that the competition is way ahead. Now, her boss is after her as well. She reads trade journals, business magazines, blogs, but feels she does not understand the terminology and how everything fits together. She has technology companies and consultants come in, but they always seem to be peddling their own wares. She wishes there was an objective view that she could read and understand the fundamental landscape of where they are and where they should be headed. ***This book is for her.***

Pete Samper is a mayor for a large city in California, a state that leads technology in the United States. Pete has read about some progressive cities using analytics and statistics to bring about data-driven policy change. He is proud of his state and wants to bring his city into the 21st century using some of the same techniques that have lead many of the businesses in his state. He is anxious because he does not know how to accomplish his goals. He has contacted several consultants, but they are expensive and seem to provide a limited view. He has thought of taking some classes, but traditional university education would take too long. There are a variety of online classes, MOOCs, but these are technical and specific to certain technologies. He wants "to know what he should know" about the fundamentals of all this stuff. He wants an objective view of the landscape. He does not have the time, nor desire to get into the weeds; he has staff for that. ***This book is for him.***

Rajiv Gupta is Chief Analytics Officer for BuyItHere.com. He has had a meteoric rise to this position. He started fresh out of high school as a junior designer developing creative content for the web site. A couple of jobs later he was performing analytics on creative, marketing campaigns and click-through analytics. Now he is leading the charge as a CAO doing predictive analytics with ML and AI. He has been working on very specific e-commerce problems for his entire career. He is at a point that he would like to broaden his knowledge to related disciplines and methodologies to problems outside the e-commerce sphere. He wants to speak intelligently. He wants to expand his scope and enter into another type of business. He feels limited in his knowledge outside of Internet retail. He is a data scientist, using some of the most cutting-edge and novel techniques (AI, Neural Nets). However, he knows there are other domains like dashboards, data visualization, BI, statistics, operations research, and mathematical programming. ***This book is written for Rajiv.***

Tom Stiles is a pricing (data) scientist and currently works for a software company. He is very knowledgeable about his company products and the types of pricing solutions they offer to solve specific problems on pricing and revenue optimization. Previously, he was a professional services consultant working with clients on distributed computing systems. Tom is considering a career change and wants to know more about data analytics, ML and AI. He did have a couple of statistics classes in college and would like to know more about careers in statistics as well as optimization and decision science. ***This book is for Tom***.

There Are Many Other Professional Stories That Are Concerned about Whether Analytics Is Important; Here Are a Few More Examples

We have heard many fears and concerns from professionals over the last few years about a lack of direction or knowledge on the topics outlined so far in this book. In this and our two sequel books in this series, we are offering answers to the following questions, which are paraphrased from actual experience. *Following is what we hope will be a representative sample.*

1) **I am in charge of informatics for a large enterprise.** There seems to be a dizzying variety of new technologies and methodologies coming into use these days. Unfortunately, most of what I see comes from vendors and consultants. We had a guy tell us that dashboards were useless and he wanted to sell us an AI platform with deep learning and convolutional networks and to replace my current staff with a data scientist (scrap the dashboards). Our dashboard initiatives have very successful: management and the board like them. Another person wanted to sell us some sort of auto ML platform that my current staff could use to create predictive models. I know I need to make some changes, but I am not sure that I am getting good advice. How can I get an objective view of where things are and where they are headed?

2) **I am a statistician, but looking at a salary survey it appears that data scientists seem to make a lot more money and are in higher demand.** I have read some articles and blogs on data science education. However, many of these seem to be pushing a specific program, a boot camp or online program. There seems to be some overlap or my training and what these programs offer and I am not sure these programs are pushing open source whereas my company has a commercial platform that I have been using for statistics and I know we can get modules for ML and AI. I just need to know more before I can make a pitch to invest in these technologies. What are the *real* differences between data science and statistics? What do I need to make a successful pitch to add value for my company and broaden my career?

3) **I am a BI developer.** I work well with IT on sourcing the data, creating relational cubes, designing reports and charts. But I want to expand my capabilities. I know there is more that I can do to take what I have created to the next level. What is the logical next step for me? What techniques should I be considering/learning?

4) **I am currently a web designer.** I consider myself creatively and technically inclined, but I have never really liked math. I can code and work on the backend with databases, and I am familiar with software development methodologies (like scrum and agile). I want to expand my horizons and I am considering some form of analytics or predictive analytics career. I know it would be beneficial to the goals of our company, for our web strategy and therefore be an easy sell to management. But what about the long run? I may want to get out of this area someday. Where else is it used? *I don't know what I don't know*. How do I get started?

5) **AI is all the rage these days, I don't get it, why?** I remember when I was a freshman in college in 1997 over twenty years ago and Deep Blue defeated Garry Kasparov. My professor said that AI had been around a long time, but this would be its new dawning as computers got powerful and fast enough to harness it. A new AI revolution was about to happen. Here we are twenty years later and it seems I am reading the same headlines. How are we supposed to believe what we read? I wish there was a source of information that was not clickbait.

6) **I have been an actuary for over ten years in a mid-sized insurance company and I have my FSA certification.** In national meetings, many of the larger insurance companies and actuarial firms are beginning to adopt ML methods. I have read in some posts. There was one forum that posted "Blog: Is Machine Learning a Threat to the Actuarial Profession?," while another has the title "Machine Learning: An Analytical Invitation to Actuaries." This is confusing. Moreover, there is deep learning, big data, and modern analytics. Should I invest time researching these fields and if so, how? Where?

7) **My friend works for an Internet company doing marketing campaign testing for e-commerce** and he tells me it is great. He says what he does is basic statistics and it can be easily learned. He loves his job and his company is investing in him, by sending him to additional training in data analytics where he will learn some more advanced stats and some data mining techniques. Where can I get basic, impartial information about this and related information? Is it something I might be interested in?

8) **I hear social networking and graph analytics/databases are hot and getting hotter** due to the rise in social media, fraud and navigation systems. Is this real? If so, what skills would I need to into this

field? What are the job titles and places that employ these types of people?

9) **I work for a large bank doing credit risk modeling for new accounts.** Basically, I assess risk based on data with predictive/prescriptive analytics. I am wanting to make a career change to another industry. I am considering getting into healthcare as I would really like to make a difference and personally I think healthcare is broken. I know there are lots of areas in the medical field, but where can I use my existing education and experience to its fullest while learning new ones and applying them to new problems? What are analytic professionals and statisticians doing in healthcare?

10) **I love computers and software, but I also enjoy working with people.** I don't want to be locked in the basement of some business or chained to my desk. I want to get out of my office and talk with people. I want to work with others to solve problems together. I think I have a lot I can teach others and I want to learn from them as well. I read about data science careers, but they sound like they spend hours and hours coding each day. Are there blended opportunities in analytics where you have time to think deeply at times, but also meet and engage others on projects?

11) **I have an ad-hoc group of "wanna-be" data scientists. We have a smart group, but we are just getting started with this and we still have our full-time jobs.** We have had a couple of informal, almost serendipitous successes in the company last year. One was reducing product returns; the other was increasing membership in our rewards program. Leadership loves what we did and has challenged us with implementing three new analytics projects this year. We are looking at projects and are realizing we need more structure around these projects. Is there a project management method out there? Should we use it or one of our IT development processes? Can I use our traditional project management program? What project management process is best for us?

12) **I know that my company's sales and marketing department is doing analytics because our CEO likes graphic results presented at our quarterly meeting.** It is no mystery that our CEO loves the way they determine their findings. She is big in the harder, data-driven results. I am in the finance department and while I get we are data driven, we are not the right kind of data driven for our CEO to pay attention. I know we could do more with forecasting our numbers and

since she likes the sales and marketing forecasts, that would probably resonate with her. What else could we do that would be more forward looking? Our reports are static; is there a way to make them more dynamic in nature? Also, we miss often miss our estimates and don't handle variability/risk well as we swing positive or negative. How can we get better with our estimates and how do we quantify the up/downside for our reports? I want our department to "find the love" that sales and marketing gets from the top boss.

13) **I am a project manager.** I have been a project manager for years, but I want to make a change to specialize in analytics projects. I need to understand the overall field and special considerations for managing analytics projects. Where should I go?

14) **I want to make a career switch into some sort of analytics.** Which should it be? AI? Statistics? BI?

15) **My CEO went to national conference and has come back "on fire" for analytics and AI.** She has given me the responsibility for bringing our company into the new age of analytics and AI, but I know there is a lot I need to learn and I am confused by all the coverage. I have to design a corporate strategy and architectural design for the entire company. We have been successful in a couple of functional areas, but how do I design for the entire organization?

Do any of the above sound familiar? Could you benefit from answers to any of these questions? Or are you already convinced that you need to know more? That you will be left behind or negatively impacted by a biased or uninformed comprehension of the subject? **Then keep reading.** This book will provide you the foundations of data-driven methodology. It is written from a broad, curated knowledge and wisdom from authors who have studied and practiced in a broad array of fields of study and application. Additionally, we will offer a level deeper on applications in our upcoming book (expected 2022) on *The Applications of AI, Analytics, and Data Science.* And for those that will be designing and architecting you will want to get our upcoming book(expected 2021), *Designing an Integrated AI, Analytics and Data Science Architecture for Your Organization.*

We will cover many of these here and then go deeper in the intersection of people, process and technology applied to analytics, data science, and AI. We provide a holistic view of the space for professionals currently involved in a dedicated area of limited scope, those seeking to enter and want to know what area most interests them, and those professionals that want to know how these shifts in technology may affect their careers.

What This Book Is Not:

This is not an academic book. It is not a scholarly pursuit. This is not a technical book or a programming book, and there are no complicated mathematical equations in this book. It is not meant to be a daily practitioner's step-by-step guide. It does not discuss low-level, nuts and bolts recipes for producing ML models or applying these algorithms. It does not discuss software vendors. This book is not complete. It is not written for a specialty area, i.e., it is not an AI book, nor a statistics book, nor a BI book. Lastly, it is not a history book.

Why This Book?

As stated previously, we have noticed a changing sea of terminology and concepts. We know that much of this is generated by companies, technologists, and consultants. We recognize software and technology have improved greatly over time, but much has just been relabeled as well and there is much confusion with leaders and practitioners. Without changing the names of techniques, it is difficult to sound innovative and fresh. Marketers, product managers, and consultants are pushed to be more innovative, to differentiate and to forge new horizons. We understand. However, we want to help professionals in the field understand some of the underlying foundations, some of the relationships and some ways to think about the subject.

Data Science – Data Analytics – Predictive & Prescriptive Analytics has a wide range of specific tools to solve problems. (Gary, one of the authors) solves these problems by subjecting a "cleaned up dataset" to many or all of the tools in "Automatic Competitive Evaluations" that rapidly spit out results that show which tool is most effective in analyzing a specific dataset (it is oftentimes difficult to predict ahead of time *which* tool will do the best job. If one works by trying "one tool at a time" an inordinate amount of time is used (wasted), when we have available automatic "competitive evaluating software" to do this in seconds for us. When Gary gets the "competitive evaluation" report he can look at what are indicated as the "best tools" and then chose among them (there may be a reason for a particular dataset *not* to use one tool, when another tool that is more appropriate for specific type of data is shown to be equally or almost equally effective in analyzing that dataset) for further modeling. MORAL OF STORY: Do *not* act in "isolation" – e.g. do *not* have a bias toward any one tool, as if one does, you may miss the most important information that can be obtained from your data.

Sure, Business, but Why Healthcare, Public Policy, and Business?

Professionals are challenged each day by a changing landscape of technology and terminology. In recent history, especially the last 25 years, there has been an explosion of terms and methods born that automate and improve decision-making and operations. One term, "Analytics," is an overarching description of a compilation of methodologies. But AI, statistics, decision science, and optimization, which have been around for decades, have resurged. Also, things like BI, Online Analytical Processing (OLAP) and many, many more have been born or reborn.

How is someone to make sense of all this methodology, terminology?

That is why we created the ***Analytics Landscape***. Even the title was difficult. How do you describe the intent in a few words that encompass terminology and practices of a wide field of methodology and practice? After 30 years in the space, in many industries and academic studies, the authors want to help the modern practitioner.

These techniques and technologies have been embraced by consumer-based businesses for years.

Healthcare has come later to the party and policy is just arriving.

We know there is a real need for the application of these techniques in all forms of medicine and government.

That is why we wanted to specifically call them out.

Here are just a few ways that innovative companies are applying the science in the healthcare domain:

■ **Improving diagnostic accuracy and efficiently predicting diseases.** AI image processing, recognition, and classification for radiology scans of all types (x-ray, CT, MRI, PET) are having a huge impact on healthcare and will accelerate in the coming years. AI can learn/train on tens of millions of images and augment the intelligence of radiologists and other care providers – something a human can never do in an entire lifetime.

■ **Training for healthcare providers will become more dynamic and interactive.** Video games with avatar intelligence enabled by AI are part of training new surgeons. This training, sometimes in the form of "Games for surgeons," but also surgical robots and data mining (Predictive & Prescriptive Analytics) will probably be making a difference in healthcare delivery sooner than later (Smith, 2017)

■ **Data science is enabling precision medicine,** medical care designed to optimize efficiency or therapeutic benefit for particular groups of patients, especially by using genetic or molecular profiling (precision medicine). This will radically change the benefits of drugs and treatments.

■ **Virtual assistance for patients.** This can radically change the process of treating patients. AI-assisted chatbots and intelligent agents can allay the costly in-person office visit as an initial consult and will greatly reduce costs. Subsequent needed interactions can be made after most of the data is collected, processed and enhanced by ML algorithms.

■ **Computer-assisted language processing** (text analytics, texting mining, which we explore in depth later) can scan millions of physician notes and text in EMR/EHR databases and learn/train from these instances. This is assisting providers with diagnoses and treatment options.

■ **Intelligent robots.** Advances in robotic surgery let doctors perform many types of complex procedures with more precision, flexibility and control than is possible with other conventional techniques.

■ **Chronic disease management** and population health specialists are applying everything from visual analytics to predictive analytics to make them more effective in providing access and information at the appropriate time.

■ **Health insurance claims** are mined to reduce fraud, waste, and abuse to more effectively distribute risk pool and insurance monies.

There are many, many more ways that data science, AI and analytics can solve problems in healthcare and we will discuss some of these in this book, and they will form more than a third of our upcoming book on detailed applications.

At the same time, the bulk of medical practice has not changed in over 100 years. The basic processes of the medical examination of physician to patient are the same as they were in the early 20th century. Yes, medical technology, pharmacology, and medical education have improved greatly. Nevertheless, much of medicine is practiced the same as it was a century ago. A physician interviews a patient, takes a few (very high level) diagnostics like blood pressure, heart rate, and temperature, and hears the patient describe the reason they are there. Most typically, the patient is prescribed a drug that was formulated for the general population, not their genetic make-up and both parties part and hope it works out. That is very much the same as it has been for many years. **Is there not a better way?**

We are not medical experts, but almost every process improves over time and often for the better. We think there is a huge opportunity in healthcare for improvement by adopting more data-driven techniques and technology. This book is applicable to all of the following professions as they are all impacted by AI, data science and analytics:

- Healthcare and hospital executives, chief medical officers (CMOs) and administrators
- Medical professionals including physicians, nurses, clinicians, and healthcare consultants
- Healthcare professionals in hospitals, medical groups, clinics, and community care centers
- Data analysts, medical informatics analysts, and technical professionals
- Health science, public health, pharma, and life science providers
- Public health, nursing, biology, informatics and other related majors seeking careers in healthcare analytics

Additionally, if you are interested in a career in data-driven medicine consider "Harnessing the Power of Data in Health," a report by Stanford Medicine (Stanford Medicine, 2017). Also, the website for UCI where both authors have affiliations and teach a couple of courses in Healthcare Analytics (UCI, 2019: https://ce.uci.edu/areas/healthcare/healthcare_analytic s/). These two links are good sources of careers in the healthcare field. Even, The Centers for Medicare & Medicare Services (CMS), the payer of more US$1.4 trillion of national healthcare expenditures in the United States, is getting into AI. CMS offered an AI competition in 2019 with up to a US$1.65M payout to competitors (www.cmschallenge.ai/).

Policy and government is a huge and wide field. We feel that at the very least, policy development should follow a system of testing and continuous improvement. This system at its root focuses on cycling a four step process – Plan, Do, Study, Act (see Deming circle/cycle/wheel, in *The New Economics* by Deming: Deming, 2018). In the United States, we tend to pass large, very expensive initiatives with inadequate testing and accountability. What if legislation was piloted and be required to prove efficacious results before being expanded? This would not be that difficult! Instead of passing a US$200 million dollar legislative bill, you pass a US$10 million pilot with 4 criteria to prove results. If these are met then you roll out the rest step of the program and as part of the program, certain criteria have to be met for continuation. This is how successful consumer and healthcare businesses are run. ***Plan, execute, measure, expand, govern, amend, rinse and repeat.***

As an example, as we wrote this chapter, then presidential candidate Andrew Yang was proposing a "Freedom Dividend" of US$1000 per month for every adult over the age of 18. We take no position whether this is a good or bad idea. However, if passed in full it would be expensive (estimate US$2.4 trillion per year) and the big question is, "would it achieve the objectives?" According to Yang's website (www.yang2020.com/policies/the-freedom-dividend/) the objective is:

> This would enable all Americans to pay their bills, educate themselves, start businesses, be more creative, stay healthy, relocate for work, spend time with their children, take care of loved ones, and have a real stake in the future.

How would you measure its success?

Again, we are not taking a side, only pointing out this example as one that is too often followed.

In general, governmental programs and policies at all levels, city, county, state and federal, lack definition and guidelines. There are too often:

- No clear objectives to be obtained; often very vague
- There is no measurement for success
- They continue without review

By adopting a more data-driven methodology, a statistical methodology in this case, the process would look more like the following framework:

1) What is the policy objective?
2) What quantifiable outcomes would be measured?

NOTE: this is where many people suggest that not all outcomes can be quantified. We recommend referring to *How to Measure Anything: Finding the Value of Intangibles in Business* (see Hubbard, 2010) which applies to objectives in healthcare and government.

3) Plan a pilot project. This would require specifics, for example:
   a. What are the objectives of the plan to be studied?
   b. What metrics would collected and by what method of collection?
   c. What are the criteria for success? What benchmarks must the metrics surpass?
   d. What is the sample for the pilot – location or subset of the population to test objectives?
   e. What is the period for evaluation, specific dates?
   f. What is the method of analysis, experimental design/plan?
   g. Who compares results to targets, presentation format and to what body?
   h. What is the plan for termination or expansion?

Obviously, there are many details in such a framework. But similar processes are used by the most successful companies in the world. Why not government?

NEXT-GENERATION MEDICAL DEVICES – HUMAN ENHANCEMENT

There is a push to augment human proficiency with ML and AI. It is taking new forms. Here are three examples:

Elon Musk, the founder of Tesla and SpaceX, is investing US$100 million into a somewhat secretive venture called Neuralink that will employ some of the leading scientists to create a brain to device network. This news was announced in the summer of 2019. Musk said the Neuralink system would allow for a chip to be implanted into the brains of willing subjects and would allow humans to achieve "symbiosis with AI."

Athletic performance is greatly being affected by the Internet of Things (IoT) where streaming information is available for training, performance, and strategy. Athletic suits can be worn and sets of sensors can model action and movement, other sets can be used for monitoring cardiac output and physical stress. These can be used to maximize training and even formulate strategies using AI and optimization. Football, MMA (mixed martial arts) and virtually any deep pocket sport are evaluating such uses.

AI and IoT are also helping gain freedom from disabilities. Whether it is assisting veterans to walk again or helping the blind see, these technologies are enhancing humans. One example is a new app that Microsoft launched in 2018 called "Seeing AI." It helps people who are blind or with other visual disabilities interact with the world by using the smartphone's camera; the phone will audibly describe what it is seeing, read written documents, scan product barcodes and even recognize faces (Microsoft, 2018; Bureau of Internet Accessibility, 2018). Even things like the Apple-enabled "Siri" allow people with spinal cord injuries and inability to use their hands to dial a phone number, communicate with others by speaking to their smart phone and verbally telling it who to call – just with a voice command. Microsoft in Australia appears to be a leader in advancing AI and IoT: Globally there are 1.3 billion people dealing with disability needing some kind of AI / IoT support. Of this 1.3 billion worldwide number, about 4 million are Australians, and thus Deloitte in Australia has estimated there is a market worth about US$1.4 billion by 2020 just for Australia (Microsoft, April 2019).

How This Book Is Organized

As readers, we love to see what is in store. Time is limited so let us explore what the rest of this book offers.

Chapter 2: Building a Successful Program. We want to provide an overview of what will make you successful in your journey. Things like what pitfalls are out there, what should you be considering, and what can thousands of hours (experienced by this book's authors) in discussions of successes and failures provide you.

Chapter 3: Some Fundamentals – Process, Data, and Models. We are covering many different programs, but there is an underlying theme. Can we address some things that tie all these methods together? Yes, please see this chapter.

Chapter 4: It's All Analytics! Yes, be it data science or AI, statistics, or reporting, it is *all analytics* and we cover the spectrum in this chapter.

Chapter 5: What Is Business Intelligence (BI) and Visual BI? Where it starts and where it ends.

Chapter 6: What Is Machine Learning and Data Mining? The RAGE 1.0 it had been getting a lot of press and it should; it can radically change your life, probably already has. What you need to know.

Chapter 7: AI and How It Differs from Machine Learning. AI is the Rage 2.0, but in many respects, it is the same.

Chapter 8: What Is Data Science? Yes, it is hot and will continue to be hot. What is it and how does it differ from everything else you are reading about?

Chapter 9: Big Data and Bigger Data, Little Data, Cloud and Other Data. All the rage and justifiably so, what does the cloud offer? Data lakes or data swamps? Does size matter or is it performance over volume?

Chapter 10: Statistics, Causation, and Prescriptive Analytics. A few things you should know about statistics. We discuss one of the most misunderstood concepts in analytics today!

Chapter 11: Other Disciplines to Dive in Deeper: Computer Science, Management/Decision Science, Operations Research, Engineering (and More). We love analytics and could go far too long, so we leave you with some endnotes and directions to pursue.

Chapter 12: Looking Ahead. A brief glimpse at our next book. We are dedicated to helping the general practitioner. Whether they are in healthcare, government or business – technology does not care or matter of the use case, stick with us.

Postscript

Hopefully, after reading this chapter, you are excited to continue our journey into the data-driven revolution. You are conscious of the sources of confusion and think critically when garnering information from **potential** sources of misinformation:

1) Consultants
2) Software vendors
3) Marketers
4) Specialists / Narrow thinkers
5) Scientific papers
6) Biased blogs

Not to say you discount the information, you just take an objective, informed view. Finally, you know the impacts of this revolution will greatly affect you both professionally and personally and you are ready to seize the opportunity!

References

Announcement of Requirements and Registration for "Artificial intelligence Health Outcomes Challenge" Authority: 15 U.S.C. 37, https://innovation.cms.gov/fil es/x/aichallenge-pubnotice.pdf. Update: June 7, 2019.

Araya, D. 2019. *Forbes*. Online January 2019, www.forbes.com/sites/danielaraya/20 19/01/04/artificial-intelligence-and-the-end-of-government/#7aad21e8719b.

BALLANTYNE, C. 2012. "22000 crunches do what?," *Men's Health*, www.menshe alth.com/fitness/a19523809/22000-crunches-do-what/.

Bughin, J., Seong, J., Manyika, J., Chui, M., and Joshi, R. September 2018. "McKinsey and Company," *Notes from the AI Frontier: Modeling the Impact of AI on the World Economy*, McKinsey Global Institute: McKinsey and Company.

Bureau of Internet Accessibility. December 15, 2018. "Accessibility and the internet of things," 9. www.boia.org/blog/accessibility-and-the-internet-of-things.

Burtch Works. September 30, 2019. www.burtchworks.com/2019/09/30/hotspots-remote-work-and-relocation-options-in-data-science-and-analytics/.

Chambers, M. 2014. *Computational Intelligence in Business Analytics*, Sztandera, L. (ed.), x–xi. Person Education LTD.

Columbus, L. 2017. "IBM predicts demand for data scientists will soar 28% by 2020, May 2017". Found in *Forbes Online*, www.forbes.com/sites/louiscolumbus/ 2017/05/13/ibm-predicts-demand-for-data-scientists-will-soar-28-by-2020/#1f 2046d07e3b (accessed July 7, 2019).

CompTIA. 2019. "IT industry outlook for 2019. (January 2019 – As Seen on August 12, 2019)," www.comptia.org/resources/it-industry-trends-analysis.

Dartmouth. 2019. "Artificial intelligence (AI) coined at Dartmouth-2056," in *DartouthEdu*, https://250.dartmouth.edu.highlights/artificial-intelligence-ai-c oined-dartmouth.

Dash, P.K., Kaminski, R., Gendelman, H.E. et al. 2019. "Sequential LASER ART and CRISPR treatments eliminate HIV-1 in a subset of infected humanized mice," *Nature Communications,* 10(2753), www.nature.com/articles/s41467-019-10366 -y (accessed August 11, 2019).

Davenport, Thomas H. April 2017. "What's your data strategy?" *Harvard Business Review*, https://hbr.org/webinar/2017/04/whats-your-data-strategy.

Davenport, T.H. and Patil, D.J. 2012. https://hbr.org/2012/10/data-scientist-the-se xiest-job-of-the-21st-century.

Deming, W. E., 2018. *The New Economics for Industry, Government, Education* (3rd ed.). MIT Press.

DHHS. 2019. Department of Health and Human Services, Centers for Medicare & Medicaid Services, Announcement of Requirements and Registration for "Artificial intelligence Health Outcomes Challenge, https://innovation.cms.gov/ files/x/aichallenge-pubnotice.pdf.

Dove, L., 2019. "Is spinach a really good source of iron or not?" in *HowStuffWorks*, https://science.howstuffworks.com/innovation/edible-innovations/spinach-goo d-source-of-iron1.htm.

Glickman,M., Brown, J., and Song, R. 2019. "Data in the life: Authorship attribution in Lennon-McCartney songs," https://hdsr.mitpress.mit.edu/pub/xcq8a1v1; DOI - https://doi.org/10.1162/99608f92.130f856e.

Green, F. 2016. "The Holy Grail of data monetization. Every-market-media," https://everymarketmedia.com/holy-grail-of-data-monetization-fran-green/ (accessed August 11, 2019).

Hubbard, Douglas, W.April 12, 2010. *How to Measure Anything: Finding the Value of "Intangibles," in Business.* Wiley.

Indeed. 2019. "Data analysts salaries in the United States (as of August 9, 2019)," www.indeed.com/salaries/Data-Analyst-Salaries.

Johnston, M. D. and Miller, G. E. 1992. "SPIKE: Intelligent scheduling of Hubble Space Telescope observations," Space Telescope Science Institute, www.stsci.edu/~miller/papers-and-meetings/93-Intelligent-Scheduling/spike/spike-chapter3.html (accessed August 11, 2019).

Johnston, M., Miller, G., Sponsler, J., and Shon, V., and Jackson, R. "Artificial intelligence scheduling for the Hubble Space Telescope," Found in Space Telescope Science Institute, https://ntrs.nasa.gov/archive/nasa/casi.ntrs.nasa.gov/1990001 7961.pdf. – Thought to be 1988 by most scientists; however another citation on this topic does provide a 1988 date: Dussud, P. H. 1988. "Lisp hardware architecture: The Explorer II and beyond." SIGPLAN Lisp Pointers 1, 6 (April 1988), 13–18. http://doi.acm.org/10.1145/1317224.1317226.

Kah, S. November 2018. "Will robots take your job? Humans ignore coming AI revolution," in *NBC News Online*, www.nbcnews.com/think/opinion/will-robots-take-your-job-humans-ignore-coming-ai-revolution-ncna845366.

Manyika, et al. 2017. "Jobs lost, jobs gained: What the future of work will mean for jobs, skills, and wages," www.mckinsey.com/featured-insights/future-of-work/jobs-lost-jobs-gained-what-the-future-of-work-will-mean-for-jobs-skills-and-wages (extracted June 11, 2019).

McKinsey. 2011. www.mckinsey.com/business-functions/mckinsey-digital/our-insights/big-data-the-next-frontier-for-innovation.

Meehan, M. December 8, 2016. "Where data goes to die," *Forbes*, https://www.forbes.com/sites/marymeehan/2016/12/08/where-data-goes-to-die-big-data-still-holds-answers-but-theyre-not-where-youre-looking-for-them/#5624533a5896.

Mehr, H. August 2017. "Artificial intelligence for citizen services and government," Harvard Kennedy School, Ash Center for Democratic Governance and Innovation. Found in, https://ash.harvard.edu/files/ash/files/artificial_intelligence_for_citizen_services.pdf.

Mester, T. January 7, 2019. "Learning data science −4 untold truths," in *Data36*, and as viewed by authors of this book on August 12, 2019, https://data36.com/learning-data-science/.

Microsoft. 2018. "Accessibility and the Internet of Things," Seeing AI. www.microsoft.com/en-us/ai/seeing-ai.

Microsoft. April 2019. "AI and cloud combine to transform opportunity for people living with a disability," https://news.microsoft.com/en-au/features/ai-and-cloud-combine-to-transform-opportunity-for-people-living-with-a-disability/.

Miller, G. (1989). "Artificial intelligence applications for Hubble Space Telescope operations," In Heck, A. and Murtagh, F. (eds.), *Knowledge-Based Systems in Astronomy.* Lecture Notes in Physics, vol. 329. Springer. DOI: https://doi.org /10.1007/3-540-51044-3_14.

Miner, L., Bolding, P., Hilbe, J., Goldstein, M., Hill, T., Nisbet, R., Walton, N., and Miner, G. 2015. *Practical Predictive Analytics and Decisioning Systems for Medicine: Informatics Accuracy and Cost-Effectiveness for Healthcare Administration and Delivery Including Medical Research.* Elsevier/Academic Press.

Molla, R. 2019. "Amazon's former HQ2 location is doing just fine without Amazon," *Vox Media,* www.vox.com/recode/2019/7/2/19102639/amazon-hq2-long-island-city-real-estate (accessed August 11, 2019).

Nisbet, R., Miner, G., and Yale, K. 2018. *Handbook of Statistical Analysis and Data Mining Applications* (2nd ed.). Elsevier/Academic Press.

Panetta, K. (February 6, 2019). "A data and analytics leader's guide to data literacy," Gartner, www.gartner.com/smarterwithgartner/a-data-and-analytics-leaders-g uide-to-data-literacy/.

Payscale. August 12, 2019. "Average healthcare data analyst salary," www.paysca le.com/research/US/Job=Healthcare_Data_Analyst/Salary.

Press, G. November 2016. "Forrester predicts investment in artificial intelligence will grow 300% in 2017," www.forbes.com/sites/gilpress/2016/11/01/forrester -predicts-investment-in-artificial-intelligence-will-grow-300-in-2017/#14e3472b5 509.

Press, G. January 2017. "6 predictions for the $203 billion big data analytics market," *Forbes,* www.forbes.com/sites/gilpress/2017/01/20/6-predictions-for-the-20 3-billion-big-data-analytics-market/#6f9abcc12083 (extracted June 9, 2019).

Reinsel, D., Gantz, J., and Rydning, J. 2017. "Data age 2025: The evolution of data to life-critical don't focus on big data," Focus on the Data That's Big. IDC (International Data Corporation) White Paper © 2017 IDC. www.idc.com; found in: https://assets.ey.com/content/dam/ey-sites/ey-com/en_gl/topics/wo rkforce/Seagate-WP-DataAge2025-March-2017.pdf.

Seagate. 2020. "The digitization of the world," https://www.seagate.com/our-story/d ata-age-2025/.

Smith, R. 2017. "Artificial intelligence: Coming soon to a hospital near you," www.s tatnews.com/2017/04/13/artificial-intelligence-surgeons-hospital/.

Stack, T. February 5, 2018. "Internet of Things (IoT) data continues to explode exponentially. Who is using that data and how?" https://blogs.cisco.com/datace nter/internet-of-things-iot-data-continues-to-explode-exponentially-who-is-using-that-data-and-how.

Stanford Medicine. 2017. "Harnessing the power of data in health," Health Trends Report, https://med.stanford.edu/content/dam/sm/sm-.news/documents/Stanfo rdMedicineHealthTrendsWhitePaper2017.pdf.

SZTANDERA, L. 2014. *Computation Intelligence in Business Analytics.* Pearson Publishing.

Tang, G. 2018. "Is spinach a good source of iron? Is cooked better than raw?" in Health *Castle*, www.healthcastle.com/spinach-good-source-iron-cooked-better-raw/.

Turner, A. 2019. "Researchers say they're closer to finding cure for HIV after using CRISPR technology to eliminate disease in live mice for the first time," *CNBC On-Line Blog*, www.cnbc.com/2019/07/02/researchers-used-crispr-technology-to-cure-hiv-in-living-mice.html (accessed August 11, 2019).

UCI. 2019. Healthcare Analytics Program, https://ce.uci.edu/areas/healthcare/healthcare_analytics/.

Wall, M. 2019. "Are you happy to share your health data to benefit others?" *BBC News Services*, www.bbc.com/news/business-48784205 (accessed August 11, 2019).

Wikipedia. August 12, 2019a. Dartmouth workshop, https://en.wikipedia.org/wiki/Dartmouth_workshop.

Wikipedia. August 18, 2019b. Computer-aided software engineering, https://en.wikipedia.org/wiki/Computer-aided_software_engineering.

Resources for the Avid Learner

1 https://hms.com/resource/hms-pods-episode-6-predictive-modeling/ (short video, population health, Vitreos – some care management, chronic disease stuff I mentioned last week)

2 short videos for population health, http://vitreoshealth.com/blog/incorporating-social-determinants-in-your-population-health-programs/#How_Your_Historic

3 Body as a machine, athletics, human performance enhancement with AI / ML www.tibco.com/blog/2019/08/05/optimizing-mma-fighting-with-tibco-spotfire-software/

4 For sports analytics fans, "All eyes on how GM Ron Francis will 'build out' the analytics department of Seattle's NHL team," August 7, 2019, *The Seattle Times*, www.seattletimes.com/sports/hockey/all-eyes-on-how-gm-ron-francis-will-build-out-the-analytics-department-of-seattles-nhl-team/

Chapter 2

Building a Successful Program

Keywords: Culture, Organizational Design, Alignment, Project/Program Success, Center of Excellence, Scale, Productivity

Preamble

In Chapter 1, we considered all the "hype" about AI (currently the biggest and hottest "hype" topic) and other "hype items," and the fact that all the tools needed for data analysis have been around for at least 20 years. Yet every year a "new name" is given to an old procedure either by some field new to analytics that does not understand the history of data analysis OR by a "new company" that wants to "hype" its product by giving an old procedure a new name, thus making the unsuspecting audience "think" that a NEW process has just been discovered, when it has not. In this chapter, we move into the basics needed for understanding AI, data science and the full analytics landscape.

The Hip, the Hype, the Fears, the Intrigue, and the Reality

The Hype

If data is the new oil, why aren't we all rich? – LinkedIn Post 7/18/19

Reality

Good point! Most enterprises are knowledge poor, not data poor.

The Hype

AI will revolutionize problem solving. In the future, we will not need data scientists.

Reality

AI cannot solve all types of problems even with future advancements in computing power. There is a class of problems called "Undecidable Problems" that AI will not solve, regardless of computing power.

The Hype

The best way to solve a problem is to use the "The New Convolutional Vortex System" just released by Skynet Corporation! "This Convolutional Vortex System can do anything, analyze anything, and is 110% accurate" – so say the advertisements.

Reality

We were seeing publicized solutions for techniques and solutions that could solve virtually all problems. Our mantra has been and will remain throughout this book that **there is no universally best or optimal method** (see the section "There Is No Free Lunch" in the next chapter). That is one of the chief motivations for writing this book. Furthermore, it is not the technique as much as it is *"are you asking the right questions"* that matters. A supreme answer to the wrong question is not as important as a mediocre answer to the right question.

Introduction

We just covered many reasons why you should be interested in AI, data science and analytics – why professionals need this book. We explained that there is a lot of confusion and misinformation available on this material, primarily hype and marketecture, and there is a need to be objective. There are objective sources of information, but they are oriented toward narrow applications or technical material.

We know there is a need to cover the broader subjects including non-technical issues, so in this chapter, we specifically address building a successful AI, data science and analytics program (to simplify terminology we generally refer to all these methods as just "analytics").

Here we will cover:

- Limitations and gaps in culture and organization
- Justifying an analytics program
- Designing (or redesigning) an analytics program

Culture and Organization – Gaps and Limitations

There are many practicing camps, educational philosophies, and professional organizations that have developed their own languages around the same topics. Or, they have created a nuanced version of core or foundational mathematical constructs to fit their unique problems. While this can be very beneficial if you belong to a given camp or group, it can limit a professional in their application of useful techniques. It also keeps practitioners isolated and lacking many useful tools and techniques that they could be using. Learning business cases from one sector, industry or function and applying that knowledge to another area can be very useful (see "Applying Engineering to Marketing" in the next gray box).

APPLYING ENGINEERING TO MARKETING

When Scott worked at Texas Instruments, his role was a consulting statistician in a large manufacturing plant. One of the groups he supported was engineering and worked with engineers on "the line." One method applied was statistical process control (SPC). SPC had been around for many years and was well known by manufacturing and engineering professionals.

A few years later when he went to work for Overstock.com, where he was supporting Internet retail marketing. A very different field from high-tech manufacturing! He learned the methods that were used for testing of marketing campaigns, and also how creative marketing was conducted for uplift. Overstock was applying A/B testing, a common method used at the time. But, knowing that the problem was essentially the same as making an "intervention" to a manufacturing line, he was able to save the company time and money by applying SPC to these problems (see Burk, 2006). This is an example of borrowing innovative ideas in one field and applying them to another field.

That is why we introduce many fields in this book.

A key objective for us in this book is to open the veil. We discuss commonalities of several of the techniques as well as open the door to many useful techniques across disciplines, at a topical level. In this book, we speak about the differences in language and process.

Gaps in Analytics Programs

There are issues that exist within organizations that cause problems in making analytics programs successful. Two of the major areas are *people* and *processes*. Or, put another way, culture, and organization structure. Weakness in these two areas cause what we will call symptoms. Some of these symptoms are:

- Lack of Adaptability
- Isolation / Disconnects and Alignment
- Gaps in Education or Knowledge
- Motivation / Incentives

Stories – Examples of these symptoms:

- Our leadership is in the Stone Ages. Everyone has been talking about being "data driven" for years, yet we operate by the seat of our pants. Leadership thinks "having been in this industry for thirty years" gives us an advantage, and maybe in some respects it does. However, there are many examples where companies with great histories died quickly. We need to quit talking about being "data driven" as we are barely scratching the surface and instead dive deep into analytics and AI. What do we need to do to finally execute this time? **Bottom Line: Lack of Adaptability, Gaps in Education**
- Bless our CEO, but he has been in this business for over 30 years. What brought us here will not keep us here and he just doesn't get that. Our competition is using a new customer targeting system that is intelligent, and for the last six months they have been bleeding us out. We better adopt something quick or we are dead. **Bottom Line: Lack of Adaptability**
- Our leadership got sold on AI when several members attended a national conference. That is great. What is not great is that they had a vendor come in and sell them a new computer platform without including the people that will actually use the system in the negotiations.

Now we are stuck into a contract for the next three years with a system that does half of what we need and the other half is poor. Now our brightest people are leaving because they want to create solutions and not consume pre-canned analytics. **Bottom Line: Poor Decisions Made in Isolation by Leadership Team. Lack of Alignment and Communication**

■ There are no incentives to work more intelligently. There are no metrics that tie my performance to that of the company or my annual review. I don't know how my job affects the performance of the company or the numbers that the board is interested in. **Bottom Line: Lack of Organizational Accountability, Poor Motivation / Incentives**

■ We get paid for doing more. We are not judged by any other measures. We always say we are acting in the patient's best interest, but in reality, if there are two alternatives with approximately similar outcomes, we often perform the one with the higher reimbursement. When I say approximate, this is ballpark so we can justify our "decision," and not necessarily the best decision for an optimal outcome. As a taxpayer I wish it were different, but that is the way it is. **Bottom Line: Lack of Organizational Accountability, Poor Motivation / Incentives**

■ Every time we get a new administrator, they have their own design. They do not learn from their superiors or the people reporting to them. They just throw out new operational initiatives and we are to execute them. They either talk a good game above them or move onto the next event, next company. There is no consistency and it seems we are in a perpetual reinvent cycle. **Bottom Line: Lack of Vision, Lack Clear Objectives and Consistency**

■ We created a BI group years ago and it has morphed into Visual BI, which has had some success. However, it stopped there. We, the practitioners, want to move forward, but leadership thinks we are doing fine with what we have; why fix what isn't broken? **Bottom Line: Lack of Leadership and Vision, Gaps in Education or Knowledge**

■ Our CIO has consultants come in and they push some innovative stuff, it all sounds great and we implement this, but the business does not get it! Yes, there are steering committees and the whole shebang, but people take it as something they have to do, something extra. Not what could actually help them do their job better. **Bottom Line: Lack of Clear Objectives and Consistency, Lack of Alignment and Communication, Gaps in Education or Knowledge**

■ We have tried several "data-driven" initiatives over the decade. Each time we have limited success. Everyone gets on board and is excited, but after 6 months or a year we hear the same thing: **the results stink because our data stinks**. So we make some efforts to fix it, but those projects are temporary or short lived. **Bottom Line: Bad Data, Gaps in Education or Knowledge**

THESE ARE CULTURAL AND ORGANIZATIONAL FLAWS – NOT FLAWS IN TECHNOLOGY OR PEOPLE

Example No 1: We tried a pilot predictive modeling project. The team was involved and we really enjoyed the project. However, the outcomes were not stellar and another corporate initiative got started. All the members got pulled into several directions. I wish we had paused to figure out how we could do it better. So much for continuous learning and improvement.

Example No 2: I am part of IT and we brought in a new analytics system. We had a big kickoff by the CEO and then IT was sent away to install and configure the system, which took 6 months. The IT team was extremely excited about the system. We rolled it out to the business, but they never really adopted it. At times they used it, but only scratched the surface of the capability – I would say 10%. The license was expensive and after two years we dropped it. And, the legacy was that analytics was the failure, not our organization's attempted adoption of it.

Example No 3: We started a data science program and hired four really bright graduates who were eager to start their careers. Everyone seemed on board, but in the end, most of the data science projects turned out to be data sourcing (DBA and analyst functions) and data quality projects. Simple reporting or pet (not data science) projects. Within 18 months, we had lost all of our original data scientists. The feedback we got was "this is not data science; I want to be a data scientist."

Example No 4: We have a very successful BI program that started years ago and has evolved into visual, interactive analytics dashboards with great capability. Out BI team wants to take it to the next level doing predictive analytics and machine learning. But, leadership thinks we have all we need. We know a dashboard is not predictive, can only address a small number of business variables at a time and can sometimes mislead decision-makers, who might decide to go a direction that is not statistically or practically significant. Maybe we have been too successful with adoption, but we can't seem to move to the next level.

Example No 5: We have hired some data scientists who are specialized in AI. My group needs some help as we deal only with small samples and the AI group says that it will not work. They say they need more data to train models. It seems our brightest bulbs cannot help with our problem. I went to a conference and I know there are statistical methods that can help, but these experts only speak ML and AI. I can't do this on my own. How disappointing.

This book can help with all these cases.

These stories illustrate difficulties that are rarely technology problems. They are problems of leadership, culture, alignment, people, and process. We can trace these issues back to a higher-level categorization.

Characterizing Common Problems

In the preceding section, we appended the example with some key words. These factors hamper organizations from getting a positive return from their personnel and financial investments. However, they are not the only factors. Following is a list of causes for shortcomings of analytics success at various organizations:

- Gaps in Education or Knowledge
- Lack of Adaptability
- Lack of Alignment and Communication
- Lack of Organizational Accountability
- Lack of Vision / Leadership
- Isolation / Disconnects
- Poor Motivation / Incentives
- Organizational Structure
- Lack of Clear Objectives and Consistency
- Organizational Policy
- Improper Planning
- Project Scope

We now briefly explore a few of these characterizations:

Improper planning manifests itself in lack of project scope containment (in IT, called "scope creep"), misalignment of people and financial assets, unrealistic project schedules, lack of concrete deliverables (what the project is intended to achieve) AND tying those deliverables to top metrics – KPI alignment. One additional issue can be throwing everyone at the problem, i.e., overstaffing, which leads to people running over each other, not being aligned and not effectively communicating.

Gaps in education or knowledge lead to many problems in the success of enterprise analytics programs. First, lack of leadership education can lead to wrong decisions in data architecture, analytics architecture, analytics objectives and goals, and impressive but unreasonable expectations. If there is an analytics project failure, it **can lead to a false negative in thinking** that analytics doesn't work, when in fact it was incorrect design and execution that caused the problems. **(See False Negatives, False Fails and Loonshots gray box below.)**

FALSE NEGATIVES, FALSE FAILS AND LOONSHOTS: HOW TO NURTURE THE CRAZY IDEAS THAT WIN WARS, CURE DISEASES, AND TRANSFORM INDUSTRIES

We will cover a false negative more deeply in the statistics chapter (Chapter 10). Nevertheless, for now, a false negative is arriving at a wrong conclusion, thinking something did not work when in fact it did. Safi Bahcall calls these "false fails" in his book *Loonshots* (see Bahcall, 2019).

Statins (drugs that lower cholesterol levels in the blood), a multibillion dollar industry, and Facebook, a social media giant that has a market cap of over US$500 billion, are two loonshot ideas that both experienced false fails.

When Akira Endo was testing the first statin, Mevastatin, to see if it would lower cholesterol, the tests failed. He was testing on rats, which were later discovered to have low levels of LDL or "bad cholesterol." When he tested the drug on chickens, which have high levels of LDL, the results were spectacular. The market for statins exploded, it has been one of the top-selling drugs of all time and is estimated to prevent half a million heart attacks and strokes each year. However, it almost did not happen. Why? Not because the drug did not work, it was simply tested with a bad experimental design.

FACEBOOK HAD A SIMILAR EXPERIENCE

Safi recalls that in the early 2000s, Facebook was seeking venture capital while competing with several other social networks. Investors believed social network sites were a fad since users would abandon established sites and join new ones. Many were leaving a social media site called Friendster and moving to other sites such as MySpace. Several investors passed on Facebook, but one investor dug a bit deeper.

This investor, Peter Thiel, found that users of Friendster were leaving the site because it was constantly crashing and although the company had received advice to fix and scale their site, they ignored it. Thiel concluded that users weren't leaving the social network because of its weak business model, but because of a software glitch. Thiel invested in Facebook and became a billionaire. If he had accepted the "wisdom of the crowd," he and Facebook would have lost out.

Analytics programs have proven themselves over and over. If you have a false start, don't discount analytics, re-evaluate your implementation of it.

Second, gaps in management- and staff-level knowledge can derail an analytics program that would be otherwise very successful. It can be associated with "buy-in," because people that do not get the right training and support get frustrated and unmoved, and then the effort falls apart and the "knowledge from data" effort is seen as not useful.

Adaptability has to do with the willingness of an organization or individuals within an organization to change. There are numerous examples of companies that were once extremely successful but are now dead: – Borders, Sears, Blockbuster, Toys R Us and many more. They were resistant or unwilling to adapt to a changing marketplace or technology within a marketplace. Analytics continues to dramatically change the way organizations operate and is a necessary condition for survival.

Alignment has to do with making sure that all the pieces of an enterprise are working together for a common good of the body. Are the top tiers pulling insight from all levels of the organization or making all decisions within the c-suite without input from the lower levels of the organization? Do staff line personnel know how their activity affects the top-level objectives? Is there a known linkage of the metrics at the top to metrics generated at the bottom? These are called *Key Performance Indicators* (KPIs; they will be discussed in Chapter 5). Finally, the structure of the organization influences alignment, and we dedicate a section on this later in this chapter.

Accountability has to do with the individual ownership of activities and the results of those activities. While today's professionals need to be fluid and often have a lot of leeway in their approach in their activities, it is important they not only adhere to policy and procedures, but also support the mission and objectives of leadership. Moreover, the performance and success of employees should be measured on how well the employee performed against these objectives. It is important that leadership designs clear roles and goals, awards alignment to them and penalizes behaviors that do not support them.

Isolation / Disconnects are islands ("Silos") in the organization that act independently of the rest of the organization. Leaders of these islands often make decisions which may benefit the local group, but do not align to the rest of the organization. In analytics parlance, this is called trying to achieve a *local optimum* versus a *global optimum*. This is often seen in policy decisions, and we will revisit this in Chapter 11, which speaks on the subject of optimization. This can be due to a functional organization structure, which we will talk more about in this chapter's "Organizational Structure" section.

A great example of silos was freight movement before shipping containers. The trucking folks loved trucks, the railroad people loved the rails, the shipping people saw only ships. When one man viewed it as "I only want to move freight," he designed the shipping container and this cross-boundary thinking revolutionized the cargo and freight industry. See Levinson for a very interesting read (Levinson, 2016).

Motivation and Incentives impact human behavior. We are all influenced and motivated by incentives. The study of economics is the study of incentives. Motivation is the fluid which creates new technology, methods, and growth in society, and is the pathway on which the company must walk, no matter what its "philosophy or camp," to achieve success.

FOR FANS OF THE TV SERIES *THE OFFICE*

Clear Objectives and Consistency. For any readers that are fans of *The Office*, you may recall an episode where Michael Scott is leaving and his replacement Deangelo has been hired. Erin, the office administrative assistant is answering the phone, so Deangelo suggests an alternative greeting when answering the company phone. Michael says he prefers the old way of answering the phone, but the new way is okay, old way preferred. Michael and Deangelo are going back and forth when the phone rings. Erin picks up the phone and is speechless; she hangs on empty air for a few seconds, then says "I'm sorry" and hangs up. The camera pans to Michael and Deangelo who are obviously dumbfounded.

This is what you get when management or leadership does not send clear signals on objectives!

Vision and Leadership. Stephen Covey (see Covey, 1989) does a great job in defining vision and the differences of leadership and management. Managing is about *efficiency*. Leadership is about *effectiveness*. Efficiency focuses on how we can get the most out of the resources we have. Leadership has to do with where these resources should apply their effort.

Don't Confuse Organizational Gaps for Project Gaps

A word of caution on failure, missteps, and gaps. You should not confuse organizational gaps, which are at a higher, strategic or cultural level, with project gaps, which are tactical. Here we provide a few reasons projects fail to live up to expectations. Bear these in mind when assessing that your project has not lived up to expectations, as you may miss your mark if you don't pay attention to all possibilities. In other words, one needs to attempt to determine if the issue is systemic in nature, or if the failure is a shortcoming in execution. Assuming there is a representative over a project who is accountable, we will assume that this person is the project manager, and thus the failure rests with this project manager. Projects can fail when project managers are not able to do to any of the following:

- Make decisions
- Manage scope
- Manage schedule
- Manage budget
- Manage risks
- Track project progress
- Measure performance
- Communicate effectively
- Resolve problems

Justifying a Data-Driven Organization

For organizations needing to start an analytics or data science program, we offer several suggestions in this section. These same arguments could be used as justification for revamping or rescaling an existing program. We start with motivating factors and a few events that might drive organizational change.

Motivations

Organizations adopt an analytics strategy to help drive business transformation, such as processes and product improvement, market growth and increased profitability. We look at the two most common motivators for analytics adoption – critical business events and adopting analytics as a winning strategy. Critical business events are sharp, sudden changes in the market. Strategic analytics adoption is more proactive and more forward thinking in nature.

Across organizations of all types, sizes, and industries, the decision to invest in analytics is often tightly connected to a critical business event. A critical business event is an incident or phenomenon that disrupts normal business activity and if left unaddressed the business will ultimately fail. The reason for this connection is that an analytics focus might uncover the real issue and thus affect knowledge and subsequent decisions based on that knowledge that enables the appropriate solution to be enacted. In fact, proper analytics technology implementation might turn a reactive response into a proactive innovation opportunity to drive growth for the organization.

Critical Business Events

- Major decline in reimbursement, payment or pricing pressures
- Regulatory compliance changes
- Mergers, acquisition, divestiture or reorganization
- Extreme competitive pressure
- Disruptive technology
- Radically new market approaches
- Critical mass of stagnant culture providing slow and poor decision-making
- Betting survival on new product
- Betting survival on new services
- Radically new marketing strategies and sales channels
- Significant drop in customer retention, loyalty

Analytics as a Winning Strategy

Part I – New Programs and Technologies

Unlike the immediate impact of critical business events that must be addressed immediately, thinking of analytics as a winning strategy is promoted by a forward-looking, long-term mindset. Some strategies focus on growth, some on cost efficiency and some on quicker innovation.

Some common paradigm and innovation drivers include:

- Preparation for new technical capabilities
- Gaining scale to meet market or geographic demands
- Cost savings
- Reduction in organizational structure complexity
- Optimization of internal operations
- Increased business agility

- Improvements to customer experiences or engagements
- Transformation of products or services
- Disruption of the market from new products or services

Part II – More Traditional Methods of Justification

Developing a clear business justification for analytics adoption with tangible, relevant costs and returns can be a complex process. First, review some common business value areas to help justify the analytics adoption journey. We consider five suggestions for an enterprise and define them below; however, factors in industry may cause you to consider areas more aligned to your unique situation.

Five suggestions to consider:

1) Positive return on investment (ROI)
2) Scale
3) Productivity
4) Reliability
5) Sustainability

Positive Return of Investment

Analytics can show positive ROI on both sides of the ROI equation by reducing costs and improving revenue. It can drive down the cost to acquire new patients, customers or constituents. It can drive down the likelihood of losing those constituents as well. Case studies of operational efficiencies abound that show solid cost reduction, from reduction in waste and obsolescence, as well as staff and operational efficiency and more. For example, on the cost reduction side (see Matthews, May 2019; Landi, March 2019):

- Predictive analytics reduce manufacturing downtime
- Hospitals reduce supply chain costs with analytics
- Predictive analytics cuts down employee turnover
- Analytics cuts customer acquisition costs
- Sales activities are more efficiently applied using analytics
- Content marketing costs are reduced using analytics

Similarly, analytics can improve revenue by helping organizations reach more patients, customers, and constituents. Analytics can enhance reimbursement, revenue or gross proceeds. Enterprises can attract more patrons and maximize the contribution per interaction involving products and services. Depending on the entity, they can optimize reimbursement, prices or fees.

In the end, you can justify investments in an analytics program when gross proceeds exceed the total cost of the program – staff resources, technology investment (capital and operating expenses) and any ancillary costs. This is one of the strongest justifications for all enterprises. For-profit entities justify existence by returning value to stakeholders, and as the saying for nonprofits goes, "no margin, no mission," meaning that if you cannot support operations you cannot support your purpose.

Scale

Scale is about being able to grow and manage that growth successfully. One benefit of careful planning of analytics programs and technology is the ability to scale elastically. That means delivering the appropriate amount of resources to the program initiatives set by leadership and management. The ability to add capacity in data, IT and staff resources based on demand, when and where it is needed, is critical in our present fast-paced environment. It prevents organizations from overexpanding or contracting for near-term objectives and thus makes them able to more proactively adapt to environmental and market changes.

Productivity

Productivity is a cornerstone of analytics, especially AI. AI is all about automation – from self-driving cars, to automated warehouses, to cashier-less restaurants, robotic surgery, and self-service healthcare. Add to this the Internet of Things (IoT) enabling smart cities and smart homes and infrastructure. With AI and IoT in place, analytics teams can spend their time on more important business goals.

Reliability

Reliability says "yes" to the question "Is it available when you need it?" Cellular smart phones are highly reliable these days if you are not in a remote location. Reliability is about the analytics infrastructure being able to perform as it was designed and do it now. Reliability is tightly integrated with IT systems and processes. It is meant to weather the storms of immediate, unforeseen short-term events. Are all incumbent data systems maintained, backed up and available when needed? Are all the relevant disaster recovery and failover mechanisms in place? Are people resources available at the time of need?

Reliability can be threatened and hampered by a misalignment of people or policy.

Sustainability

Sustainability has to do with the viability of the program for the long haul. The major threat to reliability (see above paragraph) is based on technical, structural and policy considerations. Sustainability has more to do with softer, less rigid factors. It is meant to endure the effects of unforeseen future events. For example, the knowledge and skills your staff possess greatly affect sustainability. The biggest threat to sustainability is staff turnover. It used to be the case that you could replace staff rather easily. However, now more than ever, the value in the heads of personnel is a key determinant of an organization's success. It may sound cliché, but now for an analytics program to succeed, an organization must hire and retain the appropriate staff. For an example of closing gaps in education, see the Tenure and Education gray box below.

TENURE AND EDUCATION

Enterprises that focus on the short term may have a difficult time. They lack long-term sustainability. Knee-jerk realignments and layoffs limit keeping the knowledge quotient in house. Unlike some roles, it often takes years to become a productive analytics producer. As we will see, it takes technical skills as well as business acumen. At Shopify, one of the fastest-growing tech companies in the world that supports e-commerce, they work very diligently on retaining people. Most people think they should be headquartered in Silicon Valley, but they resisted this temptation and are located in Ottawa, Canada. Unlike Silicon Valley, where the same job candidate may be interviewing with Google, Facebook, Apple and others, Shopify does not have the same competitive pressure. If someone is willing to interview, pass their extensive hiring process, get hired and relocate to Ottawa, there is a level of commitment above just moving to the Valley, where most new hires will jump ship within 18 months to go across the street. In addition, Shopify works very hard to keep its employees happy. They are very long-term and strategically focused, knowing that knowledge workers need time to be fully productive if the company is to maintain its success.

Designing the Organization for Program Success

In a previous section (Characterizing Common Problems), we covered some limitations and gaps that cause the failure of analytics projects and programs. Most of these limitations are driven by culture and organizational design. The cure is highly dependent on the area of application, the industry, and the domain. We feel this is so important to be done right; we are currently writing a book (see Burk and Miner, 2021) where we cover this and technical components of architecture. However, we feel it might be useful to cover here in this book some high-level components providing a basic framework for success. This framework should generalize to most enterprises regardless if they are in healthcare or other areas, and whether they are a public or private business.

Following are comments and recommendations which we have heard in the field:

- Analytics team fell apart.
- Project fell apart.
- Another program! Not another program! I am too busy already! What will it be next month?
- We were making things happen. Management just killed us (cost cutting because there were no visible returns).
- Leadership thought it a great idea, but when we wanted to connect with middle management, they were clueless – upper management had done no training or communication with middle management.
- Leadership / Management thought they would just hire some nerd-types, and leave them alone. We are isolated and we need guidance. We need priority and direction.

- Management was supposed to help us with the problem definitions, priority and deliverables. However, they rarely showed up to our biweekly meetings. We are frustrated.
- I know my college friend's company's analytics program is going gangbusters. This place will never adopt advanced analytics.
- I am the most likely person to lead this at my company, but I don't have a clue how to start!
- Our sector / industry is broken – healthcare. NO INNOVATION except peer review medical research.

Motivation / Communication and Commitment

Establish Clear Business Outcomes

The most successful analytics adoption journeys start with a business outcome in mind, backed up by financial reasoning and support. A business outcome is a concise, defined and observable result or change in business performance captured by a specific measure.

As it is said, success breeds success, and an early win can be a catalyst for buy-in and commitment from leadership and stakeholders.

VALUE OF THE CFO (CHIEF FINANCIAL OFFICER)

A key player in creating and landing an analytics adoption plan is the CFO. The CFO can drive the value of innovation and create a financial plan for adoption. The CFO can also work with the Analytics Strategy Team to develop cost models that compare the value add of such a program. These models should include key measurements to quantify business outcomes.

In the following section, Organization Structure and Design, we discuss organizational structure for the enterprise. To illustrate these concepts, we assume that an Analytics Oversight Team will be adopted in some form within the organization. This team will be responsible for the analysis, planning, execution, and oversight of analytics program initiatives. The Analytics Oversight Team consists of business leaders from all functional areas. It could be part of a center of excellence (COE) or may report directly to the c-suite or board.

The **Analytics Oversight (or Strategy) Team** is responsible for:

- Reviewing business outcomes and creating the business justification plan for possible use cases for the analytics program
- Building or facilitating the project rationalization process, selecting the first and subsequent projects and maintaining prioritized backlogs
- Managing communications with key stakeholders and promoting the analytics adoption journey success and learnings

Here are the key points for this section:

- The key areas to focus on when you develop your data-driven business strategy are to:
  - Define your business justification by identifying business value opportunities
  - Select the right people, processes and technology
  - Establish clear business outcomes to drive transparency and engagement
- Some common business justifications for adoption include:
  - cost
  - scale
  - productivity
  - reliability
  - sustainability

Organization Structure and Design

The Organization and Its Goals – Alignment

It is critical for organizations to be aligned in their goals, objectives, and accountability. Most organizations have some sort of mission statement or statement of purpose. Furthermore, they normally have some sort of strategic plan for the near-term horizon. If done properly this strategic plan cascades into initiatives with objectives. An organization of any size should have objectives that are supported by analytics. For example, some of these might be to maximize growth, maximize revenue, improve patient or customer loyalty, improve employee retention, reduce the cost of services and/or expand geography or markets.

**ALIGNMENT IS ABOUT GETTING EVERYONE
TO MARCH IN THE SAME DIRECTION.**

These high-level objectives start in the c-suite or the boardroom, but need to cascade and permeate the entire organization. Moreover, each functional area should be aware of how its activities impact the larger goal. More about this in the chapter on BI where we discuss alignment of KPIs. But, for now, we need:

1) Each person in the organization to know the strategic objectives
2) Each working group in the organization to discuss and know how their activities affect these objectives
3) All management and leadership to learn how each staff area across the organization will support the initiatives and how they will measure their contribution.
4) In general, decisions on staffing, technology, vendor selection, and service level agreements (SLAs) to support the **entire enterprise**. We saw the lack of this in the previous section on symptoms, Gaps in Analytics Programs, where leadership made a technology platform selection without taking the larger picture into consideration. Obviously, there may be exceptions, but in general this alleviates problems.

Organizational Structure

There are many options for organizational structure for analytics groups and staff, each with its own advantages and drawbacks. NOTE: We are specifically talking about how the analytics personnel fit within the organization, not the overall organization. We present three of the most common types:

- Centralized
- Decentralized
- Matrix or hybrid structures

Centralized Analytics

Centralized analytics groups normally exist within a COE or similar group. The leader of this group may be part of the c-suite, with a Chief Analytics Officer reporting to the CEO or president of the organization (see Figure 2.1).

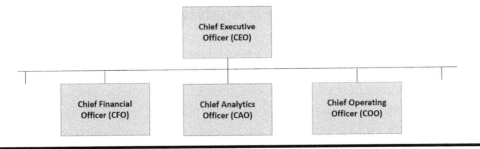

Figure 2.1 Centralized analytics organization with chief analytics officer reporting to CEO.

Alternatively, they could be a vice president or director-level position reporting to the c-level, COO, CFO or CMO. This is normally determined by the company culture as some companies are more operationally driven, others marketing driven. This group has high accountability and may often be on the board meeting agenda. The advantages of this structure are the visibility and energy it gets from this high-level reporting. Additionally, all group members have similar backgrounds: most are data scientists, statisticians, or from other data-focused backgrounds. They speak a similar language and often share similar psychological profiles. They want to make a contribution via data.

The drawbacks of this homogeneous type of group are that they do not know the business as well as people in the functional areas of finance, marketing, sales, operations, HR (human resources) and customer service. And they rely on others outside the center of excellence to identify the problems to work on. **AND, analytics projects are a team sport.** So, it is critical that members in an analytics COE have access to and support of functional personnel. Functional team members are often called subject matter experts (SMEs, we cover in a later gray box section, Putting it Altogether: An Example of the Data Science Team in Action), as they know the problem area very well. In addition, if not carefully planned for, you can run into issues with the "day jobs" of functional personnel. If you have a finance manager with limited personnel and a list of deadlines, they are responsible for and being judged on meeting these deadlines successfully, they may treat analytics projects as a secondary priority. This leads to the frustration of the analytics personnel, as they are highly dependent on these functional areas for critical education and support.

Decentralized or Embedded Analytics

A decentralized or embedded analytics structure is where the major functional areas (accounting, finance, marketing, sales, operations, customer service) each have their own analytics specialist members. These members often have started with experience in the functional area and then as their careers progress and they take on additional responsibilities they add knowledge of analytics, data science, and statistics. They are the "go-to" people when members of the team need something.

An advantage of this structure is that the analytics staff also have strong subject matter skills and therefore they are less reliant on going outside to get the needed information. Furthermore, when they need information they know exactly who to contact. Finally, the leader of this functional area is responsible for the success of the project and so this is the "day job" when the organization is structured this way.

The disadvantage of this framework is that the embedded analytics professionals often feel isolated and out of touch with other analytics types. They do not have comrades to bounce ideas off of and may become disheartened in their jobs.

Hybrid (report to both an Analytics director AND a functional boss) – **also called a MATRIX organization:**

As the name "hybrid" connotes, this is a mixture that has the advantages of both centralized and decentralized structures. The way this works is that analytics personnel report into a COE, but there are teams that move across different vertical functional areas and are project driven. This is a form of a matrix organization. It is meant to reduce the limitations of each of the previous structures, but allows analytics professionals to be within a common group for camaraderie and learning while at the same time being part of a functional team for specific projects. Another advantage is that an employee can move across functional areas – say finance, then human relations (HR), etc. This allows for a variety of different projects and learning opportunities. This can keep the job fresh and interesting. It can provide career progression that helps employee retention; this is especially true for the retention of disciplinary teams, as these groups of functional specialists are preserved from one project to the next (UpCouncil, 2019). For an example of this structure, see Figure 2.2.

You can see from this figure that there is a dual responsibility of team members. Vertically, they report into the analytics leader. Horizontally, they

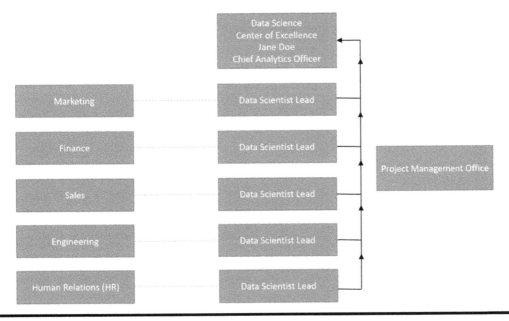

Figure 2.2   Matrix organization (Data Science Direct with cross-function reporting).

are an asset of a functional area. Here we have examples of functional areas including marketing, finance, sales, engineering, and HR. In a similar model, projects and project managers could replace these functional areas.

Multidisciplinary Roles for Analytics

We now illustrate important roles in the analytics program – remember that analytics is a team sport. Of course, it is important for any organization to hire and support the best people. In addition, retaining these people is of particular importance in deep knowledge areas such as analytics (we examined this previously in this chapter – see gray box, "**Tenure and Education**").

The size of the organization, the sector, and the mission will dictate roles for analytics. We briefly outline a few roles that exist to support analytics projects:

- Data scientists
- Data engineers
- Citizen data scientists

- Developers
- Business experts
- Business leaders
- Project managers

We are providing minimal definitions below, but note these roles can overlap and differ by organization.

Data Scientists

This term has morphed over time. It used to be a catch-all phrase for a unicorn, meaning it rarely existed as it covered a broad set of skills and the data scientist was meant to be a master of all! Now the term is used in a much more realistic fashion. There are at least three domains that a data scientist needs to understand, but not necessarily be an expert. The first is some sort of mathematical or quantitative background. This could be in applied mathematics, statistics, operations research, engineering, econometrics, computer science or similar. The second is a great use of information technology; often they are very good at scripting/coding, storage, and access technology and have a good knowledge of digitized data. Finally, they are not theorists, but practitioners, and they have knowledge of domain of application – some areas of healthcare, business, social policy or similar.

Data Engineers

This term evolved from the data scientist role. As stated above, its function was originally considered part of being a data scientist unicorn. The data engineer knows a lot of what the data scientist does but focuses on the data piping around analytics projects. They are heavily involved in sourcing historical data for analysis and modeling and then making the production data available to apply models for insight and action.

Citizen Data Scientists

Citizen data scientists are similar to data scientists, but they know a lot more about the domain they are applying analytics to than the data scientist. Creation of the "citizen data scientist" role is about the democratization of data science across the organization. It enables anyone with the aptitude and mindset to be part of the analytics fabric within the enterprise. Citizen data scientists normally start their careers in the domain and then add math and computer skills. Data scientists normally start the other way, beginning with a strong knowledge of math and computer science and then adding an area of application to their skillset.

Developers

Developers create interfaces between the back-end data to the front-end application, thus making analytics available to consumers. Developers may work closely with data scientists and data engineers to create these interfaces, or they may use tools independently and work with business users or citizen data scientists.

Business Experts

Business experts provide the context and very important domain knowledge around analytics projects. At times, they are historians, knowing how changes in the business result in changes in the data. We will see more about this in the next chapter, under **Processes Drive Data**. Moreover, without process knowledge, data is meaningless; therefore, data science or AI without business expertise will fail.

Business Leaders

Business leaders provide resources (budget and people), energy and motivation. They provide smooth access to IT and other resources external to the team. They are accountable for project results and therefore they will drive to make sure the team is on track and schedule.

Project Managers

Project managers are vital to organizations with a matrix structure and are a good idea in any analytics program. They are responsible for project goals and objectives, metrics, deliverables, and documentation. They schedule meetings that include project kick-offs with leadership, working team meetings on a regular cadence that review tasks completed and scheduled, and project results and next steps again with leadership. They are responsible for all documentation, metrics, successes and end-of-project reviews of analytics projects.

The size of the organization will dictate whether all these roles are required or whether certain people will have to fulfill the tasks of multiple roles.

MOST MAJOR CHALLENGES IN ANALYTICS ARE PEOPLE AND PROCESS

Kaggle is recognized as an online community of data scientists and machine learners. They promote many analytics competitions and host surveys of analytics professionals. These surveys have some of the highest response rates and are well done, providing valuable information.

In August 2017, they conducted "The State of Data Science & Machine Learning" survey with over 16,000 responses. There were several questions, but one very meaningful question for us was "What barriers are faced at work?" Out of the top 15 responses, almost all were people and process issues. There was only one in the top 15 that was clearly about technologies or platform, #12, limitation of tools. Most of the others we have categorized in this chapter. As an exercise, see if you can map the following list to our characteristics. These are in order, #1 being the most frequent.

1. Dirty data
2. Lack of data science talent
3. Lack of management / financial support
4. Lack of clear question to answer
5. Data unavailable or difficult to access
6. Results not used by decision-makers
7. Explaining data science to others
8. Privacy issues
9. Lack of domain expert input
10. Can't afford data science team
11. Multiple ad hoc environments
12. Limitation of tools
13. Need to coordinate with IT
14. Expectations of project impact
15. Integrating findings into decisions

See www.kaggle.com/surveys/2017.

Analytics Oversight Committee (AOC) and Governance Committee (Board Report)

We will not go into depth in this book on this topic, but make a few remarks for consideration. It should be obvious that visibility to leadership is highly correlated with results. It is therefore very important to form some oversight or steering committee with accountability to the CEO and board of directors. There should be monthly or quarterly reporting of activities with metrics of success, postmortems of projects and future plans. The committee will determine whether projects are continued or eliminated. This committee will have a say in the list of projects for the analytics team and help prioritize them. Visibility and accountability of the AOC can leverage future budgets.

It is not uncommon for analytics committees to be sister groups to IT committees, as they can share the same data governance and security policies.

Ethics in AI and data science is a very hot topic with Cambridge Analytica, Facebook and others under severe scrutiny in 2018 and continuing throughout 2019 (Gourley, March, 2018). The EU has adopted special laws to help in the ethical use of data including the General Protection Data Regulation (GDPR) implemented in May 2018 (De Groot, July 15, 2019). Ethics can roll up into an oversight committee or an ethics department.

For more information on building a successful analytics program from organizational structure to data and analytics architectures, see Burk and Miner (2021).

Postscript

We have just covered the justification for an analytics program. Moreover, we covered limitations and gaps in many programs and how you can overcome these gaps by correctly designing your program for success. Next, we looked at similarities across the different analytics domains before we dove deeper into each. In our next chapter, we lay the foundations. We take a topical look at what unites these techniques and technologies. We will start to learn a common language and at the same time we will discover there are many dialects – some of the basics of terminology of AI and data science, and also consider algorithms, mental concepts, models, paradigms, decisions and the need for additional tools that are "in vogue" today. We will show you that there is a need well beyond what is commonly presented – an analytics culture, an organization designed for success and many things that are often not considered but are paramount.

References

Bahcall, S. 2019. *Loonshots: How to Nurture the Crazy Ideas That Win Wars, Cure Diseases, and Transform Industries.* St. Martin's Press.

Burk, Scott. 2006. "A better statistical method for A/B testing in marketing campaigns," *Marketing Bulletin*, 17, Technical Note 3.

Burk, Scott, and Miner, Gary. Forthcoming in 2021. *Designing An Integrated AI, Analytics, and Data Science Architecture for Your Organization.* Rutledge/ Taylor and Francis Press.

Covey, Stephen R. 1989. *The 7 Habits of Highly Effective People: Powerful Lessons in Personal Change.* FranklinCovey Publishing.

De Groot, J. 2019. *What Is the General Data Protection Regulation? Understanding & Complying with GDPR Requirements in 2019.* https://digitalguardian.com/bl og/what-gdpr-general-data-protection-regulation-understanding-and-complying -gdpr-data-protection.

Gourley, B. 2018. *AI and Big Data: Facebook and Cambridge Analytica Are Writing New Case Studies For Us All.* https://ctovision.com/the-ethics-of-big-data-faceb ook-and-cambridge-analytica-are-writing-new-case-studies-for-us-all/.

Landi, H. 2019. *Hospital Leaders See Clear ROI for Supply Chain Analytics, But Most Use Outdated Processes: Survey.* www.fiercehealthcare.com/finance/hospital-lea ders-see-clear-roi-for-supply-chain-analytics-but-most-use-outdated-processes.

Levison, Marc. 2016. *The Box: How the Shipping Container Made the World Smaller and the World Economy Bigger* (2nd ed.). Princeton University Press. ISBN: 978-0-691-17081-7.

Matthews, K. 2019. *How to Get a Return on Your Predictive Analytics Investment: What Companies Should Know.* https://towardsdatascience.com/how-to-get-a-r eturn-on-your-predictive-analytics-investment-what-companies-should-know-74 207fced2ba.

UpCouncil. 2019. *Matrix Organizational Structure: Everything You Need to Know.* www.upcounsel.com/matrix-organizational-structure.

Resources for the Avid Learner

1 Banko, Michele, and Brill, Eric. 2001. *Scaling to Very Very Large Corpora for Natural Language Disambiguation, Microsoft Research.* Association for Computational Linguistics. Available at Microsoft, www.microsoft.com/en-us/ research/publication/scaling-to-very-very-large-corpora-for-natural-language -disambiguation/.

2 Collins, Jim. 2004. *Built to Last: Successful Habits of Visionary Companies (Good to Great).* Harper Business Publishing.
3 Do, Chuong. 2017. *What Is the Most Effective Way to Structure a Data Science Team?* https://towardsdatascience.com/what-is-the-most-effective-way-to-struc ture-a-data-science-team-498041b88dae.
4 Godin, Seth. 2018. *This Is Marketing: You Can't Be Seen Until You Learn To See.* Portfolio: Penguin Group (USA) LLC.
5 Wolpert, D.H., and Macready, W.G. 2005. "Coevolutionary free lunches," *IEEE Transactions on Evolutionary Computation,* 9(6): 721–35.

Chapter 3

Some Fundamentals – Process, Data, and Models

Keywords: Data-Driven, Process, Models, Algorithms, CRISP-DM, No Free Lunch Theorem, Signal and Noise

Preamble

In Chapter 2, we considered shortcomings of existing analytics programs – limitations and gaps in culture and organizations. We discussed building a successful analytics program by justifying and selling the concept throughout the organization, then avoiding gaps by redesigning or designing the program for success. In this chapter, we move into the basics that are shared across different data-driven techniques before we launch into upcoming chapters, where we cover each topic independently and more in-depth.

The Hip, the Hype, the Fears, the Intrigue, and the Reality

The Hype

"We don't consider customers cargo," said Jaguar's head of R&D, Wolfgang Epple, in 2015. "We don't want to build a robot that delivers the cargo from A to B."

Reality

(According to Thompson Reuters) Jaguar Land Rover has since invested US$25 million in Lyft to cash in on the autonomous trend.

Introduction

What motivated us to write the book? We have visited with people across many industries and organizations and discovered recurring themes. In the last chapter, we covered a recurring theme – *what keeps analytics programs from being as successful as they could be?* A different environment, culture, and structure make all the difference in the world toward success or failure, and we provided some guidelines.

This book covers a very broad range of topics, from business intelligence (BI) to artificial intelligence (AI). Some topics are more complex, some more intuitive, some have long histories, some are more novel. So, an obvious question is, what do they have in common? Why all these topics? **The singular underlying element in the book is using data to solve real-world problems.** Other recurring themes are data, signal vs noise, models, and algorithms.

This chapter will cover the commonalities of practice and application amongst the various methods covered in the book. What do data science and mathematical programming have in common? What do statistics and AI have in common? Is there a common process methodology that an organization can use whether the problem they are working on is a decision science problem or a statistical design? *Is there a common framework?* Let us call these various groups of practitioners as "camps." These different camps speak different languages, yet their conversations are often about the same thing. We will not translate everything, but we will try to synthesize some common practices in this chapter.

One of the most important themes of this book is the need for lots of tools in the toolbox. Why do we emphasize a list of tools when there are some very powerful ones that solve a lot of problems, take for example AI. Because **there is no universally optimal methodology or analytics paradigm that works best on all problems**. We will explore this in this chapter: **There is No Free Lunch**.

Framework for Analytics – Some Fundamentals

We now explore some fundamentals that are often overlooked when applying or consuming analytics. These are fundamental and important because many people assume them away, and when there are issues or shortcomings, they look for in the wrong direction to solve the problems. A few fundamentals here:

- Processes and systems are everywhere
- Data are generated by a process
- We collect some of this data
- We analyze data and create models
- Analytics and models provide insight
- Insights inform action
- Action improves life

Processes Are Everywhere

We often do not think in these terms, but you participate in and observe thousands of processes and systems in a day. You get out of bed and take a shower: that shower is a process. You dress and ready yourself for the day, which is a process. You fix breakfast, which is a process. Getting to work by walking, car, bus or train is a process or a multistep process.

A system is a set of interrelated processes. The bus to work contains a large number of systems – an electrical system, an engine, a powertrain, GPS and many more. These systems are composed of thousands of processes. Each and every one of these processes generates an observable result. Each observable result can be recorded. Recorded results are data.

Processes Drive Data

We will soon explore models and algorithms. For algorithms to generate models, we must feed them data. We collect data at a dizzying rate these days, as we explained in Chapter 1 and we will talk deeply about all sorts of data in Chapter 8. We collect data in a variety of ways – manual entry into smart phones, computers, and notepads. Computers collect most of the data without us even knowing – cameras, sensors, voice, electronic sensors, machines, devices, telemetry. At the heart of this collection are again systems and processes. We do not think about it most of the time, but when we do, we realize life consists of processes. Therefore, we have a great opportunity to improve life by understanding these processes via analytics.

The following are some examples of processes and systems and the data they generate.

Examples of Processes and Systems	Data Generated
Human / biological systems	EKGs, ECGs, smart watch data
Smart phone video recording	Video (MOV, MP4 data)
Book writing	Handwritten pages or word-processing files
Delivery, postal, transportation	Telematics, GPS and logistics data
Smart cities	Data from sensors, cameras (CCTV), traffic impedance detectors
Doctor's visit	Data in an electronic medical or health record (EMR/EHR) system or computerized physician order entry (CPOE)
Exercising, gym routines, workouts	Log book, smart phone app
NFL games	Video, sports statistics, play movement
Medical bill payment	Billing codes, patient info, claim adjudication, payment splits, payment processing
Customer survey process	Customer ratings, comments

Moreover, note that there are millions of things that could be collected as data but only some are collected, although the number of processes collected as data is increasing. In fact, think about video. The streets of most cities a few years ago were just as full with the bustle of activity as they are today. However, today, that bustle is captured on video, being recorded, generating data that can be analyzed.

As said by a famous statistician (W. Edwards Deming) a long time ago: "*In God we trust, all others bring data.*" We can do that more than ever today. Data has the ability if used correctly to separate anecdotes and hyperbole from facts. In this book, we explore how we can use data intelligently to build analytical models. First, we need to explore "what is a model?"

SIGNAL AND NOISE – ANOTHER CONSISTENT THEME

Data that we collect hopefully contains some signal, i.e., what we are interested in quantifying or qualifying. However, all collected data will contain noise as well. Using the techniques described in this book, we want to be able to filter out the noise and benefit from modeling the signal relationships. The best example to explore this is the concept of picking up a radio signal. We hope most people reading have experienced trying to dial in a radio station. When you are between stations, you are hearing what is referred to as "white noise" and you use the tuner to dial in the radio station you want to hear as best you can.

Another noise example is when you are talking with a person on a cell phone in a public environment like an airport. There is a lot of "background noise" and the task for the listener is trying to distinguish the signal – what is being said, what is of interest, versus the background noise, the voices and the din around the person in the airport.

For a data-driven example, assume you are trying to determine what is important to restaurant customers. One way to try to figure this out is by using surveys. There is a lot of noise in restaurant surveys. Some people take time to thoughtfully respond and some people just check boxes randomly. These random responders create a lot of noise. All data involves a measurement process and the level of signal and noise is greatly influenced by the measurement process. Measurements made by an electron microscope are much more accurate than when one of the authors measures the length of a wall with a tape measure.

Various mixtures exist of the amount of signal versus the amount of noise. Surveys are very noisy – people's opinions change daily... mood affects, etc. How much signal can you measure vs noise? Podcast – background noise – can one use a filter to decrease background noise? Some podcast hosts use filters after the program has been recorded to take out the background noise. Obviously, filtering is popular in Hollywood productions both for audio and video cleanup.

Finally, an alternative to signal to noise is looking at it the other way around, which is how much **information** is contained in data. A podcast, movie, radio – all of it is data. Information, signal, and noise will be very important concepts as we move forward. We will see that if we have a lot of information we do not necessarily need a ton of data.

It is important to know when more data is useful or not useful. We will cover this more in depth in our chapter on data (Chapter 9). For rare or infrequent events, it is useful to collect data over longer time periods and this leads to bigger data sets. However, contrary to popular opinion, "Big Data" is not the solution for many analytics problems.

Models, Methods, and Algorithms

Models, Models, Models

We will be talking a great deal about models in this book: AI models, machine learning models, statistical models and more. We will be using this in a very general sense, but what is a model? We deal with models unconsciously, all the time. Without them, we would have a hard time navigating through life. A model is just a representation of a mental concept. We provide three diverse examples. First, take a look at the following (Figure 3.1):

Yes, the number seven is a model. All numbers are models. Humans constructed the ideas of counting long, long ago. We have since created volumes about mathematics and sometimes numbers are useful in mathematical theory. Seven is also a whole number, it is an integer, it is discrete, it is halfway between six and eight, it is odd, it is prime and it pays in Vegas! All of these concepts circle around a mental model of the number seven.

When I (Scott) tell people that they have never *seen* a number, they have a hard time with it. "What? No, this is a number and it is seven, it is real and it exists." The fact is you have never seen a number! It is a concept, a model, a manmade one. You have only seen a representation of a number. While there are books on pi and epsilon and cool relationships of numbers to nature, they are still mental models, concepts. To put it another way, a number is something that man created to describe the world he lives in. ***A model is a representation of reality, not reality itself.*** It may be a very good representation of reality or a very poor representation. A quote by a famous statistician, but it applies to all models – *"All models are wrong, some models are useful"* – George E. P. Box (see the following gray box about how airplanes are based on old information).

Figure 3.1   A simple model.

**NEWS ALERT! AIRPLANES BASED ON
300-YEAR-OLD MODELS!**

Have you flown lately? Did you know airplanes are designed on old models that we know are wrong?

Airplanes, cars, almost every engineering feat that you use every day is based on an antiquated model called Newtonian physics, which most high school and undergraduate courses revolved around. But we know that Newtonian models are wrong. They are too simple when you get into the teeny tiny nitty-gritty of matter and its relationships. Einsteinian physics, quantum mechanics, etc. are much closer to the truth of the way things really work. And, it turns out that even these models have flaws.

Yet, we fly billions of miles a year, drive billions of miles a year and use kitchen and home gadgets very successfully. Engineers are not using the latest and greatest physics models to build everyday things because it does not matter. They use what works well for the problems they solve and the theory that is over 300 years old. YES, 300 years old, not the latest and greatest, not the sexiest quantum mechanics. That is consistent with our theme: know there are many tools and use the right one for the job.

Statistical Models

A simple statistical model might be estimating tomorrow's high temperature based on today's high temperature. Without any other information we would probably estimate tomorrow's temperature to be the same as today's. This is a *simple estimation model*, called a *naïve model in time series*. And, you would not expect this model to be particularly accurate. Note there are only three outcomes:

- our estimate is low
- our estimate is high
- our estimate is correct

But we would usually be wrong with such a simple estimate.

From there we can add many improvements to our model. For instance, we can use several years of historical data to make the forecast more accurate, thus creating a time series model. Alternatively, we could use other factors like airflow, pressure differences, etc. to predict tomorrow's temperature via an algorithmic or machine learning method. An algorithm is simply a process or set of rules to be followed in calculations or other problem-solving operations. It is a recipe of sorts with instructions to follow. Following the set of instructions for this problem results in a formula (sometimes it may result in a long set of computer codes depending on the problem you are trying to solve). This formula is our solution, the representation of our model for this problem. This type of model is a predictive model, because based on new inputs it predicts an outcome. Predictive models are a major topic of this book and we create them in lots of ways in upcoming chapters. In addition, it should be noted that using this model we would often be wrong, but hopefully we would outperform simple guessing or the naïve method. How do we improve results? By knowing many methods and knowing where and when to apply them – we help you do this in this book!

Rules of Thumb, Heuristic Models

Another model or concept that is very useful is a non-algorithmic model that is based upon studying the world around us, an observational model. This is sometimes called a rule-of-thumb model, or heuristic model. Vilfredo Pareto, an Italian economist, developed the Pareto Principle in 1896. He showed that 80% of the land in Italy was owned by 20% of the population. This simple rule has proven itself many times over in everything from economics, to healthcare, to natural science, to social networking. It therefore is sometimes referred to as "the law of the vital few," the "80/20 rule" or the "principle of factor sparsity."

To summarize, models are everywhere. They are mental concepts that we use to navigate our world. They can be generated by simple observation, by mathematical derivation and via algorithms. The models we will emphasize in this book will include all three. BI and visual analytics emphasize **observation and human cognition**. Predictive and advanced analytics, machine learning and AI depend primarily on **algorithmic generation** of models. Statistical, linear and mathematical programming models are normally derived by **mathematical derivation**. **Simulation** is a bit broader in that we create an algorithm to simulate a model that could be derived mathematically or simply based on a heuristic. We cover all of these and more in this book.

A Note on Cognition

Scott has a particular interest in where cognition happens. Essentially, in description, prediction or analysis of any type these days, cognition occurs in two places – a machine or *machines* and *your head*. The real benefit of cognition is two-fold: increased knowledge and improved decision-making. Today, we have access to more information via our smart phone than all the information than the Library of Congress has on its shelves. Note that the information via that phone is not curated and may be garbage, whereas presumably most of the information in the Library of Congress is valid or at least vetted. Nevertheless, information via a machine is readily accessible and may be useful.

If we use that information to make a decision, we still do the final computation for the decision in our head. There may be a layer of analytics involved in the smart phone information as well. It could be that we are trying to decide where to eat and we use the wisdom of the crowd, in other words, some sort of restaurant rating app. That app gives us a map with pins of the locations of the restaurants and distance to our location, a snapshot of cuisine offered, the customer ratings, hours and more. We mentally process that information to make a decision. So ***this decision is augmented by analytics***. We will see several examples where knowledge and decisions are shared by machines and humans.

However, there is another set of problems that are decided and acted upon solely by machines. **Self-driving cars are an example:** the sensors of the car stream data into data stores, this data is run against computer code (generated by a predictive model) and a prediction is passed to a second layer of code, where a decision is generated (by a prescriptive model – the optimal action based on the current data) and subsequently passed to the control system of the car to accelerate, brake or turn. This is done continuously and in microseconds.

We will discuss the full landscape where most or all of the decisions and actions are done by a machine as in the self-driving car example. And, we will discuss methods where most of the cognition is performed in the brain as in the restaurant selection problem. But it is very important to understand the shortcomings of each option. **There are things that humans do very well, there are things that machines do very well and there are things done best by the marriage of mind and machine.** Be careful in the selection of your technique for your problem at hand.

Algorithms, Algorithms, Algorithms

We mentioned algorithms briefly, but let's dive in a little more in this section. For simplicity, we talked about algorithms as recipes. More formally, an algorithm is a sequence of instructions typically to solve a class of problems or perform a computation. In analytics, we analyze data and build models with algorithms. We will see that we can build predictive models to, well, predict things. Consider building a predictive model to determine the length of stay in a hospital, not "in general" but with specificity for "each individual." We may use many different historical factors (age, gender, disease, comorbidity, and many others) to build our model. We will cover this specific process in detail in a later chapter (Chapter 6), but for now, suppose we have a model.

Once we have a model, we can represent that model in computer code. We now have a model that is, yes, represented by an algorithm. This algorithm is now used for a different purpose. This scoring algorithm is used to create a score, an estimate of our length of stay for a new patient given their unique characteristics. This confuses many people! The terms "model" and "algorithm" are often used interchangeably, but most of the time this does not cause major problems.

To simplify things, some people just call that executable code that scores new patients, a model. The following is a simple diagram that attempts to capture this (see Figure 3.2). The actual process will be covered in various chapters throughtout the book, depending on the application.

This is another example that, if you understand it, will put you well ahead of most people that are practicing predictive analytics today. At some point, when you feel comfortable, you might do a search and see some blog posts on the confusion. It is very enlightening and **illustrates another reason you need this book**!

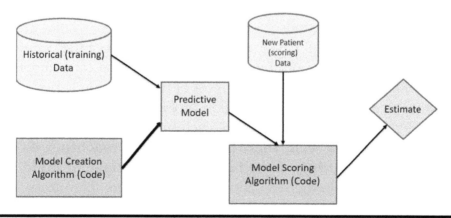

Figure 3.2 Algorithm use and model creation.

Distinction between Methods That Generate Models

We will explore several methods of analysis and model building in this book. We now make some brief comments on some advantages and disadvantages of these methods. We will provide in-depth coverage of each in subsequent chapters.

The first example is when we derive a solution from a small set of formulas or rules that are evaluated in a finite number of operations. These are called *closed-form expressions*. A very simple closed-form expression is the average of a sample. Step 1: sum up all the elements in the sample. Step 2: take that sum and divide by the number of elements in the sample. The result is the statistical mean or average of the sample. Some solutions require many more steps, but it is always a finite number of steps. At the heart of these closed-form expressions are assumptions and solving with calculus to derive the closed-form expression. So thanks, math people, for providing a much simpler set of equations or better yet a computer program implementation of these formulas that solves it for us.

The major advantages of closed-form solutions are they are less computer intensive, meaning they will run quickly. In addition, they are often transparent, meaning you can understand what the model they generate actually does when you apply them. The main disadvantage of these solutions is that they most often come with assumptions. Some statistical and mathematical algorithms are closed-form solutions. When the assumptions made are tenable, these are often the best method to choose.

The second set is algorithms that require a computer program to search for the best answer. Machine learning and other data mining methods are domains for these algorithms. This is typically done by specifying a candidate solution (model or solution space) and letting the computer run until it finds the best possible solution based on some criteria. An example could be imaging processing, where we use a model-building algorithm to generate a model to predict a brain aneurysm based on patient brain scans.

However, using these algorithms, the best answer might never be found. Why? Read on…

The main advantage of these algorithms is that fewer assumptions have to be made. They are very forgiving, whereas the closed-form solutions sometimes are not. And, machine learning algorithms often generate very good models. However, depending on what algorithm you select, they may not be transparent in how they actually do what they are doing – remember the 2008 financial crisis? Another drawback is that if these algorithms are not carefully used they could generate a local optimum, meaning that a better solution exists, but the algorithm did not find it. Finally, they may require a lot of computing time, but this is less of a constraint with modern technology and this is the reason behind their popularity.

Finally, some models are developed without any formal formula or algorithm. They are developed by experience and observation. These are **heuristic models**, or they may be called a *"rule of thumb"* model. An example is a deterministic rule based on someone's experience or expert opinion as we saw previously with the Pareto Principle. If I am working on a manufacturing line, I can posit that 80% of the defects will be caused by 20% of the process.

Another heuristic model is a rule-based model. We might formulate these rules into a computer script than can be executed on demand. For example, if someone comes into my website on a specific landing page from this zip code and also came through yesterday, then present them with this offer based on a set of rules encoded into my website. The advantages of heuristic models are they are transparent, simple and easy to create. They can also be enhanced and made more powerful via computer simulation.

There Is No Free Lunch

We just covered three classes of models, but we also have available AI models, machine learning models, linear programming models and many more. Which one is best? Everyone likes shortcuts. Shortcuts help in life by saving mental energy, time and resources. While we hope this book is useful in determining the correct method to do your analysis, we know from experience that there is no free lunch. Actually, this thought is an extension of a formal theorem. **The no free lunch theorem.** *There is no panacea for analytics.*

Certain analytic solutions are often presented as the Killer Tech Bullet. *For example, AI is all you need!* It solves everything and soon we will all not have a care in the world. We will not have to work because robots and automation will do everything for us. We will not have to drive. We will not have to think because AI will do all our thinking for us. *Unfortunately, AI is not a silver bullet either* at a grand scale. In fact, it is not a silver bullet on a minor scale.

We present many technological developments across decades:

- In many circumstances, the older ones outperform the new ones (AI is actually an old idea).
- At times, the simpler methods outperform the more complicated ones.
- In some domains – healthcare, science and ethical business practice you would like transparency of these models. You want to know how they work. You do not want a black box (see "What Is a Black Box Solution – Skynet and Wall Street" in the next gray box).

WHAT IS A BLACK BOX SOLUTION – SKYNET AND WALL STREET

In science, computing, and engineering, a black box is a system which can be viewed in terms of its inputs and outputs, without any knowledge of its internal workings. In other words, it is NOT transparent in how it works.

Skynet was a highly advanced computer system possessing artificial general intelligence in the movie *Terminator*. Because Skynet had self-generated its intelligence, no one knew what the computers and code inside Skynet really did or what intelligence it included. **The code and system were a black box**. Once it became self-aware, it saw humanity as a threat to its existence and it decided to trigger a nuclear holocaust on Judgment Day. Later, it would develop and deploy an army of terminators against humanity, whose survivors had formed a resistance group. Bottom line: black boxes and the end of humanity – not good.

2008 FINANCIAL COLLAPSE

Wall Street professionals and high-frequency traders have been using machine learning models for years for trading and optimizing portfolios. Many attribute the 2008 meltdown to financial institutions not really understanding the models they were running (Lewis, 2010; Baldwin, 2019; *Northwestern Business Review*, 2016). This led to overconfidence, which led to a cycle of overlending, leverage and risk that tanked the economy.

BLACK BOX APPEARING AS A WHITE BOX

What can be more transparent than the written word, text? Or, search results from a search bar entry? Yet, Cambridge Analytica, Facebook, Google, and Twitter, among others, all have come under fire for having algorithms that presented biased results to users. Cambridge Analytica is now defunct due to exposure by many sources of its business practices. Other tech companies have had to appear before Congress and special committees.

At the end of the day, **no method, paradigm or algorithm is UNIVERSALLY optimal!** This is an extension of the **No Free Lunch Theorem** developed by David Wolpert. In 2005, Wolpert and Macready themselves indicated that the first theorem in their paper "state[s] that any two optimization algorithms are equivalent when their performance is averaged across all possible problems" (see Wolpert and Macready, 2005). In brief, there are many things to consider. The bottom line is not to let someone sell you a solution that will only apply to a small subset of your problems. Just be cautious about separating the hype from reality.

An interesting machine learning example of this is referenced in the "Resources for the Avid Learner" section at the end of the chapter (see Banko and Brill, 2001), where they compare four machine learning algorithms to determine which meaning of a word is activated by the use of the word in a particular context (disambiguation). Let us define the "best" algorithm as the one having the highest test accuracy. They start with a training set of a half-million words and a simple memory-based learner performs the best, ranks #1. Interestingly, as the number of words used in training increases up to a billion words, the rank positioning of the four methods inverts. The algorithm that originally ranked worst, #4 (a winnow algorithm), now performs the best, and the original winner (simple memory-based learner) performs the worst of the four, rank #4. As with most situations, the best, and we have to be careful what we mean by "best," is dependent on the data!

Note something important here, in defining what you mean by best. **One of the most important takeaways of this book is to think and ask what "best" means!** What is the best mutual fund? What is the best workout? What is the best diet? Read the headlines: you will definitely see these in the title! But, best workout for what? Best workout for a body builder?

Best workout for endurance training? Best workout to improve flexibility and reduce joint pain? **One important takeaway here – do not let someone else find what is best or optimal for you – define it based on your needs and the nuances you face.**

In the example above, we defined "best" as having the highest training accuracy. We could have defined "best" as the fastest to train, cheapest, the one with the most vowels in the name, anything, any criteria. **DEFINE "BEST."** When someone is trying to sell you something by telling you it is the best, ask for comparisons with "worse" products and ask "why." When someone says XYZ is best – make them define what "best" means. We will be talking about this in detail in Chapter 11 on optimization, where we have to define carefully our criteria of what "best" means in a rigorous sense. In the meantime, whenever you read something, engage with someone or hear something and the term "best" is used, think critically about what it means!

A Process Methodology for Analytics

Professionals in healthcare know that protocols and standards are very important to improve efficiency, decrease costs and improve outcomes. Standards should serve as guidelines that are flexible, but offer a framework in which to work. The CRISP-DM (Cross-Industry Standard Process for Data Mining) was developed to provide a framework for the data mining process. While it was developed for data mining or machine learning, it is applicable to many analytics, statistical and other data-related projects.

It was developed in 1996 by analysts representing Daimler Chrysler, SPSS and NCR. CRISP-DM provides a nonproprietary and freely available standard process for feeding data mining into the general problem-solving strategy of a business or research unit. There are many references for this process; an example is seen in Larose (see Larose, 2005).

According to the standard, most data mining (data-related projects) have a lifecycle that can be broken into six phases of interrelated activities. This process is illustrated in Figure 3.3. It should be noted that the phase sequence is adaptive, meaning that the next phase of the sequence is often dependent on the results from a previous phase. It is iterative, meaning that each phase may need to be revisited based upon the knowledge discovery or results in a later phase. For example, in the modeling phase, it may be determined that certain variables need to be transformed (modified) and

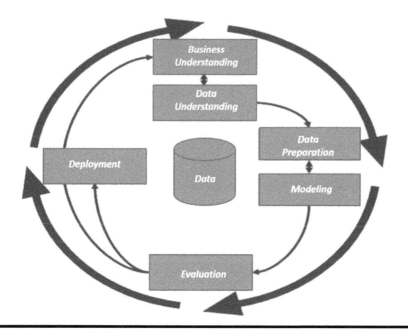

Figure 3.3 The CRISP-DM process flow.

therefore the process would revert back to the previous data preparation phase.

This process template affords continuous learning, meaning lessons learned in previous projects may be incorporated into new ones. Reiterating that the six phases of the process cycle may be directly sequential, we will provide a quick guide of the six phases of CRISP-DM.

CRISP-DM: The Six Phases:

- **Business understanding phase** (this first phase in the CRISP-DM standard process may also be termed the research understanding phase)
  - Enunciate the project objectives and requirements clearly in terms of the business or research unit as a whole.
  - Translate these goals and restrictions into the formulation of a data mining problem definition.
  - Prepare a preliminary strategy for achieving these objectives.
- **Data understanding phase**
  - Collect the data.
  - Use exploratory data analysis to familiarize yourself with the data and discover initial insights.
  - Evaluate the quality of the data.

- If desired, select interesting subsets that may contain actionable patterns.
- **Data preparation phase**
  - Prepare from the initial raw data the final data set that is to be used for all subsequent phases. This phase is very labor intensive.
  - Select the cases and variables you want to analyze and that are appropriate for your analysis.
  - Perform transformations on certain variables, if needed.
  - Clean the raw data so that it is ready for the modeling tools.
- **Modeling phase**
  - Select and apply appropriate modeling techniques.
  - Calibrate model settings to optimize results.
  - Remember that often, several different techniques may be used for the same data mining problem.
  - If necessary, loop back to the data preparation phase to bring the form of the data into line with the specific requirements of a particular data mining technique.
- **Evaluation phase**
  - Evaluate one or more of the models delivered in the modeling phase for quality and effectiveness before deploying them for use in the field.
  - Determine whether the model in fact achieves the objectives set for it in the first phase.
  - Establish whether some important facet of the business or research problem has not been accounted for sufficiently.
  - Come to a decision regarding the use of the data mining results.
- **Deployment phase**
  - Make use of the models created: Model creation does not signify the completion of a project.
  - Example of a simple deployment: Generate a report.
  - Example of a more complex deployment: Implement a parallel data mining process in another department using a completely new dataset.

It should be noted that there are some other frameworks available that have been created by commercial software vendors. However, CRISP-DM is used more than other methods according to KDnuggets (see Piatetsky, 2014), where it ranked highest in the "main methodology you are using for your analytics, data mining, or data science projects," followed by "my own," commercial and other methodologies falling way behind.

CRISP-DM is a simple, high-level process but it will not necessarily incorporate all the components of a process methodology. Depending on the questions or objectives being considered, the data, the timeline, and many other considerations, you may need a much more involved process. For example, in AI projects you should consider data validation, means of version control and model governance, model health and process stability, production control, application integration and more. We will cover some of these in more depth in the applicable chapters, but CRISP-DM is a good basis for organizations considering repeatable methodologies.

The CRISP-DM methods are meant as a framework and have been proven to be useful in many projects. And, it can help from reinventing project milestones and deliverables each time one is working on a new project. In the end, the project team should determine if it is useful for the particular project at hand.

Last Considerations

We have a lot to say about data and analytics architecture. We decided that we wanted to expand on this section greatly along with many components in Chapter 2, so we decided to write another book dedicated to this subject (see Burk and Miner, 2021). We simply point out a few considerations here.

Data Architecture

Data architecture is a framework of rules, policies, procedures, standards, and systems that govern data in the organization. Today, **data and people are the two most valuable and strategic assets in the enterprise**. Data architecture **links collected data to the business rules that translate it into meaningful contexts**. Data architecture specifies what data is accessible, whether it is stored and how it is used. It provides data governance which covers access, security, change management, scale, reliability and sustainability (mentioned in Chapter 2).

Analytics Architecture

Analytics architecture refers to the applications, infrastructures, tools and leading practices that enable access to and analysis of information to optimize business decisions and performance. It supports all current analytics needs and strategically plans for future needs and initiatives. Many organizations start with descriptive and diagnostic analytics. These are often accomplished with interactive BI platforms, dashboards and Visual BI platforms and statistical programs. It may include analytics that are embedded into functionally specific platforms for medical radiology, business finance or similar departments. Successful implementation of descriptive and diagnostic analytics often leads the organization into a new direction of predictive and diagnostic analytics: optimization. These are often accomplished with data science, machine learning and AI platforms.

Postscript

We have covered some very important considerations in this chapter. Most of these you will not see covered in other texts, as these books are more focused on the "how-to" deep dives into specific algorithms. We felt it was important to cover some very basic, somewhat philosophical foundations before we launch into specific data-driven methods and techniques.

References

Baldwin, J.G. 2019. *The Big Short Explained*. www.investopedia.com/articles/investing/020115/big-short-explained.asp.

Banko, M., and Brill, E. 2001. "Scaling to a very large ccorpora for Natural Lanaguage Disambugation," *Proceedings of the 39th Annual Meeting of the Association for Computational Linguistics*, Association for Computational Linguistics, 26–33. URL: https://www.aclweb.org/anthology/P01-1005. DOI: 10.3115/1073012.1073017; **b**https://www.aclweb.org/anthology/P01-1005.pdf

Burk, Scott and Miner, Gary. Expected release 2021. *Designing an Integrated AI, Analytics, and Data Science Architecture for Your Organization*. Rutledge/Taylor and Francis Press.

Larose, Daniel T. 2005. *Discovering Knowledge in Data: An Introduction to Data Mining*. John Wiley and Sons.

Lewis, M. 2010. *The Big Short: Inside the Doomsday Machine* (1st ed.). W. W. Norton & Company.

Northwestern Business Review. 2016. *What the Big Short Teaches Us About the 2007–2008 Financial Crisis*. https://northwesternbusinessreview.org/what-the-big-short-teaches-us-about-the-2007-08-financial-crisis-9cb30793ad92.

Piatetsky, G. 2014. "CRISP-DM, still the top methodology for analytics, data mining, or data science projects," https://www.kdnuggets.com/2014/10/crisp-dm-top-methodology-analytics-data-mining-data-science-projects.html.

Wolpert, D.H., and Macready, W.G. 2005. "Coevolutionary free lunches," *IEEE Transactions on Evolutionary Computation*, 9(6): 721–35.

Resources for the Avid Learner

1 Models are everywhere and in fact, there are mental models that contribute to our success. We recommend the book, *Super Thinking: The Big Book of Mental Models* by Gabriel Weinberg and Lauren McCann, June 2019.
2 Tiao G.C., Bisgaard, S., Hill, W.J., Peña, D., and Stigler, S.M. 2000. *Box on Quality and Discovery: With Design, Control, and Robustness* (1st ed.). Wiley Interscience.
3 Wheeler, Donald J. 1998. *Building Continual Improvement: A Service Industry Guide*. SPC Press (Statistical Process Control).
4 Wheeler, Donald J. 2010. *Understanding Statistical Process Control* (3rd ed.). SPC Press (Statistical Process Control).

Chapter 4

It's All Analytics!

Keywords: Data, Descriptive Analytics, Predictive Analytics, Prescriptive Analytics, Models, Causation, Correlation

Preamble

In the last chapter, we looked at processes that generate data and why we want to collect that data. We contrasted models and algorithms and then briefly touched on data and analytics architectures. We now look at how almost everything we do is "Analytics" and thus we title this chapter **"It's All Analytics."**

Overview of Analytics – It's All Analytics

One of Scott's (author) favorite quotes was from the movie *Sneakers* (see *Sneakers*, 1992), where Cosmo says "It's about the data… Exactly! The world isn't run by weapons anymore, or energy, or money, it's run by little ones and zeroes, little bits of data. It's all just electrons." But no, it is really more than just the data! **Data alone does nothing! Data by itself is just a cost!** Data costs include the cost to acquire it, the cost to store it, the legal liability of keeping it, the potential risk of a data breach. We normally think that data is cheap, but when you consider the total cost of ownership, it is really quite expensive. And maybe only 15%–30% of data collected is ever used (see Priceonomics, August 2019; Barrett, 2018); if it's not used, it sits there and does nothing (it is called "Dark Data"). So, it is only when your action is based on data that you gain value from it; therefore – **It's about the analytics and It's All Analytics!** You can only offset the costs of all that data if you use it to the benefit of your interests.

Another great quote that is germane to this chapter is Wayne Gretzky's quote "Skate to where the puck is going, not where it has been." It is not understanding the past, but understanding what is going to happen in the future; what's next? That is the heart of predictive analytics, as we will see in this chapter.

MUCH ROOM FOR IMPROVEMENT!

"Companies are failing in their efforts to become data-driven"; so say Randy Bean and Thomas Davenport in the *Harvard Business Review* on February 5, 2019.

Why and How?

- Becoming "Data-Driven" has been a goal of many during the past decade or longer...
- Their larger goal is "Digital Transformation" and/or "Competing on Analytics" and/or "AI First"
- BUT: managing data in all its forms is a prerequisite of the above

However, leading corporations are failing in their efforts to become "data-driven," according to Bean and Davenport (2019) and the NewVantage Partners Big Data and AI Executive Survey (2019). This survey represented very large corporations such as American Express, Ford Motor, General Electric, General Motors, and Johnson & Johnson. Results of the survey included the following statistics:

- 72% of survey participants report that they have yet to forge a data culture
- 69% report that they have not created a data-driven organization
- 53% state that they are not yet treating data as a business asset
- 52% admit that they are not competing on data and analytics
- FURTHER: the percentage of firms identifying themselves as being data-driven had declined in each of the past 3 years – from 37.1% in 2017 to 32.4% in 2018 to 31.0% in 2019

YET – many of these corporations were investing MORE in "Data Analytic type of things," as follows:

- 92% reported that the pace of their big data and AI investments were accelerating
- 88% report a greater urgency to invest in big data and AI
- 75% cite a fear of disruption as a motivating factor for big data/AI investment
- 55% of companies reported investments in big data and AI now exceed US$50MM, up from 40% just last year
- Increases in the appointment of Chief Data Officers from 12% in 2012 to 68% in 2019

WHAT are the OBSTACLES to adopting a fully functioning "Data-Driven Organization"?

- 77% of executives report that adoption of Big Data/AI initiatives is a major challenge, up from 65% in 2018
- only 7.5% of these executives cite technology as the challenge
- 93% of respondents identify people and process issues as the obstacles
  - 40.3% identify lack of organization alignment as a leading obstacle
  - 24% cite cultural resistance as a leading obstacle

Whatever the reasons for these failures in "Data-Driven Transformation," the following appears true:

- The QUANTITY of data continues to rise in business and society
- Analytical decisions and actions continue to be generally superior to those based on intuition and experience
- The companies in the survey are investing heavily in big data and analytics
- The need for data-driven organizations and cultures isn't going away (Bean and Davenport, 2019)

NOTE: It can be done! We address successful "Data-Driven Organizations" in Chapter 2. Moreover, our next book is entirely dedicated to the design (architecture) and implementation of a successful analytics program. We are writing it specifically to provide a map for program success (see Burk and Miner, 2021).

Analytics of Every Form and Analytics Everywhere

Introduction

In a broad sense almost all the subjects in this book have some overlap with analytics. For example, machine learning (Chapter 6) is the backbone of predictive analytics, where we are trying to use data to deem the likelihood of an unseen event. Another example is Visual business intelligence (BI) (Chapter 5), when data is turned into dashboards or what many term visual analytics. And we can also look at data science, statistics, optimization or other data-driven methods. ***Analytics touch them all***.

Another example is a functional form of analytics, for example, "healthcare analytics." Here we are not speaking of a discipline or type of analysis, even if the data is an image, a video or the more common spreadsheet. We are speaking across an entire spectrum of systems and processes that generate petabytes of information and in which a myriad of interesting questions and needs exist.

If you do an Internet search, you can easily find the following types of analytics. We limit this list to 50, but there are many more. We offer definitions for most of these in our expansive glossary at the end of the book.

Analytics Mega List

We start our discussion here, by providing a list of different types of analytics. Actually, this is not a full list! We went back and cut this list to the most recent, most important top 50 names in analytics. You can find many others, but many are complimentary or there is overlap.

1) Analytics
2) Healthcare Analytics
3) Government Analytics
4) Medical Analytics
5) Public Health Analytics
6) Public Policy Analytics
7) Visual Analytics
8) Business Analytics
9) Customer Analytics
10) Descriptive Analytics (part 1 of Gartner)
11) Diagnostic Analytics (part 2 of Gartner)

12) Predictive Analytics (part 3 of Gartner)
13) Prescriptive Analytics (part 4 of Gartner)
14) Advanced Analytics
15) Sports Analytics
16) Data Analytics
17) Big Data Analytics
18) Text Analytics
19) Graph Analytics
20) Social (Media) Analytics
21) Retail Analytics
22) Network Analytics
23) Link Analytics, Path Analytics
24) Modern Analytics
25) Directed Acyclic Graph (DAG) Analytics
26) Web and Digital Analytics
27) Security Analytics
28) Descriptive Analytics
29) Cognitive Analytics
30) Big Data Analytics
31) Embedded Analytics
32) Portfolio Analytics
33) Fraud Analytics
34) Marketing Analytics
35) Financial Analytics
36) Augmented Analytics
37) Customer Experience Analytics
38) Supply Chain Analytics
39) Geospatial Analytics
40) Call Center Analytics
41) Credit and Risk Analytics
42) Sales Analytics
43) Social Analytics
44) Audio/Speech Analytics
45) Video (Content) Analytics
46) Image Analytics
47) Self-Service Analytics
48) Log Analytics
49) Search Analytics
50) Automated Analytics

Whew! We provide a deeper dive into some of these later in this chapter; skip there if it makes sense for you. However, we don't want you as a reader to be lost in the weeds, so it is your preference. We first categorize some of these terms in common classifications.

Breaking it Down, Categorizing Analytics

Introduction

We provide a brief introduction here of analytic methods that classify things into categories. This is very difficult as there are methodological types of analytics, functional types of analytics and analytics that address certain types of data. To illustrate some difficulty in trying to categorize types of analytics, take "text analytics" as an example. Text is a type of data, so it could be a category of its own. Alternatively, it could be that we want to determine the author of a text. There are many manuscripts attributable to William Shakespeare, but what is the evidence, where is the specific number? Predictive analytics answers this question by learning the characteristics of Shakespeare's known works.

It could be that we want to autofill words in a search bar for Google, Bing or DuckDuckGo. These search engines will use a method of machine learning (n-grams) to attempt to guess the next word you want to enter – this is search analytics, a functional type of analytics.

Therefore, text analytics encompasses many different types of analytics depending on what you are attempting to do.

Below we describe an analytics classification scheme that is generally accepted. This scheme is ubiquitous in the analytics domain and is often attributed to Gartner. It consists of four major categories of analytics – Descriptive Analytics, Diagnostic Analytics, Predictive Analytics, and Prescriptive Analytics. This framework is not comprehensive, nor completely accurate, but it is useful. We use this as a general structure, but use our own definitions. We will also expand beyond it as we get further into this book.

Gartner's Classification

Gartner, Inc. was founded in 1979. Its purpose is to equip executives across the entire enterprise to make the right decisions at the right time, and thus stay ahead of change in the world (Gartner, Inc., 2019). It is a global company serving over 15,600 client organizations in over 100 countries around the world.

We will explore the four major groups of analytics that Gartner uses (Gartner 2019). The following chart (Figure 4.1) demonstrates the relationship of these four categories plus the concept of models that optimize a process. It contains the evolution of these across three dimensions. First, as we move from descriptive analytics to prescriptive analytics to the higher levels, we require less human cognition (see Chapter 2, section "A Note on Cognition") and more machine processing. In other words, computer processing and algorithms replace the thinking required of humans and this requires more machine processing. As we move from description and diagnosis to prediction, we are moving from looking in the rear view mirror (hindsight) to looking through the windshield (foresight). And, finally, as a general rule as we move from the lower left to the upper right the value of these projects increases.

In the following section, we go through each analytics superset in sequence starting with descriptive analytics.

Descriptive Analytics

Descriptive analytics has a very long historical foundation. These analytics are the easiest to implement, but many times do not offer the value of other methods, which are generally more complex and sophisticated. Descriptive analytics typically fall into one of the following categories:

1) Descriptive statistics and numerical summaries
2) Visual representation

According to Figure 4.1, descriptive analytics describes analytics as answering the question, "What Happened?" However, descriptive analytics go well beyond this question. They form the foundation for all the other analytics categories, meaning that diagnostic analytics, predictive analytics, etc. all start with descriptive analytics.

A simple example of a descriptive statistic is the average weight of a male living in the United States. It provides a quick summary for millions of individuals in one number. Its advantage is that it is a single number, very easy to digest. Its disadvantage is the same. It does not provide any idea of spread or nuances of the population. Spread and other nuances can be done with several complimentary statistics (percentiles, variance, max,

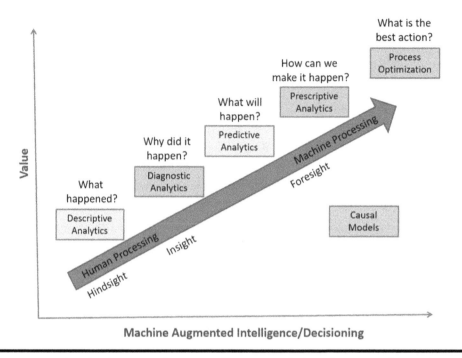

Figure 4.1   A visual reference of a generally accepted classification scheme for analytics.

min, etc.), but this also requires mental gymnastics to be able to understand them.

A **visual representation** is often better than a set of summary statistics. Humans are very good at processing visuals. This skill was developed over millions of years of evolution. It is true that a picture is worth a thousand words. We will dive much deeper into descriptive and visual analytics in chapters on BI and statistics. However, we will see them in all chapters. BI is about description – tables, reports, and Visual BI is graphs, dashboards, interactive displays of information. In classical statistics, *descriptive statistics* is one of two major divisions, the other being *inferential statistics*.

Diagnostic Analytics

Diagnostic analytics is a form of advanced analytics that examines data or content to answer the question, "**Why did it happen?**" It is causal and retrospective. It has causal meaning in that a change in an attribute (a cause) will generally or specifically result in an observable change in a second attribute (the effect). Moreover, the cause must precede the effect. It is important to note the difference in association or correlation with causation (see gray box below on "Causation vs Correlation").

CAUSATION VS CORRELATION

While the confusion over causation and correlation has improved over the last few years, you can still see many examples by journalists and other authors that mix the meaning of the two concepts. When two variables tend to run together, we say they are associated, they co-occur, they are correlated. When one category of a variable is present, a second variable category is often present. Or, in the case of numerical attributes, when one variable increases the second variable increases (positive relationship) or decreases (negative relationship).

It is very important to understand that correlations can be spurious, meaning they can be caused by factors outside the two variables of interest. On the other hand, they can be sheer coincidence. There are billions of variables so at times you can think something is correlated when in fact, it is just chance. Causation on the other hand implies that there is some sort of physical, psychological or underlying link.

If you want some fun, we recommend that you check out Tyler Vigen's website at http://tylervigen.com/spurious-correlations. You will find a lot of interesting spurious correlations! We recreated a sample of this in the spirit of Tyler's website. Figure 4.2 illustrates the relationship of U.S. Spending on Science, Space and Technology vs Suicides by Hanging, Strangulation, and Suffocation.

You can see that these two series are highly correlated, and if you found it in a newspaper you might read that **U.S. Spending is causing suicides!** Yes, this happens all the time when journalists and others confuse correlation vs causation.

Predictive Analytics

Predictive analytics answers the question, "What will happen?" Predictive analytics is about assigning a probability or likelihood to an outcome based on some type of analysis or model. The types of analysis or models that result in predictive models will be presented in various chapters of this book. Many predictive models today are generated with machine learning algorithms. These models when given a set of inputs will generate the probability of an outcome.

For example, the University of Iowa Hospitals and Clinics used patient and operating room data to generate predictive models to determine the

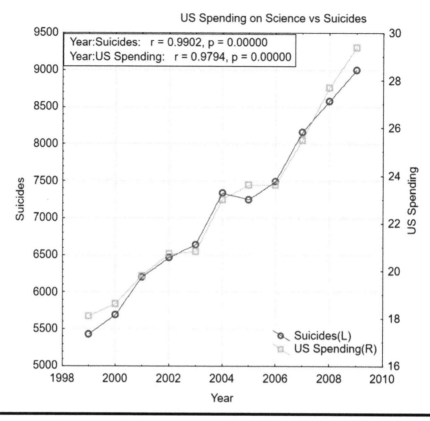

Figure 4.2 Spurious Correlations, U.S. Spending, and Suicides.

likelihood of surgical site infections developing from operations performed in the operating room. The most interesting and innovative thing about this model was that it was executed while the patient was still under anesthesia in the operating room. The resulting probability in "Real Time" gave the care team information they could use on what preventative treatment should be used – normal closure of the wound, delayed closure or negative pressure therapy (Siwicki, 2018). Relationships between targets and predictors in predictive models may be correlated or causal in nature.

Prescriptive Analytics

Gartner notes prescriptive analytics is a form of advanced analytics, which examines data or content to answer the question "***What should be done?***" or "What can we do to make XYZ happen?" This type of analytics requires good data and maybe additional assumptions. We will cover this more deeply in chapters where we apply algorithms to create prescriptive models.

The difference between predictive analytics and prescriptive analytics is often misunderstood. Prescriptive analytics requires causality. It is important to understand the differences and we created a special gray box to cover these (please see "Predictive or Prescriptive??" gray box).

Process Optimization

Optimization is a word that is overused a lot these days. I optimized my workout. We use the word optimization in a very strict, rigorous way. We will explore this concept in depth later, but in general we start with an objective function that we explicitly state. We state whether we want to maximize or minimize this function – this is optimization. We add constraints that cannot be violated. We then search for solutions that maximize or minimize our function and do not violate our constraints. The solution has the highest or lowest value of the objective function is the optimal solution.

PREDICTIVE OR PRESCRIPTIVE??

One of the most misunderstood differences is the classification of predictive vs prescriptive analytics. We have seen experienced data scientists mix this up. There is a big difference in these models. We will not get technical, but if you learn this – **you will be ahead of many professionals in the analytics space!**

First, some similarities in the method classifications:

1) Both predictive analytics and prescriptive analytics apply to unseen events (most are future or forward looking)
2) They both contain a probability of an outcome (probabilistic models)
3) Both often provide highly valuable insights

Then, some dissimilarities in the method classifications:

1) Prescriptive models are causal; predictive models may or may not be
2) Predictive models are generally easier to formulate
3) Prescriptive models require special assumptions or special data to formulate

Prescriptive models are the gold standard since they are causal, and thus manipulating factors that cause the outcome results in a higher probability of success. For example, in healthcare, it is known that prescribing antibiotics will generally reduce bacterial infections.

What is an example of a predictive model that is not prescriptive? Imagine an Internet retailer that wants to sell products or services off their website, and they have a loyalty program called "elite rewards." It turns out, not surprisingly, that a customer in their elite rewards (an annual fee required) membership is a very important variable in their predictive model to determine if they will be more likely to respond to an email offer.

Now, a naïve marketer might think – "We need to push these customers into our loyalty program so we can sell to them more frequently – they will respond more receptively to our email ads." This is the idea behind prescriptive analytics, i.e. what should I do, what actions(s) should I take? They might incentivize existing customers that are not in their elite program with a free account. Could they now expect the same results, e.g. the same likelihood of purchase as their predictive model would have suggested? No. Why? Because they have not changed the customer's behavior or mindset. Customers that are willing to pay for the "elite" program are inherently different from customers that are not. However, offering an easy path to elite membership does not change the likelihood to respond to an offer. This is an example of a confused marketer using a predictive model as if it were prescriptive.

Again, understanding the difference will make you well ahead of the pack in understanding analytics.

Some Additional Thoughts on Classifying Analytics

There are three ways to classify analytics:

1) What domain or function? Public health analytics, public policy analytics, sports analytics
2) What type of data is used? Text analytics, graph analytics, image analytics, web analytics
3) What analytics problem? Descriptive, diagnostics, predictive and prescriptive analytics

Again, in order to classify the types of analytics we are using, we need to look at many things from the domain under consideration, functions, formats of data available and the nature of the problem, whether descriptive, diagnostic, predictive and/or prescriptive. We have to think these things through thoroughly to make sure we are in the ballpark of our problem.

Fundamentals of Analytics – Data Basics

Introduction

Recall that in Chapter 3, we discussed data and processes. If we want to make better decisions and improve processes, we collect data, analyze it, model it, create insights and then use those insights.

We cover a lot of disciplines and methods in this book. We do so because you need many different tools in your toolbox so you can pull out the right tool for the right job. However, it is helpful if we can find some common elements in the problems we are trying to solve. After all, **It's All Analytics.** There are commonalities across the different analytic methods. We will cover some basic ideas of categorization / classification of data. After all, data are the building blocks, the new oil, and we will be talking about data through the book. Understanding using data helps us make good decisions.

Four Scales of Measurement

At a very basic level, data can take on four levels of measurement. These are important because they dictate the type of analysis one can use given the data they acquire. We present them in order:

1) **Nominal Scale** – by "name" only, they have no numeric value. This is the lowest scale of measurement. There is no order of elements and measurements are qualitative. An example is color – red, green, blue.
2) **Ordinal Scale** – similar to nominal in that there is no explicit numeric relationship except measurements of this type have order. Measurements are qualitative. Example, runners in a sprint place 1st, 2nd, 3rd, etc.
3) **Interval Scale** – interval data has not only order, but also in addition the relative distance between the numbers on the scale are equal

(proportional) and can be evaluated mathematically. Measurements are quantitative. Example – profit. It can be positive, negative or zero and a doubling of profit is the same if you move from US$10 to US$20 or US$2M to US$4M.

4) **Ratio Scale** – the highest scale, ratio scale has the characteristics of the interval scale and has a true zero. Measurements are quantitative. Example – Height. You cannot have a zero or negative height.

Data Formats

Data formats may refer to data types, recording and content formats, file formats and more. We will discuss a few of these here. Specifically, we would like to provide a broad brush on data formats that form the basis for certain type of analytics. The following list illustrates some **data formats that often drive the type of analytics performed**:

1) Words
2) Numeric
3) Images / Pictures
4) Video
5) Audio / Sounds

Data Format	Example of Analytics Applied
Words	Text Analytics, Natural Language, Search Analytics, Web Analytics
Numeric	Healthcare Analytics, Business Analytics, Risk Analytics, Financial Analytics
Images / Pictures	Image Analytics, Sports Analytics, Visual Analytics, Geospatial Analytics
Audio / Sound	Voice Recognition/Transcription, Security Analytics, Call Center Analytics
Video	Video Analytics, IoT and Smart Cities, Retail Analytics, Streaming Analytics

There has been a major shift in the types of data used for analysis. Forty years ago, almost all data analyzed was numerical or categorical (quantitative and qualitative) in nature. Healthcare and businesses were full of numerical data that was being analyzed by the adoption of computing technology. Ten to twenty years later, as computers got much faster, there was a greater adoption of "number crunching" and data mining, and there was an explosion of text analytics. In the last year, there has been a huge increase in image recognition, audio, video, and streaming analytics.

File formats refer to structures that a computer can read. It allows programs to identify and load different data formats from the list above as well as mixtures of these data formats. Some computer file extension examples are *.csv, *.txt. *.xml, *.mdf, *.html, *.log, and many, many more.

Data Stores

Processes generate data and we record that data. It exists in non-permanent memory sometimes called temporary memory or volatile memory, which used immediately and then deleted. For example, think of files on your computer that are created, but not saved. That data exists in temporary memory (RAM) that is only referenceable while the computer is on. If you want to access that data later, you must store it.

Most analytics data is stored at least temporarily. All analytics development can be thought of as using data storage. We just want to provide a quick list of data storage locations now, as this can dictate the type of method that is used. Here are a few examples most applicable to analytics:

1) Local files. Spreadsheets, databases, text, xml, html
2) Relational databases on premise
3) Semi-structured (non-lake) databases on premise (JSON, XML, logs, NoSQL)
4) Data lake, big data stores (Apache and Hadoop, see Chapter 9)
5) Cloud Storage options (Software as a Service, Database as a Service, Infrastructure and Platform as a service)
6) Streaming data – This is more of a connector than storage; noted here since streaming analytics is growing rapidly

The authors are in the process of writing a book dedicated to the "architecture of technology" to support data science, AI and analytics activities. The entire book is dedicated to the subject; please look for it.

Provisioning Data for Analytics

We are not going to cover all activities that should be covered in an analytics project; however, we believe it is beneficial to cover some of the basic data provisioning activities for these projects. You will hear similar names for some of these activities, like data wrangling, data munging, etc. Let us address a few activities that are common in many analytics projects.

1) Data Sourcing
   a. Identification of Project Data (led by business)
   b. Data Engineering (technical aspects)
2) Data Quality Assessment and Remediation
3) Data Integration
4) Data Cleaning of Merged Data

Once the project begins there will be additional activities:

5) Exploratory Data Analysis
6) Data Transformation
7) Data Reduction
8) Rinse and Repeat Where Necessary

The following demonstrates what we call "the data cycle" (see Figure 4.3). It is highly iterative and may be recursive at any point.

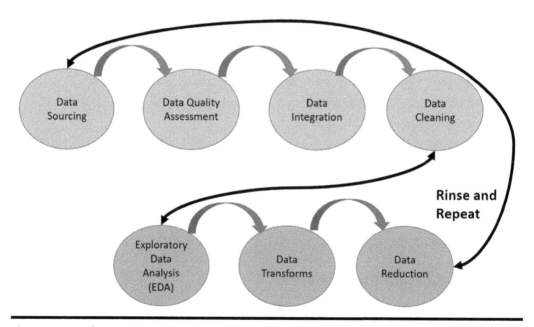

Figure 4.3   The "Data Cycle" Copyright © 2019 by Scott Burk.

Data Sourcing

There are two parts to data sourcing. **The first part** is determining the data you will need. What is the right data needed to support an analytics project? Remember CRISP-DM in Chapter 3? If not, that is okay; we will revisit the initial stages of the analytics process in the section on business understanding and project definition. What is an important result that the business would benefit from achieving? Is it attainable in a realistic time horizon? Who would need to be involved in the process, which members from what groups? IT, and which business leaders? Which technical people? What would the metrics be to support the answer? How would you know you arrived at the destination? As Dr. Tom Hill (a friend of the authors) says, "How would we know we won? How would we know we are done?"

If it helps, begin with the end in mind and work backward. What would be the decision or the action needed to bring about the final result? Then, at the next step backward: What analysis would deliver the information to determine that decision or action? Then one more step backward: What data would be required for that analysis?

Once you know what data elements are needed to support the project, you move to **the second part**, which is data sourcing, connecting and returning the data to an analytics sandbox. This sandbox could take several forms; it is normally just a database that is separated from transactional systems. First, you must ask if you can access the data you need? If so, who can source it? If not, is there surrogate data that will provide a close approximation or good enough information? If not, you might need to set this project aside for a time while you can work on getting those pipes installed and in the meantime select another target project.

Data Quality Assessment and Remediation

Scott attended a data quality conference in California in the year 2003. This conference was attended by hundreds, possibly thousands of people across the globe. It is where Scott met his first friend from New Zealand. The entire conference was entirely dedicated to data quality. THIS WAS OVER 15 YEARS AGO, and yet it is amazing that this issue of "Quality in Data" still exists and in fact, may be worse than it was 15 years ago. You would have thought that with that kind of following, i.e. hundreds to thousands of researchers around the world concerned with "data quality," and with books dedicated to the subject (see English, 2009), the problem would have gotten much better.

Once you have data in an analytics sandbox, you need to determine the quality of the data. Let's examine **five common issues in data quality** which will form your assessment:

1) Record Duplication
2) Sparsity
3) Outliers
4) Invariance
5) Redundancy

Duplication exists in transactional systems and when data is merged across systems. At this point you will have not merged data, but you should do a first pass at the sourcing and bring in the data (called staging and provisioning by data scientists). As the old quality paradigm goes, the more you can move quality toward the beginning of a system, the more time and money you can save.

Duplicates can be exact copies appearing in multiple rows. This is very easy to fix by the IT department. Or, it could be caused by "similar" records. An example for a similar record could be a patient master index that has Sarah S. Jones in one record and Sarah Sue Jones in another record, and they are actually records for the same person. Suppose that Sarah went to an out-of-network provider and filled the form out with Sara Sue Jones. When this record was brought in, the patient master was not smart enough to identify it as the same Sara S. Jones so it created a new record. Interestingly, there are systems that use machine learning to help alleviate this issue.

Sparsity is missing data. You can have row or column sparsity; this means you are missing several elements for a record across a row. You might have several missing values for a variable (column of data). If you imagine your data in a spreadsheet (see Table 4.1) with 10 variables (10 columns); then the Patient ID forms a row for the other 9 variables. In our figure, patient 3333 is missing data for two columns, for example. You must decide how to handle missing values for your modeling projects. The easiest way to handle it is to throw out rows or columns, but this may weaken the signal or amount of information you need for project success. Alternatively, there are many ways to handle missing values: replacing with averages, average frequency categories, use of an imputation model to fill data and many more methods are options to handle these issues (good predictive analytic software packages can do this "automatically," with the user having the ability to specify which type of method to handle missing data is desired).

Table 4.1 Example of Row and Column Sparsity with Patient Data

ID	Readmission	Age	Surgeon ID	EBL	Apgar_Score	HMBin60days	ASA	Gender	WND_Class	
1111	Yes	24	4	3300	5-6		2	female	00	
2222	Yes	22	1	3300	7-8		9	male	02	
3333	Yes	29		2700		2.8	2	male	03	Bad Row
4444	Yes	21	2	2400	9-10	2.2	3	male	03	
5555	Yes	41	2	2000	5-6		2	male	02	
						Bad Column				

Outliers are another problem where a few values can throw off statistics. You can test for these in a variety of ways and intelligently replace them with values more tenable for your analysis needs. All of these have drawbacks: missing data has its costs, but it does not have to derail your project unless your data is really lacking.

Invariance is when you have a categorical variable (nominal or interval) that has either all or almost all the same values. Imagine you have a column for Gender and 99% of your data is female. This would cause problems if you used this column for modeling. It is best to see if you can increase the male instances, throw out the entire variable, or apply some sort of oversampling. Or, if the variable is numeric, and it has very little wiggle (a not-so-technical term for variance), it could also be discarded, as there is not enough variance to be of much or any value in statistics and modeling. Suppose the class average is 99 with a low score of 98 and a high score of 100 – this variable will be of little use in any analysis.

Last on our list is **redundancy**. There are analytic methods that do not work well if you have highly correlated predictors. Example, suppose I want to predict annual income with four predictor variables. These predictors are age in years, highest degree completed, number of years of education and whether the occupation was science/technical vs non-science/non-technical. The highest degree completed and the number of years of education are likely to be highly correlated and contain the same information in trying to predict annual income. Therefore they are redundant and we would likely want to get rid of one of them or at least note it and not use both of them in a model that might be susceptible to problems with redundancy.

Other issues can occur in the data for your project. For example, your data can be stale, out of date. You cannot account for every possible nuance in advance, as data discovery is a process. However, with a good team working together, you can discover them and correct for them, thus adding value to your project.

Integrate and Repeat

Data integration is joining various data sets together. It is often needed to get customer demographic data from one system, transactional sales data from another system and more… Most analytics are performed on a single, monolithic set of data – wide and deep. You will typically need to join this data together. A data engineer, an IT data base guru or a savvy business analyst can help with this activity. You will stage these tables in the analytic sandbox for additional processing. Different data tables, each with different data from the same subject, can be "joined" into one table; these joins are done such that one row will represent a customer, a patient or an event.

Once you have this complete data set formulated, it is necessary to repeat at minimum a couple of the data quality steps. Once you have the process formulated it should not be difficult to repeat all steps, but it is critical to look for row duplicates, since joining several data tables or data files together increases the likelihood that you will have more of them.

Exploratory Data Analysis (EDA)

Once you have the data sourced and fixed many of the data quality issues (you should know that this is a continuing process; like parenthood, you are never done), you can start the fun stuff. We illustrate a system for most analytics at this point – note in this book we cover over a half-dozen methods. Furthermore, we are assuming a more insight-driven process rather than an automated one. Methods like autoML will be discussed in future chapters.

Exploratory data analysis is very akin to descriptive analytics. We compute summary statistics, we continue to look for outliers, but now we look at them in a different lens; we start to see data in a multidimensional way, where rather than one data point outside its neighbors, we look if it has an unwieldy effect on other variables. This *can* be very interesting and *lead to immediate wins of the analytics project. This should be underscored – you want to celebrate wins from the EDA phase.* This is the time where the analytics team can go back to the business and thus demonstrate the value of analytics to the entire enterprise – the entire membership of the company or organization. You want a place where you record all these successes. At times, the end deliverables may not be as stellar as hoped, but what might seem **small insights can have a huge payoff.** Deloitte reported in 2019 a study that increased data capture and analysis can likely save billions of dollars for the energy industry.

As with most of the analytics process, this is never complete. The initial pass may be the most time consuming and provide the greatest insights, but it usually needs to be revisited. Here are some goals from EDA:

1) What are the relationships among the predictors and what is being predicted (target)?
2) Are there any data points that highly influence/leverage a target outcome? If so, investigate, and share with the business if applicable. If this

leads to business insight or action, record this as a win for the team and try to measure the impact in a quantitative measure – money savings, money growth.

3) We need to look at interactions .
4) Are we correctly accounting for the relationships? Do we need additional data to make a more accurate prediction?
5) Are we asking the right questions? So important, we will repeat.

Data Transformations

Data transformations are formulas applied to variables or combinations of variables. A few examples are:

1) Indicator creation or dummy coding
2) Logarithmic or mathematical transformations
3) Normalization
4) Statistical standardization
5) Binning of continuous variable ranges (thus converted into categorical variables)
6) Aggregation
7) Generalization
8) Masking / de-identification for privacy

Data Reduction

Data reduction refers to eliminating variables that cannot or should not be used in the analysis. It may be discovered in the data preparation phase that certain variables should be eliminated for:

1) Ethical reasons
2) Legal reasons
3) Public relations
4) Insufficient utility for the problem being addressed
5) Future censoring – data is available historically, but not in the future
6) Expense – the data exists, but is cost prohibitive going forward

A second type of data reduction is done in the modeling or analysis phase to pare down the data set so that models can execute more timely and the analysis of the results is more efficient. Statistical and machine learning algorithms usually aid these reductions.

Postscript

In this chapter we have looked at an "overview" of the ANALYTICS PROCESS with special emphasis on getting and cleaning data. In the next chapter, we get into the specifics of BI, in particular Visual BI.

References

Barrett, J. April 2018. "Up to 73 percent of company data goes unused for analytics. Here's how to put it to work," www.inc.com/jeff-barrett/misusing-data-could-be-costing-your-business-heres-how.html.

Bean, R. and Davenport, T. 2019. "Companies are failing in their efforts to become data-driven," https://hbr.org/2019/02/companies-are-failing-in-their-efforts-to-become-data-driven.

Bill Siwicki, B. September 10, 2018. "Machine learning helps University of Iowa reduce surgical site infections," www.healthcareitnews.com/news/machine-learning-helps-ui-health-care-reduce-surgical-site-infection-74-save-12-million.

Burk, Scott and Miner, Gary. Expected release 2021. *Designing an Integrated AI, Analytics, and Data Science Architecture for Your Organization.* Taylor and Francis Press.

English, Larry P. October 2009. *Information Quality Applied: Best Practices for Improving Business Information, Processes and Systems* (1st ed.). Wiley Publishing English.

Gartner, Inc. 2019. www.gartner.com/en/about.

Gartner, Inc. January 18, 2019. www.gartner.com/en/documents/3898666/4-types-of-analytical-tools-to-support-insight-generatio.

Lasker, Lawrence, Parkes, Walter (Producers) and Robinson, Phil A., (Director). 1992. *Sneakers,* United States, Universal Studios.

NewVantage Partners. 2019. "Big data and AI executive survey 2019: Executive summary of findings," http://newvantage.com/wp-content/uploads/2018/12/Big-Data-Executive-Survey-2019-Findings-Updated-010219-1.pdf.

Priceonomics. August 2019. "Companies collect a lot of data but how much do they actually use?," https://priceonomics.com/companies-collect-a-lot-of-data-but-how-much-do/.

Resources for the Avid Learner

1 We recommend John Thompson and Shawn Rogers' book, *Analytics: How to Win with Intelligence First Edition*, July 2017, Technics Publications. There are a lot of interesting use cases and success stories related to analytics.

2 A great, classic read is *Freakonomics: A Rogue Economist Explores the Hidden Side of Everything* by Steven Levitt and Stephen Dubner. It is an extremely interesting view of the data-driven study of applied economics.

3 Written in 2007, *Super Crunchers: Why Thinking-by-Numbers Is the New Way to Be Smart* by Ian Ayers is a good read. It includes sections on data-driven government and evidence-based medicine.

4 Finally, *Moneyball* (the book, not the movie) by Michael Lewis is a great read. You get so much more information on the analytics process from the book. What the gaps were in existing data, what was needed to change the game and much more.

Chapter 5

What Are Business Intelligence (BI) and Visual BI?

Keywords: Reporting, Visual Analytics, On-line Analytical Processing (OLAP), Dashboards

Preamble

In the last chapter, we looked at all the various types of analytics – and **It Is All Analytics!** From analyzing unstructured information like text, to images, to structured information in relational databases. We now cover an old, but very important part of analytics, Business Intelligence (BI), and what is even more important these days – Visual BI.

Introduction

Let us start with an overview of where BI fits into the analytics picture. One thing for sure, people love current BI technology! An important takeaway of this chapter is that BI is not an island unto itself and it is not "old school." It fits inside an analytics ecosystem. We will see it is **extremely useful** in the beginning and end of any analytics project. And it is at the tip of the spear in most business applications meaning users are interacting with BI at the user interface even though under the covers there may be much deeper and complex things happening.

We begin this chapter with this brief introduction, then we launch into a brief history. We will need this because we are going to talk about three major evolutions in the area of BI. There are so many different ways to categorize the subject based on functionality and uses. However, we provide three broad strokes:

1) Basic Reporting
2) A View inside the Data Warehouse and Interactive BI
3) Beyond the Data Warehouse and Enhanced Interactive – Visual BI and more

NOTE: Today's BI platforms will likely include at least some advanced statistical and machine learning methods. So, while a vendor may include machine learning in their BI platform, that does not make machine learning part of the BI domain in our opinion. We are making this distinction in the core precepts of BI and its involvement, as we proceed in this chapter.

NOTE: Another distinction – there are two flavors of BI in this chapter, but we will often just say BI:

Operational BI – BI that is inserted into everyday processes and enhances business understanding and operational decision-making. It includes reports and dashboards are typically executed on a schedule or based on an event trigger.

Project-Based BI – This is where BI is used as part of the data science project to augment and improve the analytics project. Here, BI is often used in the beginning and end of an analytics project. Through this, we often come to understand the interrelationships and outside forces that act upon the enterprise by a discovery process. An old term for this that still applies today is Exploratory Data Analysis (EDA). It is also used at the end of the process to present the results of the project and then again, it is often operationalized.

BI allows professionals to explore the organization's data easily, quickly and interactively. Today it is almost as easy as Tom Cruise in *Minority Report* in the scene with the holograms (see gray box on "BI for Movie Buffs"), and in the near future it might be similar to Michael Crichton's *Disclosure*, where virtual reality (VR) can assist you with your analytic needs (see "BI for Movie Buffs").

BI FOR MOVIE BUFFS

If you have not seen it, there is a film, *Minority Report* (see Molen, 2002), starring Tom Cruise and directed by Steven Spielberg. The film is set in the future, 2054, and Washington DC's prototype PreCrime police department stops murderers before they act, reducing the murder rate to zero. The crime is predicted and police arrive at the scene before the crime actually occurs. There is a great scene where Tom Cruise is swiping holographic images before him. These images are essentially equivalent to today's visual dashboard. He easily selects a small image and twists it with his fingers and the image expands. He flicks his finger and the image is kicked off the screen. He swipes an entire image across with the palm of this hand. He is viewing a dashboard, a complete set of images, tables and more in multiple panels. The film will soon be 20 years old, so it was well before the creation of the modern dashboard. Most users of BI today cannot access holographic computer screens, but they can manipulate windows of visual data and repeat virtually every move Cruise made with a mouse rather than a hand and completely interact with the underlying data.

Another film that was well ahead of its time in capturing analytics on screen was Michael Crichton's *Disclosure* (see Crichton, 1994). Here the film shows Michael Douglas wearing a VR headset and glove and accessing databases with the help of a digital angel that assists him in his efforts. This is a 1994 film. While we are not quite there, many of these components exist and it may not be long before analytics professionals are donning VR headsets and navigating the analytics landscape in virtual dimensions.

A final comment that is very important: One of the common threads for the explosion of interactive BI was the invention of the data warehouse. Organizations in the 1980s were having problems with too many stories brought into the conference room. People were bringing their personal reports into departmental and boardroom meetings. A presentation or discussion would start and then battles would rage – "your report is junk and my numbers are right!" *This leads to a search for a "single version of the truth."* How do you do this when you have so many different systems and a lot of overlapping data? You have corporate systems, departmental systems, systems accessed on the Internet. There was a two-part solution. **The first part was** the data warehouse – it would determine the correct source system for a given data element. If a customer or patient ID was located in multiple systems it would identify how and where to source "the golden record" (a single, well-defined version of all the data entities in an organizational ecosystem). **The second part** of creating a single version of the truth is to corporately define transformations (formulas or manipulation after the data extraction). For consuming the data, this is often done within the BI system itself. If this is done properly, someone accessing the data will be sourcing the right measures (quantitative) and the right dimensions (qualitative) – thus these represent a "single source of the truth."

One note here: we are approaching BI primarily in roles that develop the end products and consume the end products of BI. We are not referring to IT or database professionals that create infrastructure for platforms.

Background and Chronology

As Christina Lago's article "150 Years of Business Intelligence: A Brief History" (see Lago, 2018) described, you guessed it: BI is old, its recording dates back to 1865 when it was written that Sir Henry Furnese had exceeded the competition by collecting, analyzing and using information to help him make better business decisions. We will not be that granular, but as we stated we will illustrate three waves of evolution which provided purpose and capability:

1) Basic Reporting
2) A View inside the Data Warehouse and Interactive BI
3) Beyond the Data Warehouse and Enhanced Interactive – Visual BI and more

Basic (Digital) Reporting

The digital revolution started in the 1950s and reporting was there along its side. At the time, we are sure it was impressive. It continued to evolve and the first BI appeared on the scene in the 1970s. Most of this type of reporting was printed reports. We will call this Version 1.0. While we moved much reporting to a digital format, if you look around you will see there are still a lot of paper reports being generated. Healthcare is a BIG paper user. Have you ever observed how many people are walking around with a clipboard in a hospital clinical setting? Government is another notorious printer of paper – see all of the reports, public records, and documents they create and disseminate. Did anyone else cringe when legislators were on TV with the 2,700 pages of the Affordable Care Act (ACA)? Moreover, this was just the ACA. If you add the associated regulations of the ACA, there were around 20,000 pages and it is likely you can find printed copies of those as well.

A View inside the Data Warehouse and Interactive BI

Then in the 1980s, the data warehouse began to arrive on the scene. While BI officially predates the data warehouse, the data warehouse was necessary to get "buy-in" because of the "multiple versions of the truth" problem we introduced in an opening section to this chapter. Once the marriage of the data warehouse and BI were shown to be so powerful, the adoption of both exploded. Bill Inmon and Ralph Kimble became famous as the "fathers" of data warehousing (while they took different approaches, they are responsible for the modern data warehouse). In addition, Howard Dresner of the Gartner Group popularized the term "BI." He described it as "concepts and methods to improve business decision-making by using fact-based support systems."

There are versions and ways to classify the chronology and evolution of BI (e.g., BI 1.0, BI 2.0, etc.) and you can find them on the Internet; we have our own categorization. From our perspective, the three major changes beyond basic reporting created a new era of BI for versions 2.0, 3.0 and 4.0. Version 2.0 consisted of marrying the data warehouse with a powerful and interactive user interface. Therefore, this section is the second wave when these two forces came into the picture. By interactivity, we mean the ability to slice and dice the data on the fly by the user. Basic reports are static, meaning once the report is generated, the user cannot change it on the fly; they have to change the base configuration. By allowing users to interact with their reports they could answer questions immediately by this slicing and dicing. For example, suppose we have a two-dimensional table of revenue. From left to right are five time periods, 2016 to 2020, and down the left are four regions in the United States (Northeast, South, Midwest, and West). Looking at this table, I might immediately have a question on what is happening in the South. I can re-query my BI tool and the tool will drill down into that zone only, showing me all the customers in that region for example.

WHAT ALLOWS A DATA MART OR DATA WAREHOUSE TO SLICE AND DICE DATA

Online Analytic Processing (OLAP) is a cornerstone of the data warehouse. It is the technology behind many BI applications. It allows for a multidimensional analysis of data – the slicing and dicing, which is sliding through a data structure, i.e., hierarchies, as well as across them. It allows for limitless report creation and complex analytical calculations. The term is attributed to Edgar Todd and first appeared in 1993. You will hear terms like OLAP Cube, which is a visual reference to the way the data is structured – a cubic structure with the dimensions along the edges of the cube and facts and measures inside the cube. The following (extremely simple) cube has different salespeople, items sold and brands and these can differ across the various branches. The cube allows for high-performance retrieval of the data (Figure 5.1).

IMPORTANT NOTE: Data mining, machine learning, and artificial intelligence (AI) model training is performed against very wide, very long data structures. OLAP requires very narrow tables for a very quick return of data. These data structures require almost divergent poles of data form. That is another reason so much of an analyst's time is spent around data processing.

OLAP is contrasted against Online Transaction Processing (OLTP). OLTP is very good at storing data, i.e., loading a database transaction by transaction – imagine sitting in front of someone inputting data in front of a computer screen. For example, sales order entries, clinical appointment systems and the DMV (Department of Motor Vehicles) are all well served by OLTP. However, pulling data out of a database quickly and easily requires a different data structure. OLAP was invented to extract data with ease, speed, and finesse.

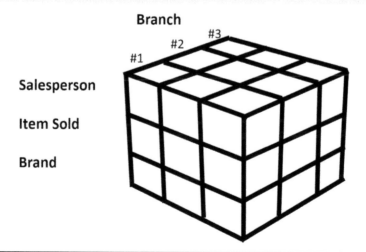

Figure 5.1   An extremely simple example of an OLAP (multidimensional) cube.

Beyond the Data Warehouse and Enhanced Interactive Visual BI and More

In the third evolutionary wave, all of what was available in Version 2.0 is also available in Version 3.0, but additionally, there are two major improvements. First, the BI in tables and basic charts becomes much more visually impactful and malleable. Secondly, visual objects are highly interactive. This means that the re-query mentioned above is as easy as clicking on a bar in a bar chart or histogram. The dashboard becomes the visual interface. To be sure, there were graphics, charts, and images available in Version 2.0, but there was a major change in the ways these became useable with the BI Version 3.0.

STORYTELLING WITH DATA

Storytelling is an important part of human existence. People love stories. People are moved by stories. When you just show people charts and graphs, it does not resonate. But, if you can tell someone a story, it helps people to relate. Florence Nightingale knew this. She had witnessed the carnage of the Crimean War and she realized most soldiers died not from combat, but infection and disease. It changed her life. It became her mission to reform nursing and the sanitation of hospitals. To convince the British Parliament and Queen Victoria to invest in better sanitary conditions she did so by telling a story with illustrations. She raised millions in today's dollars through the power of story.

With today's BI technology, storytelling with data is easier than ever. In fact, there are entire books dedicated to this skill. In *Storytelling with Data: A Data Visualization Guide for Business Professionals*, Cole Nussbaumer Knaflic provides a recipe and tips on how to create a proper story with data. But she points out it does not start with technology – "This may sound counterintuitive, but success in data visualization does not start with data visualization… time should be paid to understanding the context." And of course understanding context is fundamental to any good storytelling. See also Pettey (2018).

Business Activity Monitoring an Alert-Based BI, Version 4.0

In the final evolutionary wave, all of what was available in Version 3.0 is also available in Version 4.0. Gartner coined the phrase BAM (business activity monitoring) several years ago, but the capabilities continue to evolve. According to Gartner's online glossary (www.gartner.com/en/information-tec hnology/glossary/bam-business-activity-monitoring):

> Business activity monitoring (BAM) describes the processes and technologies that enhance situation awareness and enable analysis of critical business performance indicators based on real-time data. BAM is used to improve the speed and effectiveness of business operations by keeping track of what is happening and making issues visible quickly. The BAM concept can be implemented through many different kinds of software tools; those aimed solely at BAM are called "BAM platform products."

Two technologies that we will mention in Chapter 9 are real-time data and event-driven data. These technologies have enabled BAM. BAM is in the category of operational BI we defined at the beginning of the chapter.

This is a very short and simplistic four-version scenario for the status and evolution of BI. You can dive into the subject as deep your interests take you. We offer some interesting references at the end of the chapter as well as resources in the "Resources for the Avid Learner" section.

Strengths and Weaknesses of BI

Before we get into specific strengths and weaknesses, let us point out some characteristics could be strengths or weaknesses of BI based on the intent of the user. We will focus on the application of visual dashboards in the organization by a designer since they are currently so popular.

Transparency and Single Version of the Truth

First, visual dashboards can offer a great deal of transparency, because there are no complex mathematical models to explain. If designed properly the dashboard speaks for itself. If it is not evident what the designer is trying to demonstrate, the display can even be annotated or commented upon. Second, if the data is curated and sourced properly into the Visual BI system then it should represent the intent of the measures agreed upon by the enterprise.

However, the design and intent may totally negate these potential strengths of the BI system. Suppose I am a department manager and BI user. As a BI user, I may want to create a presentation which will bolster the chances of me getting my next year's budget increased. I can certainly game which data to use and how I construct the visuals so it distorts the truth and shores up my story. "Lies, damned lies and statistics" has been attributed (possibly incorrectly) to Benjamin Disraeli and popularized by Mark Twain. Had BI been around in his day he may have included dashboards within the quote.

The point – instead of letting **the numbers tell the story, the story is told by "cherry-picking" which numbers to use, the types of displays, the way the display is organized;** I have a story in mind and then use the visualization to try to tell "my" story. This can be done with statistics and many other methods. However, **it is really deceptive with Visual BI because people can see with their own eyes!!! How can numbers lie if I see the results** in a heat map (a type of Visual BI plot)? **The relationship is there! Yet, how many other dozens of heat maps might have been available out of the same data set? Are there configuration options chosen that enhance the intent of the author? This is extremely easy to do in Visual BI.**

NOTE: There are dozens of books on the misuse and misinterpretation of statistics. For example, Darrell Huff wrote *How to Lie with Statistics* in 1954 for the general reader. Huff was a journalist, not a statistician, and wrote many "how-to" articles as a freelance author (see also Huff and Geis, 1993).

In corporate systems where a championed dashboard of company metrics runs on a cycle, there are far fewer issues. However, for the departmental or board meeting, caveat emptor or buyer beware.

We will explain what we mean, but to summarize, there are several **strengths of BI:**

1) Humans are geared to seeing visual relationships and getting it
2) Humans love to play with things, interact
3) Many people start their analytics careers in BI
4) Tools are very mature, easy to use and powerful
5) Very little training is needed, very intuitive
6) Little processing is needed compared to machine learning and AI
7) May offer "A single version of the truth," may be transparent
8) Interlaces the analytics process, especially data science projects
9) BI is big and broad

Humans are geared to seeing visual relationships

Over hundreds of thousands of years of evolution, humans have developed the ability to see relationships very quickly. As the old saying goes, a picture is worth a thousand words. We can scan through visual dashboards and see where things tend to be pointing, and may call these the "main points" of the visualization, when in fact they may be "non-significant." We can also quickly see outliers and nuances in the visual data, but again these may be non-significant, unless error bars or confidence limits (CL) are presented as part of the visualization (which they usually are not in most of the BI tools we have seen).

Humans love to play with things, interact

We think one of the most appealing points of BI to people is the idea that you can play with the data. You can click on an object in a visual dashboard and throughout the display, every related object will be repopulated like magic. You can click for hours. This allows you to "play" with the data. You can "drill down" and "find new things" / "new knowledge" – BUT is this really new knowledge if there are no statistics of significance associated with the visualizations?

Many people start their analytics careers in BI

BI is a natural starting place for analytics professionals to begin their careers. This is interrelated with the intuitive nature of BI as just mentioned. People are great at seeing relationships in images. From this launching point, a professional can go in many directions. As we will see in the data science chapter (Chapter 8), someone may be more interested in the data engineering side or they may like the statistical side or move into other evolving BI areas like development.

Tools are very mature, easy to use and powerful

BI software has existed for 50 years. There is a lot of competition in the field and so the "ease of use" and stability are very good. They can scale to the largest enterprise and today BI systems may contain machine learning and other tools that can add significance and truth to what the user is viewing.

Very little training is needed, very intuitive

This is why many people start their careers in BI: there is a low training threshold to cross compared to many of the other analytic techniques. But if one stays at this level many mistakes in understanding "reality – truth" in the data can happen, so it is imperative that people understand that what one sees visually has to be shown to be true or false by significance measures (Nisbet, Yale, and Miner, 2018).

Little processing is needed compared to machine learning and AI

Everything is relative, and depending on the problem, the size of the enterprise and many other variables, the computing requirements will vary, but will be much less intensive than machine learning and especially AI and deep learning requirements. If desired there are many cloud options where sizing and computing can be adjusted dynamically. However, in this day and age of plentiful computer storage space and fast computing, the machine learning analysis can take place in fractions of seconds, so the "intensiveness" is not a hindrance to doing good analysis. In addition, the data preparation (which is 80–90% of the time involved in any data analytics) has to be done for the Visual BI anyway (which is the same final data that is also used for the machine learning and AI deep learning methods).

MAY offer "A single version of the truth"

We have already explained that the data warehouse and BI were created to provide a "single version of the truth." Yet, as with many techniques, it is not bulletproof. Tools in the hands of a knowledgeable user can game the system to paint the picture to justify their position or objective.

Interlaces the analytics process, especially data science projects

BI stands on its own and is a very effective tool, and therefore there are many ways to use it. However, as stated previously it is a great place to start and finish most analytics projects. And as stated previously, modern BI systems contain machine learning and other tools that we will soon explore.

BI is big and broad

There are many careers within the horizontal business dimension – all the IT and systems support, application developers (more technical development), business developers (report and dashboard creators), consumers (viewers) and more. Then you have the vertical use of BI. BI is present in virtually every industry, both private and public sectors. Careers abound and professionals have many options for upward and lateral career progression.

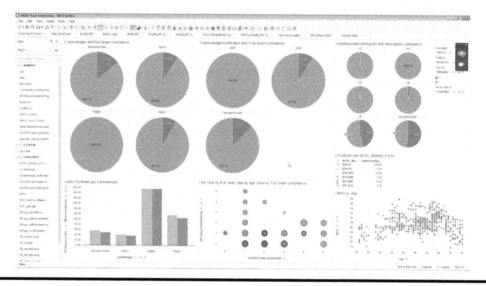

Figure 5.2 Diabetes management dashboard to explore factors affecting compliance.

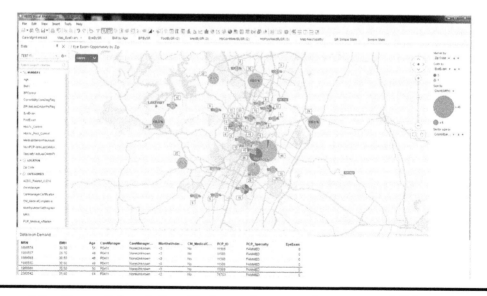

Figure 5.3 Geospatial analytics. Circles are hot, meaning you can drill into "dark gray" or "lighter gray" zones.

BI IN ACTION – POWERFUL DASHBOARDS FOR CARE MANAGEMENT OF DIABETES

The following is a brief example using visual dashboards to support operational BI:

It is important for diabetic patients to get frequent preventative care such as foot and eye exams (and more). This falls under care coordination. In addition, agencies like the National Committee for Quality Assurance (NCQA) support performance measures such as HEDIS (Healthcare Effectiveness Data and Information Set) that measure how well health plans are doing getting patients in to their doctors and clinics to take care of these preventative exams. BI systems can help these plans and care providers to raise compliance rates. We offer three sample dashboards as examples. The following dashboard provides a broad perspective of compliance across many variables ("dark gray" is noncompliant, "light gray" is compliant). Care coordinators and chronic disease managers can quickly get an analytic perspective of factors affecting compliance of exams and work toward improvement. This dashboard is interactive, meaning that when a user clicks on an element, this selection cascades through the dashboard and the relevant information is displayed (Figure 5.2).

Another useful example of this operational BI is the ability to use geospatial maps and determine zones to concentrate on. In the following figure, the circles represent zones around Austin, Texas. You can click on a "dark gray" portion of a circle and the medical record numbers (MRNs) that are not in compliance are displayed (see the bottom of the screen: MRN, BMI, care manager, primary care department and other attributes pop up). A case manager can then contact those individuals that are non-compliant and get them in for care for they need and make them compliant, thus lowering the chance they will need the emergency room and improving the HEDIS scores (Figure 5.3).

Our last example is the visual representation of the most important factors that drive a predictive model outcome. The model is built using existing data with a goal to predict whether a patient will present to the emergency room. Each dot is a patient and there are four variables displayed for each patient. Illustrated is the identification of an outlier, i.e., a patient at risk. The care manager can mark this patient in the BI system with a note, as is done below in therectangle seen in figure 5.4. This notation will persist and alert the corresponding scheduling personnel to take appropriate action and make an appointment with the correct department (Figure 5.4).

Now that we have offered some strengths and a BI example, let us explore some weaknesses of BI.

Weaknesses

1) Humans have strong imaginations and can see things in a graphic that do not really exist
2) Humans can visualize only a minimal set of variables
3) Retrospective only – except in the mind of the consumer
4) Cannot visualize higher order of relationships
5) Cognition is primarily in the head, computers are more objective and cheaper for many tasks
6) Less powerful and usually less valuable than data science and AI
7) Portability from one vendor to another may be challenging

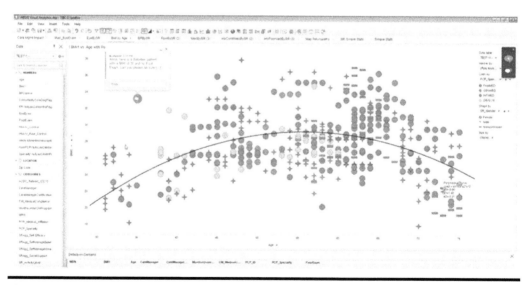

Figure 5.4   Visual representation of a predictive analytics model with collaboration/notification.

Humans have strong imaginations

People LOVE these dashboards and images; humans are great at seeing relationships (for good or evil, real or unreal). There are many presentations available like "How to Support the Budget Proposal" with Data Viz. A major university has promoted webinars where the goal is to teach you how to present toward a specific goal – creating your presentation for executive review to ensure you get next year's budget. Moreover, then the webinar points out ways to bias the presentation – ways to "cherry-pick" relationships, maximize some, minimize others in an executive presentation. While this might be good for one's career, it may not be good for the organization.

Humans can visualize only a minimal set of variables

A good analyst can consume and review the relationships across a few dozen variables in creating a few dashboard graphics and illustrations. The BI platform might be capable of supporting many more, but a professional creating dashboards is limited by time. We will see that machine learning can process tens of thousands of variables quickly. Again, this is where the marriage of the two domains really makes sense.

Retrospective only – except in the mind of the consumer

Predictive analytics is about predicting the likelihood of a future event based on conditions; it is looking toward the future or the front windshield. BI is really about looking at the past, looking through the rearview mirror – that is all the BI tool can provide. However, the human brain takes this "rearview mirror" information and projects the results into the future. While useful, there are more objective ways to handle this via machine and statistical learning.

Cannot visualize higher order of relationships

Multivariate statistics and data mining can assess dozens of variables and their interactions (how variables are interrelated) in high dimensions. You can create a model that consists of dozens of important predictors. If you look at a specific chart attempting to make an evaluation of the underlying relationships, three or four variables is about the maximum most people are comfortable in interpreting.

Cognition is primarily in the head, computers are more objective and cheaper for many tasks

We offered a section on this topic in Chapter 3. Many tasks are better served by computer processing – at least at a first pass. While exploring the data is still important, it is often helpful to use machines and CPU since they are normally a lower-cost option. Please see our expose in Chapter 3, "A Note on Cognition," where we state that cognition occurs in two places – a machine or *machines* and *your head*. The real benefit of cognition is two-fold: increased knowledge and improved decision-making.

Less powerful and often less valuable than data science and AI

This is certainly related to the previous section and the analytics maturity. In the previous chapter, in Figure 4.1 we illustrated the five distinct processes that increasingly raise the value of analytics as we go from the bottom to the top (left to right in Figure 4.1). BI is descriptive analytics and lower on the chart compared with other types of analytics. So, choose your platform judiciously as the total cost of switching platforms can be considerably higher than the difference in license cost.

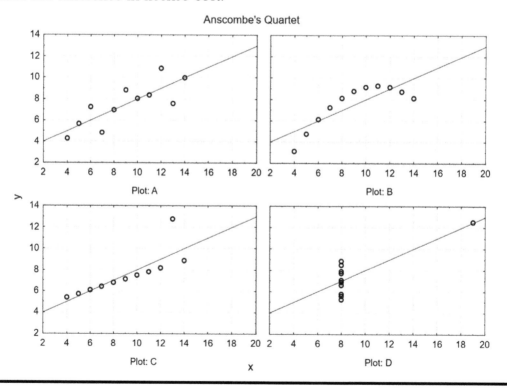

Figure 5.5   Anscombe's Quartet – Know Thy Data!

Portability from one vendor to another may be challenging

We have heard in the field that the way certain vendors approach the installation, maintenance and creation of BI assets (reports, dashboards, etc.) varies greatly. This makes moving from one platform to another platform more difficult than one would think.

AN EXAMPLE WHERE BI TRUMPS STATISTICS

Be careful of one-off exceptions. They are often used to illustrate anomalies of events; things that happen rarely, if at all. However, we will provide an interesting one here. Francis Anscombe, a statistician, synthetically constructed four sets of data. He then demonstrated these four sets of data produced virtually the exact same statistics (means, correlations, variances, etc.), but far different graphs. Figure 5.5 illustrates the differences graphically.

This supports our position that we need a combination of technologies to use when working with data. It is not just visual techniques, it is not just statistics, data science or AI, it is about a combination of the right tools in knowledgeable hands that leads to making better data-driven decisions.

Summary

We started this chapter with an overview of where BI fits into the analytics picture, and with a brief history of the development of BI over the past few decades. We provided three broad categories of BI:

1) Basic Reporting
2) A View inside the Data Warehouse and Interactive BI
3) Beyond the Data Warehouse and Enhanced Interactive – Visual BI and More

We also made it clear that today's BI systems generally include more advanced statistical and machine learning methods, thus making them more valuable than the BI of many years ago.

Some of the main points we hit upon in this chapter include:

1. Operational vs Project Based B
2. A basic history and reasons behind the evolution of BI
3. Strengths and Weaknesses of BI

Overall, we can say that while AI, machine learning and data science top the career lists, BI is very important and in demand as well. For careers listed as "the hard skills companies need most," BI ranks #20 out of the top 25 (see Petrone, 2018).

Postscript

In this chapter we have looked at BI from its earliest development decades ago to today's BI, which includes both visual and machine learning additions. These additions greatly enhance the accuracy (truth) and effectiveness of using BI in decision-making.

In the next chapter, we go into many of the methods and algorithms that actually do the data analytics to effectively understand data, namely, machine learning and data mining methods.

References

Crichton, M. and Levinson, B. (Producers), Levinson, B. (Director). 1994. *Disclosure*, Warner Bros.

Huff, D. and Geis, I. 1993. *How to Lie with Statistics Reissue Edition*. W.W. Horton and Company.

Knaflic, C.N. November 2015. *Storytelling with Data: A Data Visualization Guide for Business Professionals*. John Wiley.

Lago, C. July 18, 2018. "150 years of business intelligence: A brief history," in *CIO*, https://www.cio.com/article/3290407/history-of-business-intelligence.html.

Molen, G.R., Curtis B., Parkes, W.F., Bont, J. (Producers), Spielberg, S. (Director). 2002. *Minority Report*, 20th Century Fox.

Nisbet, R., Miner, G., and Yale, K. 2018. *Handbook of Statistical Analysis and Data Mining Applications* (2nd ed.). San Diego: Elsevier/Academic Press.

Petrone, P. 2018. "The skills companies need most in 2018 – And the courses to get them," *Linkedin*, https://learning.linkedin.com/blog/top-skills/the-skills-com panies-need-most-in-2018--and-the-courses-to-get-t.

Pettey, C. December 2018. "Use data and analytics to tell a story," https://www.gar tner.com/smarterwithgartner/use-data-and-analytics-to-tell-a-story/.

Resources for the Avid Learner

1 Inmon, W.H. 2005. *Building the Data Warehouse* (4th ed.). Wiley Publishing.
2 Kimball, R.. July 2013. *The Data Warehouse Toolkit: The Definitive Guide to Dimensional Modeling* (3rd ed.). Wiley Publishing.
3 "Useful, interesting podcast on single source of the truth," *The Data Skeptic*, http://dataskeptic.libsyn.com/single-source-of-truth.

Chapter 6

What Are Machine Learning and Data Mining?

Keywords: Models, Algorithms, ML (Machine Learning), Data Mining, Parameters, Ensemble, Regression, Classification, Natural Language Processing, Clustering

Preamble

This chapter is about two very powerful areas of analytics. *However, are they really two distinct areas?* We will explore that question as well as important, elementary foundations in these areas. We will provide a few examples of the types of problems machine learning and data mining can solve. We will explore the strengths and weaknesses of these techniques compared with business intelligence (BI) covered in the last chapter and provide a brief contrast to the next chapter on artificial intelligence (AI).

Overview of Machine Learning and Data Mining

Is There a Difference?

This is an interesting question. The short answer is today, in practice, not really. They both cover the same relevant methods and techniques. It is the maturity and morphing of the terminology that changes over time. As we have said and will continue to say throughout this book, these tidal movements are driven primarily by marketing and pressures to appear innovative. As we have said in virtually every chapter, there is hype and there is reality. There are some "net new" terminology and some "reinvented" terminology. For sure, there is improvement in technology, from the hardware to a myriad of software platforms across all the subjects we discuss, and we do not want to discount improvements in technology. We only want to help our readers with the ever-changing terminology landscape.

A (Brief) Historical Perspective of Data Mining and Machine Learning

In brief, AI precedes machine learning, just barely. AI research was first performed during a "Dartmouth Summer Research Project on Artificial Intelligence" conference in the summer of 1956. Arthur Samuel coined the term "machine learning" in 1959 while at IBM. The way Samuel coined the term implied that machine learning was a subset of AI. However, there was a major split of thought in these two fields and the AI camp separated from the machine learning camp. There was a mini-explosion of AI application and research in the 1980s. For example, Texas Instruments created a computer processing unit specifically designed to do AI.

It should be noted that *most practitioners consider AI to be a subset of machine learning.* We will see shortly that when practitioners think of **algorithmic AI** they think of neural networks, and all of its relatives – algorithms that mimic the human brain. An important note: we just said **algorithmic AI.** In the **application of AI,** you see things as simple as a light sensor on a light to be considered AI. Also, we need to make a distinction between "Weak AI" and "Strong AI." Weak AI may be as simple as the logic in a light sensor that turns a light on / off where a computer programmer writes the logic. Strong AI machines have a "mind of their own," so to speak, based on complex algorithms that allow them to learn as they go and thus enabling them to act differently in different situations (*E-3 Magazine*, May 27, 2019).

"Data mining" research came many years later, in 1995, at the "First International Conference on Data Mining and Knowledge Discovery." Usama Fayyad, a co-founder of the conference, started a new journal in 1996, *Data Mining and Knowledge Discovery.*

"Data Mining is the extraction of implicit, previously unknown and potentially useful information from data" (see Witten et al., 2016). The authors made this comment over twenty years ago in their first edition and it is true twenty years later. The term is actually a misnomer since we are not mining for data, we are mining for knowledge. Fayyad had the right idea by combing the two terms, but most practitioners referred to the area as simply "data mining" *until* about ten years later, when "machine learning" came more in vogue as the *term du jour*. We think the term is more descriptive of the actual process (teaching machines to learn by feeding them data – machine learning). And, the circle was complete. No, wait, AI started really being popular again in 2011. We should note that these terms never went away, just the emphasis on usage. In fact, the three major "Data Mining Commercial" packages that had all (or almost all) of these machine learning and neural network (AI) algorithms had been available as early as about 1996 and fully available in easy-to-use formats to industry, government, and healthcare from the year 2000; yet some of these organizations were slow to embrace the new technology. But, you are asking yourself, why did AI come back with popularity in 2011? *IBM Watson defeated two Jeopardy champions.*

PRODUCTS HYPED IN HEALTHCARE TOO EARLY LEAD TO MISSED EXPECTATIONS

IBM Watson offered "too much," however, to some areas, particularly healthcare. IBM Watson was very expensive to install and implement in an organization. Places like MD Anderson Medical Center did purchase it but after a period of time discovered that it could not do what it was touted to do and discontinued its use in 2017 after 5 years and a US$62 million cost (loss) (Schmidt, 2017).

Obviously, the AI abilities were not up to what they had been hyped to be at that time. However, the abilities of AI to change our world are rapidly increasing in scope and capacity (Miner et al., 2019).

There is another reason for the rise in AI research and usage in the last 10 years – computing power. If you look at the history of AI, there was conception in the 1950s, a big spike in the 1980s when computers became more powerful and now in the last ten years we have tremendous computing power *and tons of data!* More on AI in our next chapter.

DATA MINING VS DATA DREDGING (DATA FISHING OR DATA SNOOPING)

Years ago, there was resistance by certain camps, especially statisticians, against data mining. The misunderstanding arose from the objective of the process. It is true that if you look at a large dataset you can find relationships that are statistically significant, but are purely by chance (see an example of "Causation vs Correlation" in Chapter 4). Some researchers were misusing the process; they were data dredging by looking at hundreds of relationships, finding one that was statistically significant and reporting the results with the associated statistics – claiming that they had found some new insight.

Your 2nd author (Gary Miner) was attending the JSM (Joint Statistical Meetings) annual meeting in Canada in the year 2000, and attended the President's Banquet and talk one evening during that week. The President got up to give his talk and started by saying:

> You statisticians are going to have to do an "about face" – in this new century we are in a new age of "Modern Data Analysis – Predictive Analytics – Data Mining" and unless those of you who earn a living as "consulting statisticians" make changes you will soon lose your clients!!!

That made me take notice, as I had already committed myself to putting my efforts into data mining and text mining. I was at the meeting as an exhibitor for the company I worked with; our company gave a PRIZE AWARD to the "Consulting Statisticians" sub-group, which would have their annual "dinner meeting" on Tuesday evening of that week. Several years later, about 2005 or so, at the annual JSM meeting, Gary stopped in at the Consulting Statisticians dinner meeting, late, just as they had put up a slide showing that their clients had dropped at a 45-degree angle downward since the year 2000!!! Obviously, they had NOT gotten the message of the President in 2000; they were still trying to sell their efforts as "traditional statistics" when the market now wanted modern predictive data analytics. That is why it is important to have a well-rounded set of methods and techniques to employ based on the various problems one might be facing.

Note: When doing research to demonstrate causality, one should not simply build a predictive model and state the model as prescriptive or causal. If you want to prove that the model is causal, special care must be taken. An example of a prescriptive model that is not prescriptive can be found in Chapter 8 in a gray box – "The Most Misunderstood Concept in Data Science Today."

After 50 years of combined practice, we think most practitioners today see data mining and machine learning as essentially the same studies and AI as being a special subset of them. "Machine learning" is the more popular term today in our experience, and this is supported by a simple Internet search, with "machine learning" returning about four times as many results as "data mining." At the time of this writing, "artificial intelligence" has a slight lead over "machine learning," by about 12%, in Internet searches.

What Types of Analytics Are Covered by Machine Learning?

We mentioned 50 types of analytics in Chapter 4 and noted you will find many more if you search very hard. Machine learning applies to most of these in one way or another with a few exceptions such as descriptive analytics and visual analytics. The analytics classifications that do not inherently use machine learning (like traditional linear regression analysis and discriminant analysis) often merge into analytics that do by modifying their processes with "machine learning methods."

A NOTE OF CAUTION

As Dr. Daniel Larose (an old professor of Scott's, Larose, 2005) says "data mining is easy to do badly." For example, researchers may apply inappropriate analysis to datasets that call for a completely different approach, or a model may be developed built on wholly specious assumptions. Do you know what your software is really doing? Do you know the type of algorithm that it is applying? Documentation is typically better for commercial solutions, but it is still lacking in most cases. It is up to the user to be aware of what is happening in the background. Caveat emptor, as they say: buyer beware! Better said, you can't beat knowledge and being careful – we hope you are enjoying the book!

While we agree fundamentally with Dr. Larose, we believe there is less of a chance of misapplication of machine learning methods than many statistical methods. For example, in tests of significance and making inferences, researchers will test a number of hypotheses and never correct for multiple inferences – we will explore more of this in Chapter 10 (also see Nisbet, Miner, and Yale, 2018).

An Overview of Problem Types and Common Ground

We now cover a few of the general classes of problems that data mining and machine learning can effectively handle. We do this to help reduce the complexity of the thousands of problems that can be solved with these methods. There are some general problem types; below we discuss the classification of the most common types in data analytics.

The BIG Three!

We begin with the **BIG three problem types** that machine learning can help address:

- Regression
- Classification
- Natural Language Processing

The first two are what we call "supervised learning" methods, meaning we identify to the algorithm what we are trying to predict, call it a target, and provide some additional variables to help the algorithm learn a way to distinguish the target properties. They are "supervised" as we are specifying a prediction problem for the computer algorithm.

Let us make two quick distinctions. We will be speaking of numeric variables. Those are variables measured on either discrete counts or they may be fully continuous. Examples of continuous variables are the number of x-rays per year, per member per month (PMPM) insurance cost or the gross domestic product (GDP). The second type of variable is called a categorical variable, which are non-numeric variables that possess a distinct quality. Examples are gender, state or country of residence or medical procedure codes.

Regression

In regression problems, we are trying to predict a numeric outcome. For this chapter, we will call this outcome a "target" variable (you may also see these called dependent, outcome or response variables). We may use any mixture of numeric/categorical variables to predict this outcome. These variables used to help us predict we will call "predictors" for this chapter (you may also see these called independent variables, input variables or factors).

An example of regression would be predicting the length of a hospital stay (LOS = length of stay) using clinical and other factors. The target variable is numeric, the LOS is in days (numeric) and the inputs could be both numeric and categorical. For example, diagnosis-related group (DRG), time in surgery, wound classification, age of the patient, gender, discharge destination and many, many more including non-clinical variables like socioeconomic condition, geography and more.

Another example in government is the use of regression analysis to determine policy decisions, for example in a state or county correctional system where understanding the "average daily jail population," the number of arrests and types of crimes are of interest. This allows for having the right amount of support, police officers and jail cells available under varying environmental / societal conditions (Guynes and McEwen, 1998).

Classification

In classification problems, we are trying to predict a categorical outcome. And again, for this chapter, we will call this outcome a target variable (you will also see this called a dependent, outcome or response variable). We may use any mixture of numeric/categorical variables to predict this outcome. These variables are used to help us predict what we will call predictors for this chapter (you will also see these called independent variables, input variables or factors).

An example of classification is facial recognition. Suppose we are trying to determine via airport cameras whether any of the patrons walking inside a terminal is on a suspected terrorist list. The target variable is "on list" or "not on list." The predictor variables are all derived from data being streamed via cameras. This recording data is broken into thousands of inputs and used in a classification model to determine the outcome.

Another example of classification is credit scoring to determine who is a "good credit risk" or a "bad credit risk," hence a categorical outcome (target).

Natural Language Processing (NLP)

We will not get in too deeply here. However, it is a very important and very wide area. In short, (for most analyses) we preprocess the text and speech, converting it into data that looks more like numbers and categories. A simple example would be, in a corpus (a body of text), whether the word "friend" or some term with a similar meaning appears in the corpus. Of course, it can get very complicated, but we will keep it simple for now.

One powerful example of NLP is determining the presence or absence of disease using clinical notes. This is performed via text mining, a subset of NLP. These clinical notes are free-form text collected within a database, so instead of sending a list of structured variables we are providing notes. The algorithms go against the clinical notes and some reference data and dictionaries and determine the probability that this patient has the disease.

A very good example of how text mining can use clinical notes to provide a much more accurate prediction is the schizophrenic twin studies that are reported as tutorials No. I and No. U in the 2012 book *Practical Text Mining* (Miner et al., 2012). These two case studies (presented as complete "tutorials" showing all the steps in the data analytics) are entitled: (1) Text Mining Speech Samples: Can the Speech of Individuals Diagnosed with Schizophrenia Differentiate Them from Unaffected Controls? (Thompson et al., 2012a; on page 395); and (2) Exploring the Unabomber Manifesto Using Text Mining (Thompson et al 2012b on page 681). In these text mining analyses, a neural network (an AI-type algorithm) was able to model the data best in an initial competitive evaluation of different ML algorithms, so neural networks were used to comprehensively examine the data using Train, Test and Validation samples. An amazingly high accuracy score was obtained, greater than 90% accurate in predicting schizophrenia from the speech patterns of schizophrenics, whereas previous traditional statistical psychological studies had been only able to get predictions in the 40–50% range. Of even greater interest, when the model derived from theses schizophrenic speech studies was applied to the long written manifesto of the Unabomber (a person who had a Ph.D. in mathematics from the University of Michigan, and then disappeared but was eventually found in the Montana mountains years ago, the late 1990s, after he'd sent the manifesto to the *New York Times* in 1995 and mailed bomb packages to selected professors around the United States), it predicted that the Unabomber most likely suffered from schizophrenia.

Some (of Many) Additional Problem Classes

There are many other problem types, but we wanted to mention a couple more general classes and we want to distinguish these from the above supervised methods. These are unsupervised methods, meaning we do not specify a target variable. We normally throw in a whole group of variables and see how they interact together.

Association, Rules and Recommender Systems

Association rules are of the form **IF** "A" **THEN** "B." These can grow into very large sets of rules, because instead of a single "A" there can be an entire list. Take for example a grocery store. How should you lay out the store? What items naturally sell together? Alternatively, if you are an Internet retailer, and someone buys a smart health tracking device, what should you show him or her on the web page next – running shorts? These are called "recommender systems" and provide a way to help "lift" sales volumes and revenue. It should be noted that association rules are only one way to get a recommendation. There are many others, some quite complex as you can imagine, as there are billions of dollars at stake (see Linoff, Gordon, and Berry, 2011).

THE BEER AND DIAPER PROBLEM

A classical association rule example is called the "beer and diaper" problem. It is quoted in different ways, but it originated in the 1990s in the early days of this type of analysis. A researcher found that beer and diapers were bought within the same shopping cart very often; much higher than other shopping items. The story goes that the researcher thought the result was anomalous and described the issue to a fellow coworker who had just recently become a new father. The coworker told the researcher that he did not find the result odd at all. He responded, "a spouse is called, 'Honey, would you pick up some diapers on the way home?' The dutiful spouse complies and while they are at the store they walk by the beer cooler and say to themselves, 'sounds good' and adds it the cart." The problem is, what do you actually do with this information? Is it actionable? If so, how? It is an interesting story nevertheless.

For population health, epidemiologists and informaticists may investigate large data sets across diverse geographic and demographic populations to determine what the associations are across different factors as a starting point to understand the relationships for further investigation.

Clustering

Clustering is a very useful method, especially in the exploratory phases of data analytics, including descriptive analytics. It often progresses into predictive analytics. It is a non-supervised approach. In contrast to regression or classification, where we specify a target, there is **no target variable specified**. All variables of interest are thrown into the mix and then we see what variables' values tend to cluster together *across* variables.

A great use of cluster analysis is understanding customer behaviors. Suppose I am selling many products in many geographic areas to many different customers and I have considerable data on these customers including sociodemographic data. I can judicially add several variables into a clustering algorithm with the intent of understanding customer clusters. I can use those clusters to generate some specific customer profiles. Now that I have profiles, I have a target variable! I can next use predictive analytics to better serve my customers. For example, I can use the profile as a target to create marketing campaigns, targeted advertisements, and customer retention programs.

Another example is the public sector area. Tax assessing and collection agencies at the state and local levels need to understand all segments of their taxing base. They can use clustering to better identify small clusters (microsegments) of their population. Adding this to geospatial analytics adds real value.

These two examples have illustrated how multiple classes/categories of analytics can work together.

Some Comments on Model Types

There are many considerations when using different methods or algorithms to generate models. As we have seen above, many analytic problems are not just a one-step process. Instead, we start with a general problem, find an analytics solution and then incorporate that solution as an input into another analytic solution and so on. Kind of cool – like Lego blocks!

There are more aspects to consider than we can cover in this book, and it certainly is very industry and application specific, but we do want to mention three areas:

1) Some Popular Machine Learning Algorithm Classes
2) Transparency and Processing Time of Algorithms
3) Model Use and Deployment

WHAT IS FUN? WHERE DO MOST PEOPLE ACTUALLY SPEND THEIR TIME?

Michael O'Connell (Chief Analytics Officer at TIBCO) said: "data scientists (machine learning practitioners) spend about 80% of their time doing data prep and the other 20% of the time complaining about the time they are spending in data prep." This is actually derived from an established fact that analytics is about 80% consumed by data prep and about 20% in machine learning, modeling, and other activities.

Most people, the authors included, enjoy applying these machine learning algorithms, discovering new insights and wrapping these insights up in visual dashboards and non-data-related activities more than the data preparation. Software companies are automating machine learning processes. However, most of the automation thus far, is happening on the modeling side – not the data sourcing, data merging, data understanding, and cleansing activities. There have been inroads and these developments will improve – see AutoML in a later section in this chapter.

Some Popular Machine Learning Algorithm Classes

1) Trees 1.0: Classification and Regression Trees (CART) or Partition Trees
2) Trees 2.0: Advanced Trees – Interactive Trees (CART and CHAID), Boosted Trees and Random Forests, for Classification and Regression
3) Regression Model Trees and Cubist Models
4) Logistic and Constrained (penalized, LASSO, Ridge, Elastic Net) Regression
5) Multivariate Adaptive Regression Splines (MARS)
6) Support Vector Machines (SVMs)
7) Neural Networks in 1000 Flavors
8) K-Means Clustering Algorithm
9) Directed Acyclic Graph Analytics (Optimization, Social Networks)
10) Association Rules
11) AutoML

We will now provide some brief comments for these classes. This is meant to provide only the highest conceptual level and to provide some references for further study. We attempt to simplify these summaries as much as possible. There are great resources available and we mention several references in the following discussion as well as in the "Resources for the Avid Learner" section. However, we want to provide three definitions before we make comments on the above classes of machine learning techniques.

Parameters – Parameters are constants in a model or statistical distribution. For example, let's look at elementary math, where you have the slope (m) of a line. In the conventional form of elementary math, the slope and intercepts are both parameters. Thus in $y = mx + b$, the slope m and the intercept b are parameters, the equation is the model, and x is the independent variable or predictor variable while y is the target in the machine learning or statistical sense.

Ensemble Modeling – This is combining multiple models together. This can be done inside a machine learning algorithm (meta-algorithms, e.g., Random Forest, see below) or by a data scientist's action to enhance model performance (see Nisbet et al., 2018).

Scoring – Scoring is the process of taking characteristics from a candidate, inputting them into a predictive model and then letting that model produce a prediction. In our previous section "Regression," we would take the characteristics of a new patient and input their characteristics into a model and the model would predict (score) their LOS.

Trees 1.0: Classification and Regression Trees or Partition Trees

As we have noted, classification predicts a label (a discrete class) and regression predicts a quantity (a continuous quantity). The target variable values (categorical or continuous) are predicted from a group (usually) of both continuous and categorical predictor variables. The results are displayed in a tree-like graph where the data is split into "leaves," so to speak, of the tree. These procedures are usually provided as one package in software that can do either Classification or Regression Trees, and generally referred to as CART. Overall, the purpose of the tree-building algorithms is to determine a set of *if-then* (split) conditions that permit accurate prediction or classification of cases. These tree methods give simple, easy-to-understand results, and no assumptions for the analysis are needed, i.e. tree methods require minimal assumptions (nonparametric) and are nonlinear. Tree methods can often provide insight into simple relationships among a few variables that may go undetected by other analytic methods. CHAID (Chi-Square Automatic Interactive Detector) trees are very similar to CART but CHAID produces bushier trees by potentially creating additional splits.

Trees 2.0: Advanced Trees: Boosted Trees and Random Forests, for Classification and Regression

Boosted trees and **random forests** were developed to improve the predictive accuracy and overcome some of the problems of techniques we described in our "version 1.0" of tree methods. Both are ensemble methods, meaning they combine smaller trees together to get a better model. You may read that these trees support stronger learners by combining many weak learners together. The primary difference between boosted trees and random forests is that random forests work by "bagging" to reduce the variance. Boosted trees work by, well, boosting (resampling) methods to reduce bias.

Bagging and boosting get a number of weak learners, "N," to combine or ensemble by generating additional data in the training stage. "N" new training data sets are produced by random sampling with replacement from the original set. In the case of bagging, any element has the same probability to appear in a new data set. However, for boosting the observations are weighted and therefore some of them will take part in the new sets more often.

Regression Model Trees and Cubist Models

Two more tree-based methods we should mention are **Regression Model Trees** and **Cubist Trees**. In CART, a new observation finds its leaf, that is, the location in the tree it should fall into, based on basic "if-then" rules as described above. The prediction for a new candidate is simply the average of the observations used to train the model. So you have a number of candidates that end up with the same exact prediction (score) and this makes predictions appear coarse or grainy. Why not build a linear model inside each leaf? That is what a **Regression Model Tree** does. For a new score, it does two things. It first finds which leaf the new candidate should fall in; second, it fits a small linear model to this exact candidate and provides a score based on its unique characteristics. The results are more exact and appear finer than a CART model.

Cubist models initially create a full tree structure and collapse each path through the tree into a rule. There are intermediate linear models built at each step of the tree. A regression model is fit for each rule based on the data subset defined by the rules. These models are based on the predictors used in the previous splits. They are similar to Regression Model Trees, but instead of using the regression equation in one leaf, the prediction is mixed across leaves in the path.

Logistic and Constrained/Penalized (LASSO, Ridge, Elastic Net) Regression

Not only books but entire libraries can be filled on the subject of regression, and to add confusion to the mix, even the definition of regression in the first place. As we have said – regression problems typically denote trying to predict a numeric (quantitative) target or outcome. However, regression methods have been ADAPTED to predict qualitative targets (categories, which we would normally call classification problems). There are all kinds of regression from simple to complex. On the simplest end of the spectrum, you will see the ordinary least squares regression (OLS), which predicts a numeric target. Then on the other end of the spectrum, you will see constrained, penalized regression techniques that can predict numeric targets or that can be adapted for a qualitative target.

Ordinary least squares regression and **multiple regression** are closed-form solutions, meaning you do not need a looping or recursive algorithm to approximate a result. You simply solve with formulas. These formulas are derived by mathematical statistics via calculus to optimize the solution. Ordinary means one predictor and one result; multiple regression incorporates many predictors to come up with its predictions (see Kutner et al., 2004).

Logistic regression is a technique borrowed by machine learning from the field of statistics. It is a method-of-choice for binary classification problems (problems with two class values, such as disease/no disease, yes/no, true/false) (see Brownlee, 2016–2019).

LASSO (Least Absolute Shrinkage & Selection Operator) regression is taught in both statistics and machine learning courses. As the name implies, LASSO employs the concept of shrinkage. Shrinkage restricts the regression coefficients by applying a penalty function against them growing larger. In fact, LASSO may shrink the less important feature coefficients to zero, thus removing some features altogether. The LASSO procedure encourages simple, sparse models (i.e., models with fewer parameters). This particular type of regression is well suited for models showing high levels of redundancy in the predictors (multicollinearity) or when you want to automate certain parts of model selection, like variable selection/parameter elimination. It is a regression method that does variable selection to enhance prediction accuracy and interoperability of regression models, which is the reason it was introduced (Tibshirani, 1996).

Ridge regression is also a form of penalized regression that employs shrinkage of the regression coefficients. The technique ensures that variables with minor contribution have coefficients close to zero, but does not eliminate them entirely. It helps solve problems with variables that are measured with different scales (one variable in years, another in millions of dollars) (see Kuhn and Johnson, 2018; Ridge Regression, 2019).

Elastic Net is a form of penalized regression that combines features of LASSO and ridge regression (see Kuhn and Johnson, 2018).

Multivariate Adaptive Regression Splines

Multivariate Adaptive Regression Splines (MARS) is a method that requires minimal assumptions to be made by the modeler. It builds multiple regression models across a range of predictor variables, thus fitting a "curve" exactly. We might say that it "learns the curve." It has similarities to tree-based machine learning models. MARS makes no assumptions about the relationship between the target variable and the predictor variables. MARS is useful for relationships that change radically from linear and nonlinear across time of some other variable. It is very flexible and fairly transparent (Hastie et al., 2009).

Support Vector Machines (SVMs)

SVMs are used in regression and classification tasks by constructing nonlinear boundaries that serve as a decision point to place a new value into one of the other classes. They have a high degree of flexibility in handling these tasks. There are several types of SVM models that can be applied. SVMs are very useful in text categorization and classification of images. SVMs are now widely used in the biological sciences with protein molecules (see Alpaydin, 2004).

Neural Networks in 1000 Flavors

Neural Networks (NNs) are classification and clustering methods modeled after a hypothesized process of learning in the human brain. It is capable of predicting new observations after learning from data. One of the advantages is that NNs are able to learn and approximate any continuous function, and thus one does not need a hypothesis about one's data to begin with; however, setting up the initial conditions of the network is critical. NNs are extremely powerful but very opaque, meaning you cannot understand how a NN is actually determining its result. They are "black box" models. However, for image and video processing, they offer great solutions that provide some of the best results of any machine learning method; additionally, transparency is normally not an issue for these problems (see Larose, 2015).

Deep-learning networks are an extension of NNs but instead of having the usual single hidden layer of NN, they are characterized by depth, e.g. having many hidden layers. More than three layers (including input and output layers) qualifies as "Deep Learning" (Nicholson, 2019; Nisbet et al., 2018).

K-Means and Other Clustering Algorithms

We have mentioned clustering in this chapter several times, and there are many algorithms for clustering. Probably the most common algorithm for clustering due to its simplicity is **K-means clustering.** It is a very simple algorithm but very powerful and useful for unsupervised machine learning. Clustering is grouping data samples together into "clusters" of "like-minded samples." K is the number of clusters we want in our output, so K is selected by the modeler. The algorithm takes the data points as "input" and groups them into "K-clusters" as output. When we have a lot of data but no specific hypothesis nor specific "target variable," this type of clustering can be very useful in understanding the data, and may even bring about completely new insights or discoveries.

Directed Acyclic Graph Analytics (Optimization, Social Networks)

According to Gartner (Gartner Press Release, February 2019), "graph analytics is a set of analytic techniques that allows for the exploration of relationships between entities of interest such as organizations, people and transactions. The application of graph processing and graph DBMSs (Database Management Systems) will grow at 100% annually through 2022 to continuously accelerate data preparation and enable more complex and adaptive data science. Graph data stores can efficiently model, explore and query data with complex interrelationships across data silos, but the need for specialized skills has limited their adoption to date."

Optimization. GPS is an example of an easily understood application of machine learning algorithms applied to directed acyclic graphs (DAGs). A good example is the practical application of Dijkstra's algorithm, an algorithm for finding the shortest paths in GPS applications. Other optimization constraints such as construction and traffic can be layered upon competing candidate routes to arrive at the best solutions.

Networks of all types can be represented as a DAG. Social networks, where users are interfacing, can provide insight into fraud, terrorism or groups (clusters) of "like-minded people." Many of the algorithms covered have some application to DAGs – it is the structure of the graphs that provides valuable information to the modeling process. Bayesian statistics (networks) are often represented in DAGs, and we discuss this subject in Chapter 10. There are also networks for biological systems, computer systems and more. Any interrelated set of processes can typically be represented with a DAG.

Association Rules

We mentioned association rules earlier. The goal of **association rules** is to detect relationships and associations between categorical variables. Amazon and Netflix, among others, are champions in using association rule and recommendation engines (we mention the Netflix prize in Chapter 8 in the gray box "Netflix Prize, Kaggle and Crowd Sourcing"). However, there are a number of problems in healthcare and government that can be solved with association rules.

Algorithms that support these rules are used both in regular structured datasets and in text mining. A set of solutions around the "a priori algorithm" is available in open source and commercial versions. For big data, the Frequent Pattern (FP) growth can be enabled in-memory via Spark. More about Spark in Chapter 9.

AutoML (Automated Machine Learning)

AutoML is a fairly new development where the entire process of data analysis, from cleaning the data to competitively examining several ML algorithms to see which will handle a specific data set best, to selecting that best method and fully exploring it and developing a model and a prediction, are all done at once. This area of machine learning has and will continue to grow very rapidly as enterprises attempt to quickly scale up their machine learning services. See "Automated Machine Learning" in the "Resources for the Avid Learner" section at the end of this chapter.

Transparency and Processing Time of Algorithms

Now that we have several categories or classes of algorithms, which should I choose? Should it be a powerful neural network of some type or should it be a simple CART model? There are several considerations, but two of the most important are speed and transparency. In other words, how long will it take my model to train and can I explain to someone else how the model is coming up with its predictions?

Some algorithms run very fast in comparison to others. Of course, all of this is dependent on the number of variables, along with the number of features and rows of data. CART and linear regression are the quickest methods. NNs are the longest-running methods and everything else is in between (as a very rough rule of thumb).

Some algorithms return models that are very transparent and you can easily explain how the model is working. Again, CART and linear regression models are very transparent: they generate rules and functions that you present to managers and leadership that explain how the model is making predictions. Neural networks are very opaque or non-transparent. Following and explaining even one prediction from a very simple neural network will make eyes glaze over in a presentation. Many government and regulatory bodies, like the Securities and Exchange Commission (SEC) and the Food and Drug Administration (FDA), require model transparency!

Model Use and Deployment

This is a very large area and we will cover it in depth in our next book, which we noted previously. But, we should mention that it is important to consider at the onset how a researcher or enterprise will want to use the model once it is created. It could be small or enterprise-wide. Some models are deployed into production IT processes, some are hard coded into products, some are provided as services via a web interface (e.g. RESTful (Representational State Transfer) API) and some are used on an ad hoc basis as needed.

Major Components of the Machine Learning Process

In Chapter 3, we covered a process that is well accepted and yet adaptable to machine learning projects. It was called CRISP-DM (Cross-Industry

Standard Process for Data Mining) and includes a nice set of procedures. In Chapter 4 we talked about the data cycle, which is also useful. In general, here are the major steps involved in a project (which can vary as needed):

1) Data Sourcing
2) Data Merging
3) Exploratory Data Analysis
4) Data Cleansing
5) Analysis
6) Modeling or Reporting
7) Deployment

Advantages and Limitations of Using Machine Learning

Unlike in the last chapter, where you can effectively look at a handful of variables at a time, machine learning allows you to work with literally thousands of variables. The curse of dimensionality may still exist for some algorithms to scale, but we have ways to minimize this problem.

Contrasted to BI of the last chapter, machine learning offers **advantages:**

1) It lets the computer do the processing/cognition: please see Chapter 3 ("A Note on Cognition") where cognition happens.
2) The size of the problem is limited only by computer resources – machine learning covers very large problems.
3) Its results are mathematically verified, meaning that an established algorithm is interpreting the data rather than an analyst looking at and interpreting aggregations and statistics of visual dashboards.
4) It offers more powerful insights and value-added results.

And, some **disadvantages:**

1) It requires more education or training. A producer or analyst using Visual BI can produce output after just a few days of training. While companies are trying to make machine learning ever simpler, it stills requires a much deeper understanding to execute machine learning properly.
2) It requires more data pre-processing. See gray box, "What Is Fun? Where Do Most People Actually Spend Their Time?" in this chapter

3) The total cost will be higher. This is due to either training or software. Open source is "free," but you have to hire someone with more skills (especially coding) to operate it. Computer (hardware and software) will have higher requirements.

Please note again, visual analytics (and BI) and machine learning are not mutually exclusive! They are complementary. BI is very useful in the beginning to discover initial insights and at the end of the process to present the results of machine learning! Moreover, for departments or organizations with a smaller budget, BI can add value on its own.

Postscript

In this chapter, we compared the differences in history and application of data mining and machine learning. We looked at some various forms of different algorithms that employ these methods. We classified or grouped them into logical units. However, you should know there are many more available. Knowledge and application comprise the key to deriving value from these data-driven techniques. Some of these algorithms are in the "AI realm." In the next chapter, we will go into AI in detail.

References

Alpaydin, Ethem. October 2004. *Introduction to Machine Learning*. Adaptive Computation and Machine Learning. MIT Press.

Brownlee, J. February 2, 2016. "Logistic regression for machine learning," https://machinelearningmastery.com/logistic-regression-for-machine-learning/.

E-3 MAGAZINE. May 27, 2019. https://e3zine.com/strong-artificial-intelligence/.

Gartner Press Release. February 18, 2019. "Gartner identifies top 10 data and analytics technology trends for 2019," https://www.gartner.com/en/newsroom/press-releases/2019-02-18-gartner-identifies-top-10-data-and-analytics-technolo.

Guynes, R. and McEwen, T. 1998. "Regression analysis applied to local correctional systems," in M.L. Dantzker and Arthur J. Lurigio, et al. (eds.), *Practical Applications for Criminal Justice Statistics*, www.ncjrs.gov/App/publications/abstract.aspx?ID=175411.

Hastie T., Tibshirani, R., and Friedman, J. 2009. *The Elements of Statistical Learning: Data Mining, Inference, and Prediction* (2nd ed.). Springer Series in Statistics. Springer Verlag.

Kuhn, Max and Johnson, Kjell. March 2018. *Applied Predictive Modeling*. Springer.

Kutner, Michael, Nachtsheim, Christopher, and Neter, John. 2004. *Applied Linear Regression Models* (4th ed.). McGraw Hill/Irwin.

Larose, Daniel T. 2005. *Discovering Knowledge in Data: An Introduction to Data Mining.* Wiley.

Larose, Daniel T. March 2015. *Data Mining and Predictive Analytics* (2nd ed.). Wiley.

Linoff, Gordon S. and Berry, Michael J.A. April 2011. *Data Mining Techniques: For Marketing, Sales, and Customer Relationship Management.* Wiley.

Miner, G., Delen, D., Elder, J., Fast, A., Hill, T., and Nisbet, R.A. 2012. *Practical Text Mining and Statistical Analysis for Non-Structured Text Data Applications.* Elsevier/Academic Press.

Miner, G., Miner, L., and Dean, D. 2019. *HEALTHCARE's OUT SICK - PREDICTING A CURE - Solutions that WORK !!!!: Predictive Analytic Modeling, Decision Making, INNOVATIONS and Precision ... Correct the Broken Healthcare Delivery System.* Productivity Press.

Nicholson, C. 2019. "A beginner's guide to neural networks and deep learning," https://skymind.ai/wiki/neural-network.

Nisbet, R., Elder, J., and Miner, G. 2009. *Handbook of Statistical Analysis and Data Mining Applications* (1st ed.). Elsevier/Academic Press.

Nisbet, R., Miner, G., and Yale, K. 2018. *Handbook of Statistical Analysis and Data Mining Applications* (2nd ed.). Elsevier/Academic Press.

Ridge Regression. 2019. *Brilliant.org.* Retrieved 12:38, November 14, 2019 from https://brilliant.org/wiki/ridge-regression/.

Schmidt, C. May 2017. "M. D. Anderson Breaks with IBM Watson, Raising questions about artificial intelligence in oncology," *JNCI: Journal of the National Cancer Institute*, 109 (5), djx113, https://doi.org/10.1093/jnci/djx113.

StackExchange: CrossValidated, 2014–2019. https://stats.stackexchange.com/questions/77018/is-random-forest-a-boosting-algorithm.

Support Vector Machines. https://en.wikipedia.org/wiki/Support-vector_machine.

Thompson, J., Trumbetta, S.L., Miner, G.D., and Gottesman, I.I. 2012a. "Text mining speech samples: Can the speech of individuals diagnosed with schizophrenia differentiate them from unaffected controls?," in *Practical Text Mining and Statistical Analysis for Non-Structured Text Data Applications.* Elsevier/Academic Press. DOI:10.1016/B978-0-12-386979-1.00017-7.

Thompson, J., Trumbetta, S.L., Miner, G.D., and Gottesman, I.I. 2012b. "Exploring the Unabomber manifesto using text miner," in *Practical Text Mining and Statistical Analysis for Non-Structured Text Data Applications.* Elsevier/Academic Press. Doi: 10.1016./B978-0-12-386979-1.00029-3.Y

Tibshirani, Robert. 1996. "Regression shrinkage and selection via the lasso," *Journal of the Royal Statistical Society.* Series B (methodological), 58(1): 267–88.

Wikipedia; Automated Machine Learning. https://en.wikipedia.org/wiki/Automated_machine_learning.

Witten, I., Frank, E., and Hall, M.A. January 2016. *Data Mining: Practical Machine Learning Tools and Techniques* (4th ed.). The Morgan Kaufmann Series in Data Management Systems. Morgan Kaufmann.

Resources for the Avid Learner

1 A great book for machine learning and data mining is Kuhn, Max and Johnson, Kjell. March 2018. *Applied Predictive Modeling.* Springer. Scott currently uses this book in his Predictive Modeling class in the Masters of Data Science Program at City University of New York (CUNY).

2 Here is a short, nice overview of the machine learning (modeling process). We found it on the **Toward Data Science** website. It is a good resource for data scientists and analytics developers. *"How to Develop a Machine Learning Model From Scratch"* by Victor Roman, December 23, 2018, https://towards datascience.com/machine-learning-general-process-8f1b510bd8af.

3 A useful guide to understanding popular machine learning algorithms (including some AI) was published by Jason Brownlee (last updated September 3, 2019, on his **Machine Learning Mastery** website, *"A Tour of the Most Popular Machine Learning Algorithms,"* https://machinelearningmastery.com/a-tour-of-machine-learning-algorithms/.

4 A very complete and interesting machine learning project for medicine is described in a journal article, "Model-Based and Model-Free Machine Learning Techniques for Diagnostic Prediction and Classification of Clinical Outcomes in Parkinson's Disease," by team members from the University of Michigan and Tel Aviv Sourasky Medical Center, published May 28, 2018. The paper covers the application of many of the methods covered in this chapter as well as sample selection and cross-validation. It not only covers the medical study, but provides a resource into additional topics such as non-parametric statistical tests, sensitivity and specificity, effect size, exploratory data analysis and more. The results can be found in *Scientific Reports*, on Nature.com, www.nature.com/articles/s41598-018-24783-4.

5 Automated Machine Learning, www.tibco.com/resources/product-demonstr ation-video/automated-machine-learning and https://en.wikipedia.org/wiki/Automated_machine_learning.

Chapter 7

AI (Artificial Intelligence) and How It Differs from Machine Learning

Keywords: AI (Artificial Intelligence), Artificial Neural Networks, Deep Learning, Image Recognition, Hadoop, Spark, In-memory Computing, Weak AI, Strong AI, LISP, Expert Systems

Preamble

In the last chapter, we looked at data mining and machine learning. We discovered the history, some nuances, and applications – and in the end, **It's All Analytics!** From constrained regression to support vector machines to artificial intelligence (AI), we looked at it all. We now cover an exciting area of analytics that has been exploding in practice and use over the last several years. Its application, benefits, and drawbacks are often misunderstood, and our goal here is to clear up those misunderstandings of artificial intelligence or as is now common in everyday vernacular – **AI**.

Introduction

Let us start with an overview of where AI fits into the analytics picture. **First, AI is all the rage these days!** From a consumer standpoint, you can get AI in almost everything. From coffee makers to virtual/intelligent personal assistants (VPAs), from the simple to the very complex. We talk about this in the *weak AI* section. In fact, a very successful entrepreneur said they had 1,000 new startup ideas! What were they? Just add AI to existing products and services!

Then there is a second AI: *strong AI*. This is the formation of AI models using algorithms. This is where data scientists play. They can build analytic workflows that contain thousands of features (variables, but a term that is more common in the AI space is features).

Let Us Outline Two Types of AI Here – Weak AI and Strong AI

Weak AI (narrow AI) is what many people think of when they hear AI, because it is embedded into products and services that they commonly use. We just mentioned VPAs. Siri, Alexa, and Cortana are three examples of VPAs. Weak AI is a collection of technologies that rely on algorithms and programmatic responses to simulate intelligence. VPAs sound very smart, but the program they execute simply listens for key sounds in your speech and when it detects them, follows its programming to execute certain actions (like cross-referencing a database for responses to certain queries/questions).

Strong AI (true AI) is what futurists think of when they hear the term AI. Strong AI is intended to think independently. These systems are built to mimic the human brain and they are designed to be cognitive. They do not merely execute scripts, but are built to be aware of context and nuance and to make decisions that reflect actual thought. Strong AI is adaptable, meaning that it will learn and make better decisions over time. *Terminator* is an example of strong AI, but there are many other examples as well, including ones that do much simpler things!

The data scientist is interested in building models using AI algorithms. The application of these models could be either weak or strong AI. For simplicity, we will use the concept of weak AI and that the goal for modeling will be to embed our model in a product or service, or to execute at will (ad hoc). This is our perspective for this chapter. We are primarily focusing on the application of algorithmic AI to build models and produce code that can be embedded in analytic processes as well as products. We are focused on the development of AI from a machine learning perspective.

In brief, AI is popular and there is a lot of confusion and *hype* about what it actually does. Our goal in the chapter is to help clear up some of the confusion.

Another way to look at AI – it is both the intelligence of machines and the branch of data science or computer science used to create it. We will be focusing on the latter in this chapter. And, we will cover four major evolutions (as we see it) in AI over the last 50-plus years and a glimpse into the future.

There are other ways of "slicing and dicing" (or understanding) AI, and as an example please see the next gray box on "Four Types of AI":

FOUR TYPES OF AI

There are four types of AI:

- Reactive Machines
- Limited Memory
- Theory of Mind
- Self-Awareness

Reactive Machines: IBM's Deep Blue chess-playing supercomputer is an example of this. It beat the international master chess player, Garry Kasparov, in the late 1990s. Deep Blue (now called IBM Watson, as IBM has developed it for medicine and other industrial uses) can identify pieces on a chessboard, know how each piece moves and make predictions about what moves may be made next and thus, by rules of logic, "decides" which move is most advantageous. BUT, doesn't have any concept of the past, nor any memory of what has happened before.

Limited Memory: These types of AI machines can look into the past. An example is self-driving cars that do some of this now by observing other cars' speed, position, and direction. The AI machine has to observe the other cars over time, in order to calculate speed, etc. The AI machine has to have things like lane marking, understanding of curves, etc. programmed into its memory, and programmed to interact with what it is "seeing" at the moment. These limited (simple) pieces of information are not saved into the car's library of experience (like *human* drivers do "automatically") but instead are only temporary (transient). So the self-driving car does *not* have the ability to learn how to handle new situations because it cannot "remember" what it experiences (as humans do).

Theory of Mind: This is where we have "hit a wall" in AI development. "Theory of mind" means that the AI machine needs to be able to form an understanding about things in the world – the understanding of "motives" and "intentions" of other entities (the cars and the humans in the cars, in addition to other creatures and objects in the world). If AI "creatures" are to work and interact with us humans, they will have to "understand" human emotions and feelings and be able to adjust their "robotic behavior" to adjust if they are to be fully successful.

Self-Awareness: Fully successful AI machines will have to have a "consciousness;" this means that the AI researchers will also have to fully understand consciousness in order to be able to build this into their AI machines. Consciousness is "self-awareness." Humans waiting in traffic may experience someone behind them honking their car's horn; the human understands that the person in the car is probably "angry" or experiencing some other emotion like "impatience" because they have an emergency and have to get to a hospital, for example. Humans understand that other humans probably have those same or similar feelings. Therefore, AI scientists building "consciousness" or "self-awareness" into their machines will be essential, if we are to ever get to a fully functioning robot.

From: Hintze, Arend, Michigan State University, 2016.

AI Background and Chronology

One of the premises of this book is to clear up the confusion, in both substance and terminology, in the analytics, data science, and AI domain. We feel it is always useful to consider historical perspectives so we can understand the advent and evolution of the terminology and study the practices and use of these technologies. We covered a rich history of machine learning and data mining in the last chapter. We review the history of AI now. Some of these overlap, but as we have said we want each chapter to be free-standing and available for reference.

We view AI history in five major stages, and believe AI is poised for a bright future. So first, let us explore these five stages:

1) Short History of Digital AI
2) Resurrection in the 80s
3) Beyond the Second Winter
4) Deep Learning, Bigger and New Data
5) Next-Generation AI

Short History of Digital AI

The philosophy of AI and AI as a concept have been around for centuries. We cover the major digital perspectives.

As we said in the last chapter, AI precedes machine learning, just barely. AI research was first performed during a "Dartmouth Summer Research Project on Artificial Intelligence" conference in the summer of 1956 (University of Washington, 2006; Lewis, 2014; Anyoha, 2017). Arthur Samuel coined the term "machine learning" in 1959 while at IBM (see Machine Learning Definition; Samuel, 1959). The way Samuel coined the term implied that machine learning was a subset of AI. However, there was a major split of thought in these two fields and the AI camp separated from the machine learning camp. While AI may be an overarching term that encompasses machine learning, that is not often the way practitioners view it. It is often useful to think specifically. If you use the term "AI," most practitioners will think of automated neural networks and deep learning or one of the many derivatives or applications of these two domains. When you say "machine learning," a data scientist will think more broadly to the techniques we covered in the last chapter. So, there is a distinction between history and practice.

Why the 1950s? Because it was the birth of the digital age and computers were becoming (barely) powerful enough to start bringing new technologies to bear. Spoiler alert – every major reinvention or stage change is due to a bump in computer processing power and adjunct technology, as we will soon see. The UNIVAC was introduced in 1951 and IBM took over the market with a long series of releases of mainframes and increasingly more powerful machines (History, 1951).

AI research and development continued in the 1960s, but slowed in the 1970s and then began to take another revolution in the 1980s. There are two periods in AI history considered "AI winters." The first was from 1974 to 1980 (Schuchmann, 2019). Figure 7.1 illustrates the history of AI development with an emphasis on the "AI winters" and the deep learning revolution. The AI winters are lightly shaded.

Resurrection in the 1980s

AI had a major resurrection in the 1980s with the advent of expert systems. An expert system is a computer system that emulates the decision-making ability of a human expert. These systems did not approach AI the way

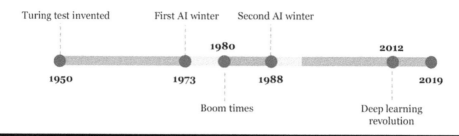

Figure 7.1 History of AI development with emphasis on the "AI winters" and the "deep learning revolution" that started about 2012 (adapted from Schuchmann, 2019).

procedural languages would or the way it is commonly handled, but did so with more simple "if-then" rules.

There were two factors that gave rise to expert systems. First was the adoption of the LISP language. The LISP language was developed in the late 1950s by John McCarthy. LISP is the second-oldest high-level programming language in widespread use today. Only Fortran is older, by one year. Dialects of LISP are still relevant with Hy for Python being introduced in 2013.

Second was the construction of actual hardware to support LISP – the LISP machines. LISP machines had an optimized method of execution and clock speed for processing. Specific LISP chips were developed as it appeared AI would revolutionize it all. There were many of these machines developed. The Texas Instruments Explorer and the Apple Lisa are examples of PCs developed for LISP. However, the resurgence of LISP also had its problems (Cummins, 2018).

Beyond the Second AI Winter

Another AI winter occurred from about 1987 or 1988 to 1993. After this winter, there was a slow, then progressive expansion of AI. These expansions were somewhat linear in nature. With more computer power some of the promises of early AI could now be achieved. Adoption was slow but steady. There were concerns for lack of transparency of AI as it produces what are considered black box models. Unlike many of the methods we saw in the last chapter, such as trees that can easily be interpreted, black box models cannot be procedurally followed to understand the outcomes it is generating. These concerns still exist today. In fact, as we discussed in our first chapter, there is an increasing regulation of machine learning models.

Deep Learning, Bigger, and New Data

This period started about 2010–2011 and is the current state. Unlike the last period, which was linear, this period has been exponential. Some of the forces involved include:

1) Even More Computing Power
2) Deeper Learning
3) The Rise of Big Data Technology Adoption
4) The Rise of IoT (the Internet of Things)
5) A Sharp Interest in Pattern Recognition (Audio, Video, Images)

There should be no surprise that computing technology grows ever faster, and memory gets cheaper; this allows for more widespread adoption of techniques that were relegated to only those organizations with large budgets and resources to handle them. In short, **processing and memory** are now cheap enough that it does not present a barrier to anyone wanting to perform AI.

Deep learning has been around for a long time. Deep learning is really just an extension of the artificial neural networks we saw in the last chapter. In simple terms, there are just more hidden layers. They require more time to train, but in the end, can produce very powerful models. Research into deep learning has exploded and given open source and other technology, professionals many more options to apply these algorithms.

Figure 7.2 illustrates a simple artificial neural network. This neural network has one hidden layer. A deep learning model would have more depth and more hidden layers. More than one hidden layer qualifies as "deep learning" (Nicholson, 2019; Nisbet et al., 2017).

The **rise of big data technology adoption** has to do with the development of the open source Apache Hadoop. Hadoop is available in open source and commercial versions. It provides a highly scalable way to perform data storage and machine model building. We will talk in depth about this technology in Chapter 9, along with Spark (in-memory computing), which enables faster deep learning, but briefly here are some advantages:

1) It can be built on commodity hardware so businesses that wanted to create data lakes often used Hadoop to do so.
2) It is open source and so some consider it free *(we know better; there is a total cost of ownership, which we will cover in depth in our next book).*

A simple neural network

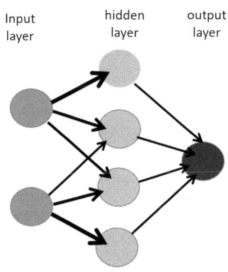

Figure 7.2 Simple artificial neural network model.

3) It enables in-cluster model development.

Before Hadoop, the machine learning flow was to process and structure all your data and bring it into the machine learning platform. This meant bringing large amounts of data across the network, and executing the machine learning algorithm inside the machine learning platform. With in-cluster machine learning, the algorithms were instead passed across the network from the machine learning platform to the cluster where the data lived. Passing algorithms is much faster and more secure than moving loads of data.

The **Internet of Things (IoT)** has been growing expansively, and is expected to double from its value of US$235 billion in 2017 to US$520 billion by 2021 (Columbus, 2018). Think about Smart Cities where there are CCTV and video cameras all over the city and streets. There are sensors buried inside and along the roads. All these devices are collecting data around the clock. Transportation companies have multiple geospatial and telemetry devices in every vehicle of their fleets. They collect this data continuously. Factories have thousands of sensors collecting data on all of the manufacturing devices, along the factory floors and in the warehouses. Even passenger planes are equipped with thousands of sensors and telemetry devices.

Pattern recognition has really taken off over the last several years where AI deep learning is a very well-suited methodology for these types of problems (Swathi, 2019). AI produces highly reliable predictive results for everything from images in hospitals (x-rays and various scans) to face recognition (airports and social media) to video (traffic cameras).

Given this great expanse of technology and almost "unlimited" data, AI has become more of a "plug-and-play" solution for image recognition. Moreover, the fact that many of these types of problems do not need a great amount of transparency makes AI a great solution: for example, **pattern recognition** as used by social media platforms where users opt in and sign away rights or are considered just content brokers and not content police. Alternatively, airports (see the interesting example in the "Resources for the Avid Learner" section at the end of this chapter with Justin Smith and Liliana Petrova) and other public areas that in the United States do not have deep privacy restrictions are great places for image recognition. AI is hands-down better than any other technology at producing the best predictive models for image recognition. In addition, AI is valuable in IoT, telemetry, and transportation, where the predictions are done inside a business with tight controls.

Next-Generation AI

We are primarily focusing on algorithmic AI in this chapter and algorithmic data science in general. However, to be fair, how AI will affect us in the future has more to do with adoption and application of models into nearly everything around us. Some of this will not be driven by algorithmic AI (artificial neural networks and deep learning) but more by applying rules and programming into products and services. Products around the world are being filled with sensors and these sensors are becoming intelligent with programming and embedded models inside them.

The major advancements in algorithmic AI are next-generation deep learning (see gray box – "Beyond Catastrophic Forgetting"), enhancements in multi-agent machine learning and computational creativity. A multi-agent system is a computerized system composed of multiple interacting intelligent agents (an autonomous entity that directs its activity toward achieving goals). Computational creativity is used to model, simulate or replicate human creativity using a computer toward goals or objectives (see Colton et al., 2009, 2015)

An interesting and powerful quote can be found by Ramon López de Mántaras (see López de Mántaras, 2018):

> No matter how intelligent future artificial intelligences become, they will never be the same as human intelligence: the mental development needed for all complex intelligence depends on inter-actions with the environment and those interactions depend, in turn, on the body – especially the perceptive and motor systems.

BEYOND CATASTROPHIC FORGETTING

One of the downsides of deep learning is something called catastrophic interference, also known as catastrophic forgetting. It is the tendency of an artificial neural network to completely and abruptly forget previously learned information upon learning new information. This phenomenon was identified many years ago. It has been and continues to be the subject of research in artificial neural networks and deep learning.

THE IMPORTANCE OF AI FOR GOVERNMENT AND HEALTHCARE

Government is getting into AI in a big way. Of course, the intelligence and defense areas of government are pushing the envelope with the help of commercial and academic partners.

But now, the Department of Health and Human Services Centers for Medicare & Medicaid Services (CMS) is embracing AI as well. CMS in 2019 announced the requirements and registration for the "Artificial Intelligence Health Outcomes Challenge," which offered US\$1,000,000 in prizes. It opened in June and there were over 300 applicants from academia and corporate America; many were partnerships of the two.

The last day of October, they announced 25 entrants (of more than 300 submitted) that made it to the second round – www.cmschallenge. ai/. This demonstrates three things:

1) The government is getting smarter by adopting a crowd-sourcing model to improve its operations and effectiveness.

2) CMS is opening up to new methods and willing to pay real money to get help.
3) Healthcare, while ahead with several successful machine learning applications, is still very far behind consumer-based businesses. Seeing CMS commit may bolster stronger investment and inroads into analytics.

The two objectives are expressed by CMS as follows:

Use AI/deep learning methodologies to predict unplanned hospital and skilled nursing facility (SNF) admissions and adverse events within 30 days for Medicare beneficiaries, based on a data set of Medicare administrative claims data, including Medicare Part A (hospital) and Medicare Part B (professional services).

Develop innovative strategies and methodologies to explain the AI-derived predictions to front-line clinicians and patients to aid in providing appropriate clinical resources to model participants, and increase use of AI-enhanced data feedback for quality improvement activities among model participants.

The competition will conclude in September 2020, but we look forward to the results and more competitions like this where the spirit of competition drives great, innovative results.

Differences of BI, Data Mining, Machine Learning, Statistics vs AI

We covered the historical perspective of data mining, machine learning and AI in the last chapter and earlier in this chapter. We found that AI is the overarching term and that data mining was part of AI, but broke off into a separate arm of research and then machine learning came into vogue. However, history is a little different than the current vernacular. We want to make you fluent in today's terminology (and it is likely to change tomorrow as the hype cycle spins). From a **current practitioner perspective,** we offer the following summary.

Data mining and machine learning incorporate the majority of the same methods. The latter is a more popular and descriptive term for what these algorithms are doing, so one could use a single term: "machine learning." For most practitioners, machine learning encompasses AI models, so it is bigger and broader (see Kuhn and Johnson, 2018; Nisbet et al., 2017). AI refers to mimicking the human brain to teach machines to think. The human brain is made up of neurons connected by synapses, and cognition is performed by linkage and firing of various neurons creating a neural network. So, artificial neural networks (neural nets for short) and deep learning (which is an extension of neural networks) are the cornerstones of AI. So when someone mentions a k-means clustering algorithm or a k-nearest-neighbors algorithm (and many more; see Chapter 6), a data scientist or practitioner will most likely think in terms of machine learning. If you mention an artificial neural network or deep learning algorithm to the same person, they will likely think in terms of AI.

Strengths and Weakness

Algorithmic AI can be extremely powerful at creating highly predictive models using very complex data not amenable to many other machine learning techniques. It handles problems of complex, highly nonlinear systems very well.

Some Weaknesses of AI

1) Requires much more data to train/build models
2) Requires more processing power and time
3) Models are not transparent or readable
4) Encodes correlation and not causation
5) Easily overtrains (shallow)
6) Trains to narrow applications, very sensitive to population stability
7) Models may think locally (greedy)
8) Models may be brittle and unpredictable

Requires much more data to train/build models

Unlike some of the techniques and methods we are covering in this book, AI requires relatively large amounts of data. Business intelligence (BI) and statistical techniques are favored for certain types of analysis and be useful with much less data. Certain domains just do not produce enough data to make these models useful. Healthcare is a prime example where small to midsize organizations may not observe enough cases each year to make AI a viable option.

Requires more processing power and time

Computing power has opened up the wide use of AI across industries and applications. AI has reached all areas of business. It is in healthcare and government. However, that does not mean it is cheap. Depending on the algorithm, size of data and complexity (e.g., how many layers / deep learning), it can be expensive. Companies like Google can support very deep models; smaller organizations are limited by the cost of computation. AI algorithms can take a lot of time and processing power to train, especially with high-dimensional, deep data (very wide and long tables of data). This can be expensive and sometimes cost prohibitive. Moreover, AI models take longer to train than most machine learning, statistical and BI methods. This is an additional cost or burden.

Models are not transparent or readable

AI models are traditionally "black box" and as we have mentioned several times are not acceptable in certain industries and applications (Bathaee, 2018; Rudin, and Radin, 2019; Airhart, 2019; Guidotti, Monreale, and Pedreschi, 2019). Areas of research, medicine and government regulation require transparency, along with the ability to read and interpret how the model is determining its outcomes, and therefore AI is not an appropriate solution. In contrast, many machine learning algorithms like decision trees, statistical methods, and BI can produce models that are very transparent.

Encodes correlation and not causation

We covered the differences between correlation and causation in Chapter 4, "Causation vs Correlation." This is the **MOST misunderstood and abused area of data AI and machine learning**. AI algorithms are very good at finding correlative factors and generating models that represent these correlations. However, that does not mean they are causative (see Leetaru, January 2019). More about these subjects with examples in Chapters 8 and 10.

Easily overtrains (shallow)

AI models can easily overtrain without proper cross-validation. This means that they perform very well on the data they are built with, but do not extend well into unseen or future data. AI can learn the training set too well. Without controls, AI will learn the data exactly. This will prevent the model from being useful/extensible with future data.

Trains to narrow applications, very sensitive to population stability

The deeper and more complex the model, the more apt it is to train to specific nuances in the data. So, a model might be thought to be useful in a business case with a slight permutation or over time will not perform as expected. This is a type of overtraining just mentioned. Data can change over time (population stability). Models need to be retrained periodically, and the more complex the AI model the more frequently they need to be retrained.

Models may think locally (greedy)

AI models may only search a limited, local space for their solution. We have to "bound" the search space for these models; otherwise they would take too long to train and require too much computation. And the optimal point for a model input may occur outside our bounds, thus limiting the optimal utility of the model.

Models may be brittle and unpredictable

AI can lead to very unpredictable results. Because they can be powerful and precise, they use the data in very special and complex ways to compute their outcomes. If new cases are introduced to the models that are outside the bounds of data that the model ever saw when it trained, it may produce a highly unexpected result (see the gray box, "AI Solves Difficult Challenges, but Comes Up Short on Simple Ones?" and Leetaru, June 2019). Statistical models are typically "more general than AI models," meaning that when a new observation comes to be predicted, AI is often more predictive: the outcomes predicted are closer to reality than those from statistical models. Yet the statistical models will typically not fail in outlier cases in which an AI model might.

AI SOLVES DIFFICULT CHALLENGES, BUT COMES UP SHORT ON SIMPLE ONES?

In 2017 Google's AlphaGo **defeated** Ke Jie, the world's number one Go player, in the first game of a three-part match. About a year before this, AlphaGo became a well-known term when Korean legend Lee Se-dol demonstrated the power of AI (see: Byford, 2017). Whether IBM Watson or Google's AlphaGo are equally powerful or can "do the same things equally well" is problematic, but it appears it is like comparing "apples and oranges," as it they probably have different purposes. At least there is one area where these two are different: Watson is excelling better in commercialization, whereas AlphaGo seems to be doing better in academia (see: Tak, 2017). But even in that, IBM Watson was purchased by M.D. Anderson Hospitals and after 5 years and a cost of US$62 million, M.D. Anderson discontinued it in 2015 because it was "not performing as they had expected" from what they had been led to believe from all the "Hype." And in fact it does a poor job of diagnosing individual patients, probably one factor being that good patient medical databases are not yet available for input.

Perhaps the most important lesson we have learned over the last sixty years of AI is that what seemed most difficult (e.g., playing chess or Go at the highest level) have turned out to be relatively easy, while what seemed easiest has turned out to be the most difficult of all. The explanation for this apparent contradiction may be found in the difficulty of equipping machines with the knowledge that constitutes "common sense." Without common-sense knowledge, among other limitations, it is impossible to obtain a deep understanding of language or a profound interpretation of what a visual perception system captures. Common-sense knowledge is the result of our lived experiences. Examples include "water always flows downward," "to drag an object tied to a string, you have to pull on the string, not push it," "a glass can be stored in a cupboard, but a cupboard cannot be stored in a glass," and so on. Humans easily handle millions of such common-sense data that allow us to understand the world we inhabit (López de Mántaras, 2018).

Some Strengths of AI

1) Extremely powerful for nonlinear and patten recognition
2) No need for labeling for many problems
3) Great results with unstructured data
4) Feature extraction can often be inherently covered
5) Now available to the citizen data scientist or analyst
6) Can process thousands of variables

Extremely powerful for nonlinear and patten recognition

Solving certain problems that are difficult in other machine learning and statistical algorithms can be competently handled with AI. Specifically, pattern recognition and highly nonlinear problems are a breeze for AI. Pattern recognition may include images, audio, video and streaming data. Many statistical and machine learning algorithms were designed for problems with approximately linear or piecewise linear (can be broken into a bunch of contiguous linear) solutions. These methods do not perform as well as AI when these assumptions are violated.

No need for labeling many problems

Imagine a classification problem where you are trying to label the data in a large set of photographs and you need to specify the contents of each picture – maybe wildlife like moose, deer, duck, etc. Or, in the medical industry where you are having a radiologist labeling CT scans as having a disease or non-disease. This is quite tedious and very expensive, in the latter case where the radiologist is quite expensive and would need to label thousands of images for the classification model to predict accurately. AI is very forgiving in this regard, as it can classify the images into clusters with high precision and the data can be post labeled.

Great results with unstructured data

Most data is unstructured: for example text in documents, email, texts (some estimates put it at 80%, others higher at 90% [Mukhyala, 2019; Grimes, August 2008; Beal, 2019]). AI is very useful in text analytics and data mining tasks, outperforming many statistical and other machine learning methods.

Feature extraction can often be inherently covered

Feature extraction is one example of using formulas, rules or even models to take data and add structure to it for use in modeling to make the models have higher predictive accuracy. One example might be using a combination of variables to define a business rule. Imagine your organization has a formula/rule for classifying a "Gold, Silver or Platinum" customer. You may apply this rule to the data set prior to the modeling process. Or, you might use a statistical method such as principal components analysis, where you reduce dozens or hundreds of variables into a few important components. You may start with 200 raw variables and compress the information in these variables down into the six most important components. AI can do some of this work automatically by learning these relationships within the algorithm, requiring no explicit task of feature extraction.

Now available to the citizen data scientist or analyst

With some of these items just mentioned like powerfully modeling nonlinear relationships and not needing up-front feature extraction, along with new easy-to-use interfaces and automatic solution search capabilities for model parameters, what was once only available for the sophisticated user or data scientist can now be used by a business analyst or what is called the citizen data scientist. More about the citizen data scientist in the next chapter.

Can process thousands of variables

Another strength of the AI and machine learning methods is that they can handle thousands of variables. The constraints are computational power and memory. Contrast this to BI, which can handle only a handful of variables at a time. Additionally, some statistical models are designed for smaller subsets of variables as well.

AI's Future

"How 'Rosy' is the FUTURE for AI?"

AI at its highest level can be defined as the "simulation of human intelligence" by machines. This means that machines would (will...) be able to demonstrate things like:

- Learning
- Reasoning
- Self-correction

The growth of AI has been phenomenal in recent years. The future growth of AI is not clear: there may be another "winter phase," no one knows. Yet AI is starting to invade all aspects of our lives, and soon may have invaded almost everything that occupies our daily lives as human beings.

Listed below are some of the many ways AI may be in our lives in the future:

- AI will transform how we do and the output of science
- Use of AI in cybersecurity may finally prevent all hacking
- Facial recognition may go beyond physical structure to understanding emotions
- AI may be able to perceive patterns in data that humans cannot
- Real driverless car and trucks (with NO human inside) may happen in just 2–3 years
- Robotic process automation will be the norm in our workplaces

FROM: Viswanathan, December, 2018

But could another "winter phase" occur before AI reaches its highest levels? Please take a look at the following gray box for some ideas on this.

WILL THERE BE ANOTHER "AI WINTER"?

The self-driving cars that we are currently hearing about and seeing tested appear not to be happening as fast as were predicted. Tesla founder Elon Musk had announced that a fully autonomous car would be on the roads in 2018 (he made this prediction in 2015). And, General Motors predicted 2019 – but it is early December 2019 as we are writing this chapter and we doubt this goal will be realized by the end of the month. Ford has been more cautious, predicting 2021. Well, that is up to 2 years from now, so maybe it will happen? Or maybe not? In March of this year (2019) a pedestrian in Arizona was killed by an Uber in "driverless mode" (a person was in the car, but was not attending to the driving process). So what does this predict?

Deep learning has hit some walls: The neural nets seem to stop learning after a certain point and there is a problem with "generalization." An example of this is that a machine trained to recognize housecats couldn't recognize larger wild cats like tigers and lions. AI winters of the past have probably happened because people have predicted that certain things would happen, but they did NOT happen because the science was not yet "ready." So are we at a stage here in late 2019 and 2020 where we have again come up against a "wall"? The next 2–3 years will probably answer this, if these "blockages" continue and a third winter sets in (Cummins, 2018).

Postscript

This has been a small chapter on a very big subject. We have provided some historical perspectives and ideas for useful applications as well as some drawbacks to the use of AI. We have covered some strengths and weaknesses of AI and some areas of application. In the next chapter, we cover the discipline of data science and the data scientist. **Both are big users of AI!**

References

Airhart, M. 2019. "DEEP learning: Explainable AI helps thwart risks of black box in deep learning," https://lucidworks.com/post/explainable-ai-and-risks-black-box/.

Anyoha, R. 2017. "Can machines think?," Harvard University, http://sitn.hms.harvard.edu/flash/2017/history-artificial-intelligence/.

Bathaee, Y. Spring 2018. "The artificial intelligence black box and the failure of intent and causation," *Harvard Journal of Law & Technology*, 31(2): 890–998.

Beal, V. 2019. unstructured data. www.webopedia.com/TERM/U/unstructured_data.html.

Byford, S. May 2017. "Google's AlphaGo AI defeats world Go number one Ke Jie," www.theverge.com/2017/5/23/15679110/go-alphago-ke-jie-match-google-deepmind-ai-2017.

Colton, S., Halskov, J., Ventura, D., Gouldstone, I., Cook, M., and Pérez-Ferrer, B. 2015. "The painting fool sees! New projects with the automated painter,"

Proceedings of the Sixth International Conference on Computational Creativity (ICCC 2015), 189–96.

Colton, S., Lopez de Mantaras, R., and Stock, O. 2009. "Computational creativity: Coming of age," *AI Magazine*, 30(3): 11–14.

Columbus, L. 2018. "IoT market predicted to double by 2021, reaching $520B," https://softwarestrategiesblog.com/2018/08/23/iot-market-predicted-to-double-by-2021-reaching-520b/.

Cummins, E. 2018. "Another AI winter could usher in a dark period for artificial intelligence: It's happened before," www.popsci.com/ai-winter-artificial-intelligence/.

Grimes, S. August, 2008. "Unstructured data and the 80 percent rule," http://breakthroughanalysis.com/2008/08/01/unstructured-data-and-the-80-percent-rule/.

Guidotti, R., Monreale, A., and Pedreschi, D. March 2019. "The AI black box explanation problem,' www.kdnuggets.com/2019/03/ai-black-box-explanation-problem.html.

Hintze, A. November 14, 2016. "Understanding the four types of artificial intelligence," Government & Technology, Michigan State University, www.govtech.com/computing/understanding-the-four-types-of-artificial-intelligence.html.

History. June 14, 1951. "UNIVAC, the first commercially produced digital computer, is dedicated," www.history.com/this-day-in-history/univac-computer-dedicated.

Kuhn, Max and Johnson, Kjell. March 2018. *Applied Predictive Modeling*. Springer.

Leetaru, Kaley. January 2019. "A reminder that machine learning is about correlations not causation," *Forbes*, www.forbes.com/sites/kalevleetaru/2019/01/15/a-reminder-that-machine-learning-is-about-correlations-not-causation/#79a3b4106161.

Leetaru, Kaley. June 2019. "We must recognize just how brittle and unpredictable today's correlative deep learning AI is," *Forbes*, www.forbes.com/sites/kalevleetaru/2019/06/24/we-must-recognize-just-how-brittle-and-unpredictable-todays-correlative-deep-learning-ai-is/#349291f25bb1.

Lewis, T. 2014. "A brief history of artificial intelligence," www.livescience.com/49007-history-of-artificial-intelligence.html.

López de Mántaras, Ramón. 2018. "The future of AI: Toward truly intelligent artificial intelligences," in *Towards a New Enlightenment? A Transcendent Decade*. BBVA. www.bbvaopenmind.com/en/articles/the-future-of-ai-toward-truly-intelligent-artificial-intelligences/.

Machine Learning Definition. unknown date. www.contrib.andrew.cmu.edu/~mndarwis/ML.html.

Mukhyala, C. February 22, 2019. "Market insight: How to dominate the unstructured data market," www.gartner.com/en/documents/3902670/market-insight-how-to-dominate-the-unstructured-data-mar.

Nicholson, C. 2019. "A beginner's guide to neural networks and deep learning," https://skymind.ai/wiki/neural-network.

Nisbet, R., Miner, G., and Yale, K. November 23, 2017. *Handbook of Statistical Analysis and Data Mining Applications* (2nd ed.). Elsevier/Academic Press.

Rudin, C. and Radin, J. November 1, 2019. "Why are we using black box models in AI when we don't need to?" *A Lesson from an Explainable AI Competition.* MIT-Press, https://hdsr.mitpress.mit.edu/pub/f9kuryi8.

Samuel, A. L. 1959. "Some studies in machine learning using the game of checkers," *IBM Journal of Research and Development*, 3 (3): 210–29.

Schuchman n, S. 2019. "History of the first AI winter," https://towardsdatascienc e.com/history-of-the-first-ai-winter-6f8c2186f80b.

Swathi, Y. January 2, 2019. "10 trends of artificial intelligence (AI) in 2019," https:// becominghuman.ai/10-trends-of-artificial-intelligence-ai-in-2019-65d8a373b6e6.

Tak, L.G. March 2017. "Difference between Watson and AlphaGo?... 'Decision making support vs self decision making'," *The Digital Times*, http://eng.dt.co.kr/ contents.html?article_no=20170317101057000179.

"The history of artificial intelligence." 2006. University of Washington, https://co urses.cs.washington.edu/courses/csep590/06au/projects/history-ai.pdf.

Viswanathan, V. December 2018. "Future scope of artificial intelligence," www.s pringpeople.com/blog/future-scope-of-artificial-intelligence/.

Resources for the Avid Learner

1 https://courses.cs.washington.edu/courses/csep590/06au/projects/history-ai.pdf
   Expert Systems (referenced in the above course)
      [1]. Expert systems in medicine: academic illusion or real power? Metaxiotis, K. S. and Samouilidis, J.-E. February 2000. *Information Management & Computer Security*, vol. 8, pp. 75. [2]. Report on a general problem-solving program. Newell, A., Shaw, J.C., and Simon, H.A. 1959. Proceedings of the International Conference on Information Processing, pp. 256–64. [3]. Recursive Functions of Symbolic Expressions and Their Computation by Machine (Part I). McCarthy, John. 1960. Communications of the ACM, pp. 10–13. [4]. The over-selling of expert systems. Martins, G. 1984. Datamation, vol. 5, pp. 76–80. [5]. The payoff from expert systems. Enslow, B. January–February 1989. Across the Board, p. 54. [6]. AI: industry's new brain child. Cook, B. April 1991, Industry Week, p. 57. [7]. The reality and future of expert systems. Goel, A. Winter 1994. Information Systems Management, vol. 11, p. 1.

2 Short article on Three Types of AI, https://medium.com/predict/types-of-arti ficial-intelligence-and-examples-4f586489c5de.

3 KD Nuggets is a great resource. Here is an example of an automated neural network (ANN) with the Python code. Garbade, M. J. October 2018. "How to create a simple neural network in Python," in: KDnuggets News. www.kdnugg ets.com/2018/10/simple-neural-network-python.html.

4 Justin Smith has a high-level (non-technical) podcast called "What is AI?" One session that is consistent with our comments on facial recognition is the one with Liliana Petrova from JetBlue about a very interesting use of AI: www.p odcastrepublic.net/podcast/1454573693.

Chapter 8

What Is Data Science?

Keywords: Data Engineering, Subject Matter Experts, Citizen Data Scientists, Computer Science, ML (Machine Learning), AI (Artificial Intelligence), BI

Preamble

In the last chapter, we covered AI and how it differs from the other methods covered in this book. We have now covered many of the techniques that data scientists use – data mining, machine learning, and AI. We will explore the use of big data in the next chapter and finally statistics in Chapter 10. This will complete the major tools in the toolbox of the data scientist that we feel should be "the essentials that every data scientist should know."

Now, we explore the fundamental questions:

> So, what is data science?, and
>> What does a data scientist do?

Introduction

Data science is not nearly as old as AI, machine learning or data mining. In fact, the term is attributed to a statistician, William S. Cleveland, who worked at Bell Labs and Purdue University. Dr. Cleveland defined data science as it is used today in a talk at the 1999 biennial meeting of the International Statistical Institute, and in a 2001 paper (see Cleveland, 2001). The paper was republished in 2014 (see Cleveland, 2014) together with a discussion and with another paper about Divide and Recombine (D&R, a statistical technique) with Tessera (see Cleveland, 2014, described next, which requires research in all technical areas of data science. For avid readers, see the "Resources for the Avid Learner" references, Tung et al., 2018) for more on D&R.

According to Cleveland:

> The technical areas of data science that have an impact on how a data analyst analyses data in practice are: (1) Statistical theory; (2) Statistical models; (3) Statistical and machine learning methods; (4) Algorithms for statistical and machine learning methods and optimization; (5) Computational environments for data analysis; and (6) Live analyses of data where results are judged by the findings, not the methodology and systems that were used.
>
> The implications for an academic department are that it is not necessary that each individual be a researcher in all these areas. Rather, collectively, the department needs to have people who do research in all these areas. There must be an exchange of knowledge so that all department members have at least a basic understanding of all technical areas.

We considered leaving the second paragraph above off, but we feel it important to clarify the unicorn misnomer. When the term "data scientist" first came out, it gave the impression to many that it required a very rare breed of professional: someone that had a deep understanding in all the areas of data management, data manipulation and cleansing, computer science and machine learning expertise, statistical and mathematical skills, and was a subject matter expert (SME) of the industry or application of the technology (e.g., finance, operations, marketing, healthcare). Or, according to Gil Press, who stated in a great article, "A Very Short History of Data Science" (see Press, 2013) in September 2005, the National Science Board published "Long-Lived Digital Data Collections: Enabling Research and Education in the 21st Century." The latter report stated:

> The NSF, working in partnership with collection managers and the community at large, should act to develop and mature the career path for data scientists and to ensure that the research enterprise includes a sufficient number of high-quality data scientists.

The report defines data scientists as: the information and computer scientists, database and software engineers and programmers, disciplinary experts, curators, and expert annotators, librarians, archivists, and others, who are crucial to the successful management of a digital data collection.

However, this definition created unicorns because you could not find anyone who checked every box. The expectations nowadays are more realistic, realizing that **data science is a team sport** and that you bring together a team that in concert can execute on all related activities.

A blog post on a very popular website for data science, Data Science Central, begins by stating that "Data Science can be practically defined as the process by which we get extra information from data" (see Seif, July 2018). That may be true, but you could replace data science with business intelligence (BI), statistics, machine learning, data mining, data engineering, decision science or operations research. Does that mean that data science overarches all of those domains? The short answer is "yes," a data scientist should be aware and may use knowledge of all those domains to complete their analytics activities. Thus, **data science is more of an accumulation of knowledge across the primary, traditional scholastic domains of computer science, applied mathematics and statistics, and engineering, as well as domain specific-knowledge** (to what area or field they apply this knowledge). Data science **applications reach across virtually every sector of the economy**. Data scientists apply methods that are well beyond what might be considered traditional data science. *Why primary scholastics domains?* Because it is pervasive in virtually all university programs in one way or another.

WHAT'S IN A NAME? APPARENTLY A LOT FOR MASTER DEGREE PROGRAMS

Many programs that were labeled as Masters of Science in Data Analytics, Business Analytics or Predictive Analytics are changing their names. Scott worked previously with Northwestern University in the School of Professional Studies (SPS), Masters of Science in Predictive Analytics. The university has since renamed the predictive analytics program in the SPS to the Masters of Science in Data Science (although they still have an analytics program in the McCormick School of Engineering). Scott currently teaches in the Masters of Science in Data Science at City University of New York (CUNY), part of the SPS. When he started with CUNY the program was called Masters of Science in Data Analytics.

Why all the name changes? Chasing the most in vogue terms. Yes, the curriculum changes a bit and of course it should, even without a name change. Another interesting dynamic that is responsible for these name changes, is that the university wants to stay innovative and with the times.

Mushing All the Terms – Same Thing?

In the book *Data Science for Business: What You Need to Know about Data Mining and Data-Analytic Thinking,* Foster Provost and Tom Fawcett (see Provost, 2013) state in the opening of Chapter 1:

> The terms "data science" and "data mining" often are used interchangeably, and the former has taken a life of its own as various individuals and organizations try to capitalize on the current hype surrounding it. At a high level, data science is a set of fundamental principles that guide extraction of knowledge from data.

We do *not* agree that data science and data mining are the same. In fact, the primary reason for writing this book was to distinguish and clarify the use of all these terms. Just as engineering uses mathematics, but is not mathematics, and electrical engineering uses physics, but is not physics, *data science uses data mining and machine learning but is not data mining.* In fact, data science is the broadest term in this entire book – data scientists may apply BI and visualization, statistics, data mining, machine learning and AI methods, big data, linear and mathematical programming, computer science and engineering as well as subject matter expertise! That is the reason we are covering these domains to help clarify differences, strengths and weaknesses and not just a morphing terminology based on hype.

We strongly agree with Provost and Fawcett when they declare: "At a high level, data science is a set of fundamental principles that guide the extraction of knowledge from data." In addition, we also agree with authors that declare that decision-making should be data-driven.

EXAMPLE OF FAKE NEWS

One reason we wrote this book is to clear up some confusion and hype in the analytics space. We are not perfect and we are sure there are some mistakes in our work, but we go a long way to vet references by cross-referencing with other sources or our own writing. You will find a lot of unreferenced opinions around analytics (and other) topics. We ran across a lot of this "fake news" on the Internet and provide a couple of examples here (we will not cite references to avoid any embarrassment). One opinion article in a popular ezine stated that data science started in 2008: "Coined by Jeff Hammerbacher and DJ Patil in Silicon Valley in 2008, the data scientist is facing new challenges." This, of course, is not true; there are credible, published references to the term in 2001 as we have noted. Another source is a popular international news website: "Interestingly, the term data scientist, coined in 2008, has often been credited to Patil and Jeff Hammerbacher, who back then were leads of data and analytics efforts at LinkedIn and Facebook respectively." One of the very interesting things about the Internet is that fake news gets propagated very quickly and cycles and cycles as if the more times it is repeated the more accurate it is; of course, however, this is not so. It is true that the White House announced Dr. Patil as the first U.S. Chief Data Scientist (Deputy Chief Technology Officer for Data Policy and Chief Data Scientist) on February 18, 2015. Also, Dr. Patil was coauthor with Thomas Davenport of an important article on data science – "Data Scientist: The Sexiest Job of the 21st Century" in *Harvard Business Review* (see Davenport and Patil, 2012).

There is truth in replacing those terms in a rotation, because at times a data scientist will be a data engineer, at times a statistician, at times a machine learning or AI developer, at times a storyteller. The job is multifaceted and that is what makes it so interesting and rewarding. We have covered many of the "most desired jobs" in Chapter 1, and data science is one of the hottest careers out there – Glassdoor rated it as the #1 Job for 4 years in a row in their 50 Best Jobs in America Report. Zhang reported in InfoWorld that data science openings have grown 256% since December 2013 (see Zhang, August 2019).

So, *what is the key difference between a BI developer and a data scientist? Or, a statistician and a data scientist?* A BI developer has one key domain (and yes, there may be other activities such as data sourcing and some advanced analytics activities), but the majority of their time is spent in BI. A statistician may be versed in a few areas, but their primary trade is performing statistical analysis or developing statistical theory. A data scientist is more of an application generalist, meaning, depending on the project they are working on, they may apply the entire spectrum of BI, machine learning, AI and statistics (and others such as decision science and mathematical programming discussed in Chapter 11).

"Data science" was created as a new term to encompass several of the new challenges. Early on, it encompassed some broad areas of the business domain, visual analytics, advanced statistical and machine learning algorithms and data sourcing, processing, broad architecture and deployment (sourcing and cleaning of data and at the end of the process, deployment of models, which may be done by data engineers). Because these skills are both deep and wide, very few people possessed all of them. Thus, data scientists were called "unicorns," as some people did not think they existed or at a minimum, they were so rare that they were rarely, if ever, seen.

The field has evolved and data engineering has now become a field of its own. Simply put, data engineers are very skilled at data management and areas of computer software engineering. To put it bluntly, they are very good at piping and processing data for the modeling work and taking the analytic models and pushing them out for production / operational systems. Today, as part of the team you will see members that are more quantitatively and algorithm focused, certainly with knowledge, if not at an expert level, of the business or the data piping. You will have members that again have some knowledge of the algorithms and data engineering, but are more business focused in their expertise. In addition, of course, you will have some that exhibit data engineering as their superpower, but they have a level of understanding of the other components. We see this as an ideal team for midsized to large companies.

As best we can tell, by today's definition, a data scientist is someone with knowledge and experience in at a minimum a combination of a few of the following (the more the better):

1) Data Engineering (Database and Software Engineering)
2) Computer Science and Coding
3) Subject Matter / Domain Experts – Healthcare, Government or Business Function

4) Applied Mathematics, Econometrics, Informatics or Statistics
5) BI or Visualization

Today's Data Science?

As we have stated, the new term "data science" was created to encompass several of the new challenges. And, to focus on something important that Dr. Cleveland said, "Live analyses of data where results are judged by the findings, not the methodology and systems that were used." We want to clarify or correct this statement by Dr. Cleveland. We believe data science should embrace all relevant techniques and methods that present relative information. This requires knowledge and appropriate application. What this means is that it does not matter if it is a BI technique, a statistical technique, a machine learning technique or an AI technique that is applied by the data scientist, as long as it used correctly.

Data Science vs BI and Data Scientist

We like the following statement in an opinion piece on "Dataversity" by Paramita (Guha) Ghosh (see Ghosh, 2018):

> Data Science, as used in business, is intrinsically data-driven, where many interdisciplinary sciences are applied together to extract meaning and insights from available business data, which is typically large and complex. On the other hand, Business Intelligence or BI helps monitor the current state of business data to understand the historical performance of a business.

We like it because it does describe the difference between data science and BI while at the same time suggesting another important differentiator. Just because BI may not be strictly part of data science, it does not mean that data scientists do not use BI tools.

Data Science vs Data Engineering vs Citizen Data Scientist

We covered the evolution of the term "data science." In the "unicorn" days, data science included what is now considered a separate discipline, data engineering. In researching many definitions and descriptions, we think

Dhiraj Rajaram (see Rajaram, 2018) has delineated some key differences between these two domains:

Data engineering is the application of technology to help collect, store, process, transform and structure data to enable it to be used for decision support.

Data science is the application of math and technology to solve focused business problems. This involves analysis, visualization and algorithmic/mathematical computations to extract insights in response to clearly defined business problems, and questions and hypotheses using clearly identified data elements.

We add that data science integrates and builds on data engineering by adding data exploration, analytics, and modeling. As part of the continued evolution and the unicorn problem, another role has emerged: the **citizen data scientist**. The citizen data scientist normally comes from a business or functional role within the organization. They know the processes, the data and the problems encountered in this functional area very well. They typically start gaining more technical expertise in data management or one of the other forms of analytics (see Chapter 4). They are similar to "business analysts." However, traditionally, business analysts sit between IT and the business. The citizen data scientists sit between the functional unit and the analytics center of excellence group (Chapter 2), or between the functional area and a data scientist or data science group.

PUTTING IT ALL TOGETHER: AN EXAMPLE OF THE DATA SCIENCE TEAM IN ACTION

We have mentioned that data science is a team sport. So, let's look at a fictitious but realistic data science project and what the team roles might look like in a clinical initiative. Dr. Susan Becker is a chief medical officer at a large integrated healthcare system. She knows that hospital-related costs associated with delirium are estimated to range from US$143 billion to US$152 billion nationally (see Leslie and Inouye, November 2011) and that it is a major concern for their health system. She puts forth a proposal to reduce costs and negative outcomes within the hospitals in the system. Her proposal is detailed and focuses on high-impact areas (cardiac surgery, neurosurgery, trauma; see Schubert et al., July 2018) and while the team would use data across the system to build the solution, the results would be piloted in two hospitals so the impacts can be measured. Her proposal is approved and funded by the board. She is the **executive sponsor** of the project with **board oversight**. She now puts together the following team to support the project.

SMEs – Nurses, physicians, and paraprofessionals from cardiac surgery, neurosurgery, and trauma in a representative sample of the hospital system. These SMEs will serve a vital role in the team providing context, process knowledge and experience in the entire care spectrum and treatment of these patients.

Data Engineers – Experts in the sourcing and initial preparation of the data with the help of SMEs, citizen data scientists and data analysts. They will also help push the analytic models into production. They will work with software developers to provide model results into a user-friendly interface that care providers will use at the point of care. If an organization does not have dedicated data engineers they may draw expertise from IT such as database administrators (DBAs), data architects and data modelers.

Citizen Data Scientists – Work within the team and help bridge gaps between the SMEs and data engineers and data scientists. Since they are knowledgeable in the general process as well as some of the technical components, they can translate between the groups. They can also prototype, provide intermediate analysis and work with the developers to design appropriate interfaces for action.

Data Scientists and **Data Modelers** – Work on a broad spectrum of the project. In projects that do not have a complete team (unlike what we have here) a data scientist may "pinch hit" or fill in for missing roles, since they typically have broad skillsets. For Dr. Baker's team, since she has a full spectrum of team members, the data scientist will serve primarily in the data analysis and machine learning modeling roles.

Software Engineers – Work with the team and very closely with data engineers to develop interfaces and embed machine learning, AI and analytic models into related systems. These might be as simple as a computer user interface or as complicated as an edge device or IoT (Internet of Things) device.

Team construction is highly variable, but we hope this provides some insight into what a team might look like. We cover these concepts deeply in our book on designing an integrated AI, analytics and data science architecture for your organization (see Burk and Miner, 2021).

WHAT IS THE DIFFERENCE BETWEEN DATA SCIENTISTS AND PREDICTIVE ANALYTICS PROFESSIONALS?

We want to point out there are nuances in how professionals are categorized in the job market. Burtch Works, a recruiting company for both data science and predictive analytics professionals, and one of Forbes' 2019 America's Best Executive Recruiting Firms markets both types of domain professionals. In their June 2019 study of salaries for these two types of professionals (in *The Burtch Works Study* – see Burtch, 2019), they define data scientists to be a specific type of predictive analytics professional. So there is a significant overlap where both roles garner insights and prescribe action, but data scientists have additional skills. These additional skills may include focusing on cleaning and analyzing unstructured or streaming data, and using sophisticated computer science and programming (coding) skills that are not typically seen in the profiles of other predictive analytics professionals. We cover what we mean by streaming data in the next chapter, but it is a fairly hot and novel topic. Unstructured data may include video streams, audio data, social media web scrapes, sensor data, raw log files or long blocks of written language. We also cover these data types in the chapter on data (Chapter 9). So, according to the Burtch study, data scientist job descriptions often include additional specifications above and beyond predictive analytic professional requirements. But, they also say: "The distinction between roles in predictive analytics and data science [is] growing fuzzier by the day." This is further confirmation that even professional recruiters in the industry see significant overlap between the fields.

CHALLENGES AND SUCCESSES IN DATA SCIENCE TEAMS

CHALLENGES: We are at the peak (maybe?) of "AI Hype," so one of the challenges for data science teams is understanding "where" and "how much" each of the components of "data science" fit and what role they play. AI is not for every problem; it is only useful for some. Companies look toward data science with big expectations, and thus invest in it; BUT it has been reported that up to 77% of businesses report challenges, and do not complete their "data science projects"; thus ¾ of all projects are dormant – collecting dust. And such disappointments mean that the team loses its energy for pushing for more data science projects. Thus, we'd have to say that overall most projects are unsuccessful, unfortunately.

SUCCESSES: The use of "data science" and "data analytics" is essential for any organization's growth in the new age. And about 25–30% of data science projects in organizations and businesses are successful. There are no shortcuts for success. But there are five things that appear to considered and applied carefully for success, and these are the following:

1. **Motivation and Vision:** The organization needs MOTIVATION and VISION about the use of data science, not for the short term, but as a long-term goal.
2. **Infrastructure:** The data science team needs both "quality data" and "suitable infrastructure" that allows successful working with that data.
3. **Hiring:** There are as few experienced data science "unicorns" out there as before. The supply of qualified people has not yet reached the need. THUS, to attract data scientists with experience one needs to look beyond salary, but at such things as: a) curiosity needs, b) use of new technology needs, and c) their need to be challenged by new opportunities and new business objectives, and given the atmosphere to "go after it unhindered."
4. **Delivery:** Overcoming "technical challenges" is the most important consideration here, as "deployment of models" appears to be the biggest bottleneck for success. For a data science team to be commercially successful it needs a delivery pipeline which meets the following requirements:
   - Evaluate a large number of incumbent and challenger models in parallel
   - Manage the model life cycle
   - Handle an increasing heterogeneity of data science toolkits
   - Allow experimentation in production without impacting the user experience and decouple the business objectives from the data science objectives
   - Decouple enterprise requirements like SLAs (Service-Level Agreements) and GDPR (General Data Protection Regulation) from the data science models
   - Scale this to peaks of 50+K page loads per minute without hiring armies of DevOps engineers

5. **Employee Retention:** The "culture" of an organization can be the most important thing for retaining good employees. Company perks and benefit packages just "do not do it" for the creative people that are good "data scientists." Instead this type of person needs to feel that their work makes a "real impact." If the CEO and decision makers are slow to understand and respond, the "team" can become very frustrated, good work grinds to a halt and eventually people leave. Delivery, adopting new technology and forward thinking are all important to employee retention, which leads to long-term success of the data science program.

Above adapted from Jan Teichmann. 2019. "How to make a success story of your data science team," KDnuggets, www.kdnuggets.com/2019/06/success-story-data-science-team.html.

Backgrounds of Data Analytics Professionals

Previously we have commented about the job responsibilities of analytics professionals in data science. We need to emphasize that since there is a dearth of candidates that fully meet the job descriptions, hiring people are looking more for skills and "skillsets" regardless of education. However, it is useful to take a look at the suggested qualifications of study for some of the jobs, so we briefly cover that, as follows:

◼ Data Engineers
◼ Data Scientists
◼ Citizen Data Scientists

Data Engineers: TRAINING AND PREPARATION: Typically, one needs a bachelor's degree in computer science, software/computer engineering, applied math, physics, statistics or a related field and a LOT of real-world experiences (internships, etc.) (2U, Inc., 2019; Vohra, 2019).

Data Engineer definition: "A data engineer is a worker who primarily prepares data for analytical or operational uses" (Rouse, 2016).

Data Scientists: TRAINING AND PREPARATION: A data scientist needs training/skills in programming, statistics, machine learning, linear algebra and calculus, data wrangling and software engineering (Talari, 2018). Others think these skills can be obtained by earning a bachelor's degree in IT, computer science, math, physics or related field; AND earning a master's degree in data or related field; AND FINALLY gaining experience in the field **you** intend to work in (e.g., healthcare, physics, business). All are essential to be seriously considered by an HR hiring official (Get-Educated, 2019).

Data Scientist definition: "A ***data scientist*** is an individual, organization or application that performs statistical analysis, ***data*** mining and retrieval processes on a large amount of ***data*** to identify trends, figures, and other relevant information" (Techopedia, 2019).

Citizen Data Scientists: TRAINING AND PREPARATION: You will not find a job listing for "citizen data scientist" even though the term has existed for a couple of years. A successful "analytics – data science program" involves a "hybrid organization structure," as we have discussed at length in Chapter 2 of this book. A "citizen data scientist" will function in making predictive / prescriptive analytic models even though they have not been primarily educated in statistics and analytics. "Citizen data scientist" is not yet fully defined, but it involves "skills needed" and if the company hiring cannot find a "data scientist" with the right skills, but finds a person with another job title but having the skills, they will hire "for the skills." Gartner also predicts that citizen data scientists will surpass data scientists in the amount of advanced analysis produced by 2019 (see Gartner Press Release, 2017; Arora, 2019).

Citizen Data Scientist definition: "A person who creates or generates models that use advanced diagnostic analytics or predictive and prescriptive capabilities, but whose primary job function is outside the field of statistics and analytics" (Idoine, 2018; Arora, 2019).

Again, let us emphasize here that in Chapter 2 of this book we make a strong case that "Data Science Is a Team Sport." This means that is a group of people all working together, each having different skillsets (some with overlapping skills), to form a "hybrid organization" that is able to get the job done!!

NETFLIX PRIZE, KAGGLE AND CROWD SOURCING

It started with the Netflix Prize, an open competition offered by Netflix for the best collaborative filtering algorithm (a technique used by recommender systems; see "Association, Rules and Recommender Systems" in Chapter 6). Netflix started the competition on October 2, 2006. Netflix offered a million dollars for the team that could beat Netflix's current algorithm by 10% among other rules and stipulations. Within days, there were teams beating Netflix's algorithm (Cinematch), but not by a wide enough margin to win the prize. The prize was awarded on September 21, 2009 to BellKor's Pragmatic Chaos team, which beat Cinematch by 10.06%. Netflix was to offer a second prize in 2010, but canceled it on March 12, 2010 due to Federal Trade Commission (FTC) privacy concerns. The Netflix Prize was a great example of teams competing against each other to improve their techniques and the entire field of data science. With every iteration of development, teams improved their recommendations from 2006 to 2009.

Kaggle was founded in April 2010. It is an online community of data scientists and machine learners. It allows collaboration and sharing of data sets, exploring and building models and much more. It got its start by allowing team-based competitions in machine learning. Many of these competitions are hosted by companies and foundations with the goal of solving difficult and meaningful problems. One interesting and representative example was a competition hosted by the Michael J. Fox Foundation. The foundation offered a US$10,000 prize to the team with the best plan to leverage an existing data set collected from a group of Parkinson's patients and controls using a basic smartphone application. The competition challenged research teams to develop the best way to improve diagnosis, treatment or therapeutic development in Parkinson's through analysis of these passively collected, objective data points. The development of the app and collection of the data were led by researchers, collaborating entrepreneurs and industry experts at Gecko Ventures and MIT. Researchers from LIONsolver, Inc. won first prize on April 24, 2013.

These two examples illustrate the power and efficacy of invoking the wisdom of the crowd. The wisdom of the crowd is the collective opinion of a group of individuals rather than that of a single expert. By allowing teams to compete for these prizes, innovation is accelerated and enriched. See about the CMS AI challenge in Chapter 7, in the gray box, "The Importance of AI for Government and Healthcare."

Young Professionals' Input on What Makes a Great Data Scientist

To get the current pulse of young professional students, Scott has open forums in his Master of Science in Data Science classes at CUNY. All students that post are working professionals in their early careers, typically with 3 to 10 years of professional experience. They live and breathe data science in the program. Here are a few selected excerpts from discussion posts in 2019.

> To me, what makes a Data Scientist great is an array of both technical skills and soft skills. Soft skills include communication, time management, problem-solving skills, multitasking and being able to convince the audience why your model works and have the data tell a story. Technical skills include programming, Mathematics, Statistics and domain knowledge of the problem you are trying to solve.
>
> A Data Scientist must have knowledge of concepts such as elementary Algebra, Linear Algebra, Probability and Statistics, Calculus... Next, programming/Computer Science. The great Data Scientist must not only be a good programmer in the languages he or she uses, but also Computer Science topics like Machine Learning, Deep Learning, Algorithms, Databases be it relational like MySQL or NOSQL like MongoDB. Other important topics such as Natural Language Processing, Web Analytics, Artificial Intelligence, and Cloud Computing may have to come into play depending on the industry he or she is in.
>
> Finally, the data scientist to be great should be an SME in the industry they are in be it in health, finance, energy, education or social sciences to name a few. You can get great scores in your Kaggle competition or walk out of this program with a 4.0 GPA, but if you don't know your domain, chances are it will be difficult to explain the findings to your customers or peers. This brings me to the next set of qualities of a great Data Scientist: soft-skills.
>
> Soft skills are applicable anywhere in life in general but in the workforce, platform or academia, a Data Scientist must be a good communicator. Being able to communicate and be clear in your analysis and findings is crucial as this is what others will base your work and value on. The great Data Scientist must be able to answer the right questions and convince people. Also, it is vital for people to understand what it is you are trying to convey. You can't assume everyone is a Data Scientist so breaking things down for the layperson to understand will pay off. It also helps to use proper grammar and punctuation to get your story across...

Time management and multitasking are also important as a Data Scientist may have to juggle multiple projects and deadlines and should know when to prioritize their workload.

For me, I think the core of who a data scientist is a person that correctly uses data to solve data-related problems. The "correct" comes from knowing and then applying the proper math, applications of algorithms, appropriateness of visualizations, etc. to provide a solution.

The "research data scientist" will likely be very deep in the technical nitty-gritty details, but won't need to be an SME in a field. And they may only need to be really good at visualization, math or algorithm development, especially when working as part of a team of data scientists or other researchers that together can cover all of the bases you mentioned above.

Having a SME is crucial, but I don't think the data scientist needs to be it [implies the team sport approach and it is becoming evident that data science is indeed a team effort – author's note]. …To this end, I would say that the data scientist needs to be able to at least translate what is happening in the modeling/visualization/etc. into the business speak, and the SME (or somebody else) will need to translate the business requirements into the technical data requirements. It's great when the SME and the data scientist are the same person, but I don't think this happens much or is necessary.

THE MOST MISUNDERSTOOD CONCEPT IN DATA SCIENCE TODAY

It is amazing how many articles that are written today that describe prescriptive analytics as just a different business case of predictive analytics with no additional requirements from the data side or the modeling side. It is absolutely one of the least understood paradigms out here. **YOU CANNOT SIMPLY USE OBSERVATIONAL DATA AND A MACHINE LEARNING ALGORITHM AND GENERATE A PRESCRIPTIVE MODEL. NO. We are sorry to be so belligerent here, but there are hundreds of articles and references out there that imply you can!!** We have even had conversations with people that know that causation is not correlation, but still think they can guide results based on inputs. We will not cite anyone or any article in order not to discredit anyone. Without getting too deep in the weeds (we will dive a bit deeper into statistics in Chapter 10), just be aware there are many reasons you cannot take a predictive model and then declare it as a prescriptive model. We will now describe a simple example illustrating what statisticians call a "lurking variable." A lurking variable can falsely identify a strong relationship between variables or it can hide the true relationship. Let's look at the latter case, where a variable hides a true relationship. Consider a simple five-variable model to predict obesity by measuring BMI (body mass index). BMI is a weight-to-height ratio, calculated by dividing one's weight in kilograms by the square of one's height in meters and used as an indicator of obesity and underweight. Suppose we use the following five variables to predict BMI:

1) Sex (male/female)
2) Number of hours per week in the gym or fitness center
3) Amount of diet soda intake per week
4) Age
5) Geographic location (place of residence)

Those five factors would do a decent job **predicting BMI** via a machine learning model given that we can train the model correctly and with enough data. This model will likely generalize, meaning that it will predict BMI of individuals with future data (given ordinary, common assumptions). **Good predictive model – PASS!** Now, if you believe the many posts, articles, and misdirection out on the Internet and in some books, you can use this model to **PRESCRIBE** actions to lower your BMI. **NO!** You cannot relocate someone to Colorado or Hawaii and expect it to have a practical effect. Colorado and Hawaii have lower BMIs on average due to culture and genetics – not geography. **Culture and genetics are lurking variables (they relate to location and BMI) and they are causal, NOT geography. Good prescriptive model – FAIL!** This is just one reason a predictive model may not be prescriptive: more on that in the next chapter.

There are two more potentially incorrect levers that you might try to pull – the amount of soda and number of hours per week in the gym or fitness center. We will leave that as a thought exercise as to why that may be the case. Pulling these levers may have either have no effect or the opposite effect of what might be predicted in this case.

We will talk about making the appropriate assumptions as well as methodologically sound ways to turn predictive models into prescriptive models in Chapter 10.

Summary

"Data science" is an umbrella term; it is useful in sourcing knowledge and applications across various domains. A data scientist may pull knowledge from virtually any technical or economic sector to solve real data-driven problems. What these problems have in common is they are all data driven. We say *It's All Analytics*, because the benefit of analytics is that you can specify what type analytics – e.g., predictive analytics – based on the objective of the method. Or, you can specify sports analytics, for example, to describe a particular area of application. Furthermore, the term "advanced analytics" applies to a broad class of predictive and prescriptive models that use AI, machine learning and data science – a superset of all forward-looking methods.

Postscript

In this chapter, we looked at what "data science" is and tried to place it among all the terms surrounding data analytics. In the next chapter, we will look at DATA – "big data," "little data" and "other data." Data is the essential ingredient for data analysis, and how to get "good data" is critical to making good decisions and eventual success.

References

2U, Inc. 2019. https://www.mastersindatascience.org/careers/data-engineer/.

Arora, S. November 2019. "Role of citizen data scientist in today's business," https://www.simplilearn.com/citizen-data-scientists-article.

Burk, Scott and Miner, Gary. Expected release 2021. *Designing an Integrated AI, Analytics, and Data Science Architecture for Your Organization.* Taylor and Francis Press.

Burtch, Linda. June 2019. "The Burtch Works study salaries of data scientists & predictive analytics professionals," https://www.burtchworks.com/wp-content/uploads/2019/06/Burtch-Works-Study_DS-PAP-2019.pdf.

Cleveland, W.S. 2001. "Data science: An action plan for expanding the technical areas of the field of statistics," *ISI Review*, 69: 21–26.

Cleveland, W.S. 2014. "Data science: An action plan for the field of statistics," *Statistical Analysis and Data Mining*, 7: 414–17, reprinting of 2001 article in *ISI Review*, vol. 69.

Davenport, T.H. and Patil, D.J. 2012. https://hbr.org/2012/10/data-scientist-the-sexiest-job-of-the-21st-century.

Gartner Press Release. 2017. "Gartner says more than 40 percent of data science tasks will be automated by 2020," https://www.gartner.com/en/newsroom/press-releases/2017-01-16-gartner-says-more-than-40-percent-of-data-science-tasks-will-be-automated-by-2020.

Get-Educated. 2019. "How to become a data scientist," https://www.geteducated.com/careers/how-to-become-a-data-scientist/.

Ghosh, Paramita (Guha). March 2018. "Data science vs. Business intelligence," Dataversity, https://www.dataversity.net/data-science-vs-business-intelligence/#.

Idoine, C. 2018. "Citizen data scientists and why they matter," https://blogs.gartner.com/carlie-idoine/2018/05/13/citizen-data-scientists-and-why-they-matter/.

Leslie, D.L. and Inouye, S.K. November 2011. "The importance of delirium: Economic and societal costs," *Journal of the American Geriatrics Society*, 59(Supp. 2): S241–43.

Maria Schubert, Schürch, Roger, Boettger, Soenke, Nuñez, David Garcia, Schwarz Urs, Bettex, Dominique, Jenewein, Josef, Bogdanovic, Jasmina, Staehli, Marina Lynne, Spirig, Rebecca, and Rudiger, Alain. July 2018. "A hospital-wide evaluation of delirium prevalence and outcomes in acute care patients—A cohort study," *BMC Health Services Research*, Volume 18. 550. https://doi.org/10.1186/s12913-018-3345-x.

Press, G. 2013. "A very short history of data science," *Forbes*, https://www.forbes.com/sites/gilpress/2013/05/28/a-very-short-history-of-data-science/#6cbd8eb655cf

Press, Gil. January 2017. Extracted June 9, 2019). "6 predictions for the $203 billion big data analytics market," *Forbes*, https://www.forbes.com/sites/gilpress/2017/01/20/6-predictions-for-the-203-billion-big-data-analytics-market/#6f9abcc12083.

Provost, Foster and Fawcett, Tom. August 2013. *Data Science for Business: What You Need to Know about Data Mining and Data-Analytic Thinking* (1st ed.). O'Reilly Media.

Rajaram, Dhiraj. 2018. "Executive edge: Why some data scientists should really be called decision scientists," *Analytics Magazine*, http://analytics-magazine.org/executive-edge-why-some-data-scientists-should-really-be-called-decision-scientists/.

Rouse, M. 2016. "Data engineer," https://searchdatamanagement.techtarget.com/definition/data-engineer.

Seif, George. July 11, 2019. "5 useful statistics data scientists need to know." https://towardsdatascience.com/5-useful-statistics-data-scientists-need-to-know-5b4ac29a7da9

Talari, S. May 2018. "Top skills every data scientist needs to master," https://towardsdatascience.com/top-skills-every-data-scientist-needs-to-master-5aba4293b88.

Technopedia. 2019. https://www.techopedia.com/definition/28177/data-scientist.
Vohra, B. February 2019. "How to become a data engineer: A guide," https://dataflo q.com/read/how-become-data-engineer-a-guide/6040.
Zhang, Vivian. August 2019. "Stop searching for that data scientist unicorn," *Infoworld*, https://www.infoworld.com/article/3429185/stop-searching-for-that -data-science-unicorn.html.

Resources for the Avid Learner

1 Cleveland, William S. 1993. *Visualizing Data*. Hobart Press.
2 "Great podcast series of hundreds of related podcasts," The Data Skeptic, www.dataskeptic.com.
3 Krishna, Praful. July 16, 2019. "How to build disruptive data science teams: 10 best practices," KD Nuggets, https://www.kdnuggets.com/2019/07/disruptive-data-science-teams-best-practices.html.
4 Tung, W., Barthur, A., Bowers, M.C., et al. 2018. "Divide and recombine (D&R) data science projects for deep analysis of big data and high computational complexity," *Japanese Journal of Statistics and Data Science*, 1: 139.
5 Cleveland, W.S. and Hafen, R.P. 2014. "Divide and recombine (D&R): Data science for large complex data," *Statistical Analysis and Data Mining*, 7: 425–33.

Chapter 9

Big Data and Bigger Data, Little Data, Cloud, and Other Data

Keywords: Hadoop, Spark, Cloud, Big Data, Streaming Data, Messaging Services, Relational Data, Unstructured Data

Preamble

In the last chapter, we covered data science. A data scientist cannot work without data and data is the subject of this chapter. We explore data of all types, but in particular, we view big data, cloud data and the emerging importance of streaming, geospatial and event-based messaging data. These are the essentials of analytics today. And It's All Analytics!

Please remember / review where data comes from – **processes** (see Chapter 3).

Introduction

As the saying goes, data is the new oil! That is true in many ways. Just as oil is a commodity, data is more so and it is ubiquitous. It can be taken in its raw form and be turned into something useful. It must be used with care and purpose or it can cause problems. One of the differences between oil and data is that oil is a finite resource and data seems to be limitless (see

Marr, 2018). Others including *The Economist* have said, "The world's most valuable resource is no longer oil, but data."

It is All Analytics! And, you cannot do any form of analytics without data. Even if that data is based on subjective knowledge, which we discuss at the end of this chapter (also see "Bayesian Statistics" in Chapter 10 and "Simulation, Sensitivity and Scenario Analysis" in Chapter 11).

Big data was the rage for several years and we will explore the reasons behind this and the forms of big data. We will also discuss recent moves away from some on-premise big data structures to offsite data held in the cloud. We will demonstrate the value of small data and note that it is not going away any time soon.

We will provide some context for different data forms – structured, unstructured and semi-structured. We will discuss two forms of data that are receiving much more attention these days – "streaming data" and "event messaging data." The popularity of analytics is driving much of the growth in these areas.

Three Popular Forms and Two Divisions of Data

If we categorize data as it is used in practical ways in analytics, we normally encounter it in one of three forms – *structured, unstructured* or *semi-structured*. We provide some quick definitions in the next three paragraphs.

If you think of columns and rows in a spreadsheet or a relational database, you are thinking of **structured data**. Structured data is highly organized, indexed and amenable to computer languages (e.g. Structured Query Language (SQL)). There are dozens of commercial and open source databases that support the creation and use of SQL databases and tables. When creating a database the creator defines the relationships, data types, and form of the database. When working within relational databases users can input, search and manipulate structured data relatively quickly. This is the most attractive feature of structured data.

Unstructured data, you guessed it, does not have a defined structure. Unlike the creation of a relational database where the creator defines the relationships, data types and forms, in unstructured the data is freeform. The most common form of unstructured data is text. Other examples include video, audio, images and generally analog data in any form. It is estimated that text alone (structured and semi-structured) accounts for 75–80% of the entire world's data (see Miner et al., 2012). This number may well continue to rise with the prominence of the Internet of Things (IoT).

Semi-structured data is a form of structured data that does not obey the formal structure of data models associated with relational databases or other forms of data tables, but nonetheless contains tags or other markers to separate semantic elements and enforce hierarchies of records and fields within the data (see Buneman, 1997). Semi-structured data does not have the same level of organization and predictability of structured data. The data does not reside in fixed fields or records but does contain elements that can separate the data into various hierarchies. Most people are familiar with CSV files that can be imported into databases and spreadsheets. They provide a minimal structure to the data. XML is a format that has been around for twenty years, but its use has really taken off in the last five to ten years. JSON (JavaScript Object Notation) is one of the most popular forms of semi-structured data today.

Last, in this section, we discuss qualitative data and quantitative data (also see Chapter 4, where we discussed the four scales of measurement and data formats). **Qualitative data** are observed, but generally cannot be measured with a numerical result. Examples might be color, breed of dog, state of residence and phone brand. **Quantitative data** can be measured on numeric scales such as the number of readmissions per year, per member per month (PMPM) insurance rates, Gross Domestic Product (GDP) and revenue per year.

What Is Big Data?

There are various reports of who officially coined the term "Big Data" and of where it actually started. Part of the confusion revolves around the question, "Is Big Data a descriptive term or a technology?" We cover both in this section. We like the following as a descriptive term:

Big Data – a massive volume of data that is so large it is difficult to process using traditional technology (as of about 2005). In most enterprise scenarios the volume of data is too big or it moves too fast or it exceeds current processing capacity.

From a technology basis, the following are some (there are others) of the technologies created to support big data:

- Data Lakes
- High-Performance Relational Database Technologies (Massive Parallel Processing (MPP))

- Hadoop, HDFS, and MapReduce (see following gray box, "Quick Note on Apache, Hadoop and Spark")
- Data Hubs
- Cloud Data Warehouses
- Data Virtualization (DV)

These technologies are sometimes defined as big data, but they support big data rather than describing what big data is. Additionally, the description of big data may include the **3 V's or 5 V's**. Initially, there were three:

1) Data Volume – the sheer amount of data
2) Data Variety – disparate types, different structures, and formats of data
3) Data Velocity – how fast data is being added to systems, refreshed

Then two more qualities were added to make it the 5 V's of Big Data.

4) Value – What is the return on investment for sourcing this data?
5) Veracity – What is the quality, reliability, and trustworthiness of the data?

QUICK NOTE ON APACHE, HADOOP AND SPARK

The Apache Software Foundation (www.apache.org) was incorporated in 1999 as an American nonprofit corporation. Our focus on the foundation in this section has to do with big data systems that support scalable in-database and in-cluster processing of big data – Hadoop and Spark as examples.

Hadoop was initially released in 2006 and was widely adopted (with its commercial derivatives) by 2012. According to the Apache Foundation (http://hadoop.apache.org/):

> The Apache Hadoop software library is a framework that allows for the distributed processing of large data sets across clusters of computers using simple programming models. It is designed to scale up from single servers to thousands of machines, each offering local computation and storage.

It offers a software framework for distributed storage (HDFS, Hadoop Distributed File System) and processing of big data using the MapReduce (a parallel, distributed algorithm) programming model.

Spark was initially released in May of 2014. It was developed by the University of California, Berkeley's AMPLab and was later donated to the Apache Software Foundation. Spark and its resilient distributed dataset (RDD) were developed in response to limitations in the MapReduce cluster computing paradigm (e.g., Hadoop). Spark's advantages over Hadoop are speed and performance. The main way it accomplishes this is by using its in-memory data processing. In-memory data processing means slower disk access is eliminated and replaced by random access memory (RAM) or flash memory. This is more expensive, but according to the Apache website, it can run up to 100 times faster (see http://spark.apache. org/ for logistic regression in Spark vs Hadoop).

Why the Push to Big Data? Why Is Big Data Technology Attractive?

The technologies of big data came about to support the massive collection and lengthening of processing time when dealing with these huge volumes of data. Users needed to access the data, and analyze and model the data more expediently. From an analytics and data science perspective, there was a major technology and practice shift when adopting Big Data technology. Traditionally, most analysis and machine learning involved moving data from large data repositories (and most of these distributed) into a single "sandbox" for analytics. This involved increasingly more time as the volume of the data increased; it was taking more and more time to move the data across the wire. It also was a security risk since you were moving this data across a network, thus making it easier for someone to tap into sensitive data.

You were also creating a duplicate copy of all this data on another server or servers, which increased costs and added additional security risks. What if you could instead move the algorithms (machine learning and other) to where the data lives in the first place? Move the algorithms instead of the data? This was the brilliance of big data technology. We will call this in-cluster, in-database or in-memory machine learning for short. A cluster refers to a group of servers that are grouped together to work on the same computational set of problems and can be viewed as one computer resource. Our examples will focus on Hadoop and Spark, two open source technologies available as part of the Apache (see gray box on "Apache, Hadoop, and

Spark") scalable in-database and in-cluster processing. For in-cluster, in-database computing, we are referring to moving the algorithms to the cluster where the data lives (Disk, Hadoop HDFS, and MapReduce). In-memory computing refers to moving the algorithms to faster, volatile/RAM, which is much faster (Spark).

We address near-memory computing in the "Other Important Data Focuses of Today and Tomorrow" section of this chapter.

The Hype of Big Data

For many years "big data" was the rage, it was a major hype cycle (see gray box, "Big Data and the Gartner Hype Cycle"). You will still hear the term, but it is now considered part of the landscape and not the technology that will ever "change the world," as it once was. In machine learning, it is still important to qualify the difference in technology as to where the models are trained. Are you moving data from a database into an analytic system or moving the code / algorithms to the data?

BIG DATA AND THE GARTNER HYPE CYCLE

We have mentioned Gartner several times. Gartner Inc. is a global research and advisory firm providing information, advice, and tools for businesses in IT, finance, HR, customer service and support, legal and compliance, marketing, sales, and supply chain functions (see www.gartner.com). It is a member of the S&P 500. According to Gartner's Website:

> Gartner Hype Cycles provide a graphic representation of the maturity and adoption of technologies and applications, and how they are potentially relevant to solving real business problems and exploiting new opportunities. Gartner Hype Cycle methodology gives you a view of how a technology or application will evolve over time, providing a sound source of insight to manage its deployment within the context of your specific business goals.

There are 5 phases of the Hype Cycle:

Each Hype Cycle drills down into the five key phases of a technology's life cycle:

Innovation Trigger: A potential technology breakthrough kicks things off. Early proof-of-concept stories and media interest trigger significant publicity. Often no usable products exist and commercial viability is unproven.

Peak of Inflated Expectations: Early publicity produces a number of success stories — often accompanied by scores of failures. Some companies take action; many do not.

Trough of Disillusionment: Interest wanes as experiments and implementations fail to deliver. Producers of the technology shake out or fail. Investments continue only if the surviving providers improve their products to the satisfaction of early adopters.

Slope of Enlightenment: More instances of how the technology can benefit the enterprise start to crystallize and become more widely understood. Second- and third-generation products appear from technology providers. More enterprises fund pilots; conservative companies remain cautious.

Plateau of Productivity: Mainstream adoption starts to take off. Criteria for assessing provider viability are more clearly defined. The technology's broad market applicability and relevance are clearly paying off.

A hype cycle graph would look like the following with expectations in the y-axis and the five key phases would be along the bottom (see Figure 9.1). Each technology would appear somewhere on the continuum and labeled as to when the technology would reach the phase of "Plateau of Productivity." Here we have provided one technology (normally there would be a few dozen) for Big Data. This approximates where Big Data was in 2014.

It is interesting to note that Big Data dropped off the hype cycle early – in 2015. In 2014 it had been listed as "Peak of Inflated Expectations" (see Woodie, August 2015) – "as big data-mania set in, the technology was near the 'Peak of Inflated Expectations.' A year later, as the shine started wearing off, big data started slipping down into the 'Trough of Disillusionment.'" It would have been expected to be near the bottom of the trough in 2015, but instead, it was totally absent. "I would not consider big data to be an emerging technology," Betsy Burton (Gartner Analyst) said: "This hype cycle is very focused. I look at emerging trends." So in 2015 Big Data had lost its emerging technology status and was considered mainstream.

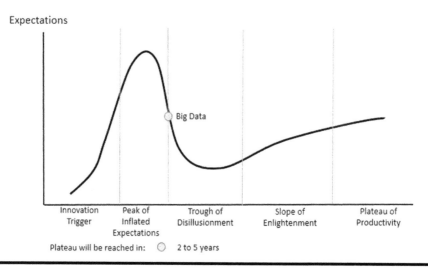

Figure 9.1   Example of Gartner Hype Cycle with Big Data Location in 2014.

To look at the pressure on CEOs and CIOs to adopt Hadoop and Big Data we can see what views were being expressed in late 2011. Dan Woods, in *Forbes* (see Woods, 2011), explains how to pitch the pros and cons to the CEOs. Big Data was all the rage and organizations had a real fear of missing out; letting competitors leapfrog them with the mysterious wonders of big data that would revolutionize business models – or so went the hype! Big data technology was hot!

Pivotal Changes in Big Data Technology

We should note that in the last year, we have witnessed some major changes in big data technologies, particularly Hadoop and commercial vendors supporting Hadoop-based infrastructures. We have talked with colleagues that are shutting down their open source Hadoop clusters (and commercial analogs) and opting for cloud and other technologies. We do not think this is the end of Hadoop as many companies have realized the value of their investment. However, it has meant the shuttering or downsizing of commercial providers, and some companies that had not realized the value of their investment are making sharp pivots into cloud and hybrid cloud (see Park, July 2019, for names, trends, and consolidations). We have seen other writers and bloggers offer the same sentiments. See Sivalingam (July 2019) for his perspective on whether the death in question is that of Hadoop or of Big Data.

Brief Notes on Cloud

Cloud technologies have been growing rapidly and this growth is expected to not only continue but accelerate. In fact, Gartner predicts the worldwide public cloud service market will grow from US$182.4B in 2018 to US$331.2B in 2022, attaining a compound annual growth rate (CAGR) of 12.6% (see Columbus, April 2019). There are various aspects discussed in this report, but the point is that cloud is huge and getting bigger. Another point made is that when it comes to data storage, cloud is shifting storage from inside the data center, i.e. on-premise, to hosted services.

Options to store data in the cloud are diverse and support all the various types of data we discuss in this chapter – structured and relational, semi-structured and non-structured and even streaming data which will be discussed soon. All of these options are supported in cloud repositories, so virtually any analytics application consuming data can keep their data in the cloud.

So why are people moving data to the cloud? Here are just a few examples:

1) **Cost Savings** – There are no hardware investments with cloud. You can normally expense rather than capitalize these costs. No long-term commitments required, except human capital to change strategies. Service costs are offset by fewer highly specialized personnel.
2) **Scalability** – Your enterprise can scale up or scale down your operation and storage needs quickly to suit your situation, allowing flexibility as your needs change.
3) **Business Continuity** – Specialized human resources are taken care of by the cloud provider so losing a key data base administrator or similar role is not the issue it can be with owning all aspects of the data center.
4) **Data Security** – Cloud offers many advanced security features that guarantee that data is securely stored and handled.
5) **Mobility** – Employees who are working on the premises or at remote locations can easily access all the could services. All they need is an Internet connectivity.
6) **High Reliability** – Cloud environments are distributed across the globe and have near 100% availability. The cloud provider handles disaster recovery, backups and more. However, you must consider your network and Internet connectivity (see #1 drawback of cloud).

It would be unfair not to mention a few of the drawbacks with cloud:

1) **Requires Connectivity** – ***This is a big one***. No Internet connectivity with public cloud, or network connectivity with private cloud, makes cloud technologies useless.

2) **Security** – While cloud offers some security advantages, it opens up other disadvantages. There have been examples where administrators of cloud services have created data breaches.

3) **Control** – Since the cloud infrastructure is entirely owned, managed and monitored by the cloud provider, it limits control of the customer. If you have technical issues, you can be at the mercy of the provider.

4) **Unexpected Charges** – If (virtual) machines are left running the meter is running. Also, you may be charged for data movement and other fees. Companies that do not manage these services can be surprised by expenses.

5) **Vendor Lock** – of course, this can happen with any IT product or service, but it should be considered up front. If you move everything to a specific cloud provider, there is a lot of inertia and it takes a lot of effort to move to another vendor.

CHIEF DATA OFFICER (CDO) – IMPORTANCE OF THIS NEW ROLE IN DATA SCIENCE / DATA ANALYTICS:

Many today see the role of CDO as mainly defensive, ensuring compliance with regulations. However, many see that in the future the CDO will drive innovation and "data culture," as evidenced by the references/statements below:

Is innovation with data the future role of the CDO?

Chief Data Officers will be expected to step up to lead the data innovation charge. A majority of firms report having appointed a Chief Data Officer (55.9%). While 56% see the role as largely defensive and reactive in scope today – driven by regulatory and compliance requirements – 48.3% believe that the primary role of the Chief Data Officer should be to drive innovation and establish a data culture, and 41.4% indicate that the role of the CDO should be to manage and leverage data as an enterprise business asset. Only 6.9% suggest that regulatory compliance should be the focus of the CDO.

(New Vantage Partners, 2017)

WHY DO YOU NEED A CDO?

In order for businesses to become **data**-driven, they **need** to empower their CDO to ensure quality information that **can** be used in a meaningful way throughout the organization. Empowering **Chief Data Officers** ultimately leads to a successful business. Why? **Data** comes in high volume and variety.

(Experian, 2019)

What is the difference between CIO and CDO?

Clear reporting lines are also critical. Depending on the sector a **CDO** can implement digital transformation which can free a **CIO's** time to focus on operating IT. The **CDO's** responsibility is to experiment with new business tools and develop digital skills across the workforce. Typically the **CDO** would report to the **CIO.**

(Dobinson and Williams, 2019)

"Not Big Data" Is Alive and Well and Lessons from the Swamp

While much of the hype and focus was on "Big Data," *"Not Big Data"* was having a huge impact on organizations. It was allowing for better decision-making, and it allowed for action across a huge set of business problems. It provided useful machine learning, data science, statistics and business intelligence (BI).

In fact, most analytics problems are not solved with Big Data technology!! Big Data technology was just a very hyped, built-up marketecture that sold many hours of consulting and licenses of software. We are not saying that all dollars spent on big data were wasted. Definitely not. There are many, many examples of valuable, successful implementations of Big Data and they continue today and will tomorrow. What we want to again point out, is *watch out for the hype cycle*. Here are a few pointers:

1) *Be wary of white papers, posts, and blogs* on technology that will rapidly change the world. Who/why is this person writing this? The writer may be correct. They may be early or late. They may have an immediate bias. Think critically about the credentials and intent of the writer.

2) While certainly not perfect in their predictions or opinions, we have mentioned *Gartner* several times. It would be good to check what some of these analysts are saying. No one is completely unbiased, but they are more objective than many other sources. Gartner, Forrester, Dresner are our top three, but there are many more out there with different methodologies. Some rely directly on customer feedback, others on the wisdom of the crowd, others on analyst/expert opinion.

3) *The crowd can be wrong.* If you look back in history, and big data is a great example, you will see hyper hype – like the hype around big data. Big data was real; big data was and will continue to be important. However, people that skipped the hiring of a bunch of data scientists and data engineers and spending millions on Hadoop and commercial clusters, but instead went straight to the cloud, saved a lot of money. There are good reasons for recessions like the dot com bust and the financial crisis – fear of missing out! Look for the value, be realistic.

4) *Experiment, rather than diving in.* One of the tenets of any technology solution is: "Is it scalable?" Meaning as my enterprise grows larger or into new geographies or markets, will my solution easily expand to support it? Therefore, scalability should be a requirement and you should be easily able to do a pilot project to test out the results. For Hadoop, many customers were creating data lakes by throwing in every piece of data. What should we put in our lake, how should we tag or label it – "just throw it all in, all history as well as everything coming in, we will figure out how to structure and use it later, we will use this data someday!" They now have stagnant data that cannot be used for analytics without huge effort – these lakes have become data swamps! What if they had started with a pilot with specific measurable objectives, a timeline to meet these objectives, a phase II for expansion if they reached success or a termination plan if they failed?

Data is valuable everywhere it is meaningfully applied to real problems, i.e., where good analytics are performed. We need big data, small data and everything in between. However, the view "just throw it all in and we will use it someday" is a losing proposition. This "throw it all in" applies in data warehousing as well as data lakes. One more time – if data is not used it is just a cost and of no value. It costs money to store it, secure it and back it up and this becomes a liability. To paraphrase Ben Franklin – "an ounce of planning is worth a pound of success."

Many business processes do not generate large volumes of data. Not every problem is a big data problem. In our experience, large volumes of data are not required to provide significant value. We will see in the next chapter that many statistical methods do not require large volumes to provide insight.

A Brief Note on Subjective and Synthetic Data

We have been talking about data that is stored in a repository or database. However, there are powerful analytic methods that do not require tables or spreadsheets of tables. We will call this **subjective data,** meaning data that lives in our heads, based on our experience and our past observations. There are many uses of subjective data. We mention four methods of working with subjective data at this point, and will elaborate more in upcoming chapters:

1) **Bayesian Statistics** – We will dive into Bayesian statistics in the next chapter. Simply put, Bayesian statistics combines subjective knowledge of a researcher or data scientist (prior knowledge) with data observed (e.g., database, etc.) to formulate probabilities of events (posterior knowledge) happening in the future.

2) **Simulation** – Based on our subjective knowledge of a process or phenomenon we can generate computer-based models via computer code to formulate and augment our intelligence. No formal data is required; instead, it is generated/synthesized from a statistical or mathematical model. We will talk more about this in Chapter 11.

3) **Mathematical Programming** – The rich disciplines of computer science, management science, operations research and engineering often use mathematical programming, linear programming (LP) or optimization procedures. These techniques are formulated without databases or tables. Instead, an objective and some constraints are specified and input into an LP model and then data is run against the framework. We will talk more about this in Chapter 11.

4) **Sensitivity or Scenario Analysis** – This is really a subset of simulation. Due to its wide use and relationship to other analytic model results, we mention it separately. Sensitivity analysis is a process of

varying input parameters of a model (maybe a subjective model) within an allowed area and observing the resulting changes in the model solution.

Other Important Data Focuses of Today and Tomorrow

We briefly mention some technologies that are shaping the data and computing landscape today and will play a prominent role in the future. These are not necessarily new in concept or practice, but they will be playing an important role in analytics of all types:

1) Data Virtualization (DV)
2) Streaming Data
3) Events (Event-Driven or Event Data)
4) Geospatial
5) IoT
6) High-Performance In-Memory Computing Beyond Spark
7) Grid and GPU (Graphics Processing Unit) Computing
8) Near-Memory Computing
9) Data Fabric

Data Virtualization (DV)

DV was created not to supplant the data warehouse, but to extend the reach and capabilities of the data warehouse. By virtualization, there is no physical recreation or copying of data. An apt, concise definition on which we agree was provided by techopedia:

> Data virtualization is the process of aggregating data from different sources of information to develop a single, logical and virtual view of information so that it can be accessed by front-end solutions such as applications, dashboards, and portals without having to know the data's exact storage location (https://techopedia.com/de finition/1007/data-virtualization).

We would add that there are several other desirable characteristics for DV – we mention two key ones here. The first revolves around improved security. With DV you are not moving data so it is less likely to be compromised. You also have an added security permissions layer for role-based or user-based security that allows for both column- and row-level access that is easily governed outside the database. You also have a business-centric metadata repository or catalog where users can search, collaborate and understand the enterprise data.

Streaming Data

Streaming data to a consumer might mean streaming services that provide content such as iTunes, Netflix, Hulu or any other of the many streaming services available. Here is a simple useful example: a device, Roku Streaming Stick, Google Chromecast or Amazon Fire TV Stick connects to a server via the Internet. The server responds to a request and provides a continuous transmission of audio to these "client" devices and loads their "cache" or memory over a period of time, pausing when the cache is full, but providing the data in real time, until the request has been completed.

This is not a new technology, but the technology is constantly improving and moreover, the application of the technology is spreading at a faster and faster pace with IoT (see below), with telemetry, video, and sensors tapping into more and more real-time data. The promise of 5G technology will connect the world in new and amazing ways. The application of analytics to this technology is crucial. Streaming data enables what Gartner calls "Continuous Intelligence" (see Gartner Press Release, February 2019).

Events (Event-Driven or Event Data)

While event-driven data can be streaming or real time, it is not required. Life is full of events and we can qualify and quantity data around these events. John Spacey very simply and clearly provides 12 examples of event data. These event data are things like analytics, e-commerce, home automation, infrastructure, transport, IT, business processes, AI, complex event processing (CEP) and more (see Spacey, 2018). Event-driven technology has been around for many years and is very useful in BI and business activity monitoring (BAM, see Chapter 5). However, it is receiving more attention these days because data science and machine learning are expanding the reach and value of traditional BI and BAM. Instead of using simple rules or alerts in event messaging, we can now place machine learning predictive and prescriptive models at the point of decision-making or action taking via event messaging.

Geospatial

With technology in smart phones and smart apps, geospatial applications have really taken off and will continue to flourish. Traditional maps are a thing of the distant past as consumers use apps of every sort. Transportation and logistics companies are building intelligence in all their geospatial systems. The granularity/specificity is amazing these days. For shoppers that elect to opt in, retailers can follow their movement inside stores and provide location-specific offers to their customers at the right time. Geographic Information Systems (GIS) are streamlining supply chain management, reducing crime, improving economic development and more by embedding AI and machine learning models inside them.

IoT (Internet of Things)

Technology is enabling a more widespread adoption of IoT, from pill-shaped micro-cameras that can pinpoint thousands of images within the body, to smart sensors that can assess crop conditions on a farm, to the smart home devices that are becoming increasingly popular. We have already discussed IoT in several chapters and it is not an independent technology or methodology. For example, take **Smart Cities**, which use the concept of interconnecting cameras and sensors and sources of previously stored data that can be integrated and acted upon with a variety of analytics. We just mentioned streaming data, which is an important technology that enables IoT; additionally, event-driven messaging goes hand-in-hand with IoT. IoT has had a big impact on the way we live today, and similar impacts will be accelerated in the coming years. Please see gray box, "New Stanford IoT Hospital," for how Stanford is using IoT-based technologies to create a hospital of the future. (reference: https://online.stanford.edu/courses/xee100-introduction-internet-things).

NEW STANFORD IOT HOSPITAL

More than ten years in the making and at a cost of US$2.1 billion, Stanford opened the doors of a new 824,000-square-foot medical facility on October 23, 2019. The hospital includes a variety of new technologies from patient-centric controls in rooms to modular architecture, to a robotic pharmacy and IoT-based technology. According to the *Wall Street Journal* (see Rosenbush, November 2019)

> Sensors will track the location of staff and equipment in real time, improving efficiency and inventory control. The infrastructure can support 120,000 connected devices streaming 4K high-definition video. The infrastructure will be able to accommodate upgrades such as 5G wireless. Magnetic resonance imaging equipment and other systems will be integrated with one another in new ways.

> Doctors and nurses will be able to monitor multiple patients from a single remote location. Alerts and alarms will go directly to secure mobile devices carried by nurses and doctors, instead of sounding at nursing stations—reducing noise levels… *[What's Next]*… Two patient rooms will test a bedside computer-vision system that uses depth and thermal sensors to improve patient safety.

High-Performance In-Memory Computing Beyond Spark

There are commercial platforms and technologies that extend beyond Spark. These are extremely powerful in-memory databases. Most are based on Apache Spark and related Apache platforms and are completely compatible with Apache open source. However, they outperform Spark on benchmark tests by optimizing the architecture and database throughput, and at the same time offer low latency and high concurrency.

Grid and GPU Computing

While grid computing originated in the 1990s it is important to mention so readers are aware of its continuing relevance to AI and machine learning. **Grid** incorporates widely distributed computer resources to solve complex problems. Each node in the grid is set to perform a different task. A **GPU** is a chip (semiconductor package) specifically designed to perform rapid mathematical calculations, primarily for the purpose of rendering images. However, they are often used in grid computing, AI and computationally intensive methods because the chips are relatively cheap due to their ubiquitous application in graphics cards, smart phones and elsewhere.

Near-Memory Computing

We spoke about two paradigms in this chapter for machine learning and AI modeling:

a) the conventional approach of moving stored data to the CPU for computation (slow and a performance bottleneck for emerging scale-out data-intensive applications) and
b) in-memory computing, where we move the algorithms into fast, volatile, flash or RAM memory.

The next generation in the acceleration of computational speed is near-memory computing (NMC), which couples compute units close to the memory (see Singh et al., November 2019; Singh, August 2018). Memory-centric chip technologies are emerging that help solve bandwidth issues. Essentially the idea is to bring the memory closer to the processing tasks to speed up the system (see Lapedus, 2019).

Data Fabric

In the last couple of years, there has been a lot of buzz about data fabrics. In February 2019, Gartner noted "Data fabric" as one of the data and analytics technology trends (see Gartner Press Release, February 2019):

> Data fabric enables frictionless access and sharing of data in a distributed data environment. It enables a single and consistent data management framework, which allows seamless data access and processing by design across otherwise siloed storage.
>
> Through 2022, bespoke data fabric designs will be deployed primarily as a static infrastructure, forcing organizations into a new wave of cost to completely re-design for more dynamic data mesh approaches.
>
> **(Gartner, 2019)**

It will be very interesting to see how data fabric technology plays out and fits in with existing technology such as data virtualization.

Future Careers in Data

Careers in data engineering and data management have been bright for many years and will only get brighter. We are generating data at a dizzying pace and this is accelerating with no end in sight. Technologies to capture data are expanding – especially video, audio, streaming, sensors, telemetry and IoT. IDC predicts that the global datasphere will grow from 33 zettabytes in 2018 to 175 zettabytes by 2025 (a zettabyte is 1,000,000,000,000,000,000,000 bytes, 1 billion terabytes). If one person downloaded this amount of data at 25 megabytes per second (average speed in the United States today) it would take 1.8 billion years to download it. If everyone on the planet joined in 24 hours a day it would still take 81 days. See Figure 9.2

We have covered many data concepts and illustrated many technologies in this book, but will dive more in depth in our upcoming book, *Designing an Integrated AI, Analytics, and Data Science Architecture for Your Organization* (see Burk and Miner, 2021). You can count on data access getting faster; data will continue to get bigger. Many of the challenges that have persisted for years remain today because the data is always changing. As data volumes grow, the data variety expands; data velocity increases and existing technology cannot handle it. Technology must respond and adapt to

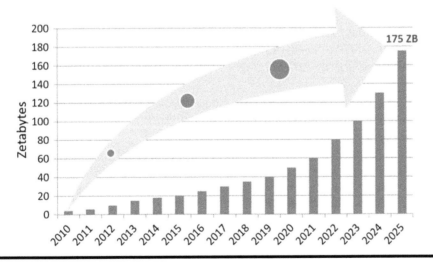

Figure 9.2 Annual size of global data (adapted from Reinsel et al, Data Age 2025; The Digitization of the World (IDC November 2018)).

these changes. The search for the **"single version of the truth"** is an ever-present reason for new concepts and solutions. Technology will continue to enable all growth. Data sourcing via APIs (application programming interfaces) will continue to grow and diversify, creating larger volumes. Network speeds and 5G will increase velocity; cloud and cloud-related technologies will expand data variety. The use of analytics is the only way to prove the value of data, otherwise, collecting data is just a cost.

Postscript

We have covered many data-related concepts and technologies in this chapter. We have provided information on Big Data to Small Data, from structured to unstructured, from old data technologies to new ones. **Data has replaced oil as the most valuable resource, that is – if we use it, to do that – It's All Analytics!**

In the next chapter, we will cover statistics, a much feared subject, and one that is often very misunderstood. However, it is a very important subject for all forms of analytics. We will also cover prescriptive analytics and causal models.

References

Buneman, Peter. May, 1997. "Semistructured data," in Proceedings of the sixteenth ACM SIGACT-SIGMOD-SIGART symposium on Principles of database systems, 117–21, https://doi.org/10.1145/263661.263675. https://dl.acm.org/doi/10.1145/263661.263675.

Burk, Scott and Miner, Gary. Expected release 2021. *Designing an Integrated AI, Analytics, and Data Science Architecture for Your Organization*. Taylor and Francis Press.

Columbus, Louis. April 7, 2019. "Public cloud soaring to $331b by 2022 according to Gartner," *Forbes*, www.forbes.com/sites/louiscolumbus/2019/04/07/public-cloud-soaring-to-331b-by-2022-according-to-gartner/#6d3066d35739.

Dobinson, Chloe and Williams, Hannah. November 21, 2019. "What is the difference between a CIO and CDO?" www.cio.co.uk/it-leadership/cio-cdo-differences-3644709/.

Experian. 2019. The Chief Data Officer, Powering business opportunities with data, www.edq.com/resources/data-management-whitepapers/the-chief-data-officer-powering-business-opportunities-with-data/.

Gartner Press Release. February 18, 2019. "Gartner identifies top 10 data and analytics technology trends for 2019," www.gartner.com/en/newsroom/press-releases/2019-02-18-gartner-identifies-top-10-data-and-analytics-technolo.

Lapedus, Mark. February 2019. "New approaches are competing for attention as scaling benefits diminish," Semiconductor Engineering, https://semiengineer ing.com/in-memory-vs-near-memory-computing/.

Marr, Bernard. March 2018. "Here's why data is not the new oil," *Forbes*, www.f orbes.com/sites/bernardmarr/2018/03/05/heres-why-data-is-not-the-new-oil/#3 9b12ecf3aa9.

Miner, Gary, Elder, John IV, Hill, Thomas, Nisbet, Robert, Delen, Dursun, and Fast, Andrew. January 2012. *Practical Text Mining and Statistical Analysis for Non-structured Text Data Applications* (1st ed.). Academic Press.

NewVantage Partners. 2019. "Big data and AI executive survey 2019: Executive summary of findings," http://newvantage.com/wp-content/uploads/2018/12/B ig-Data-Executive-Survey-2019-Findings-Updated-010219-1.pdf.

Park, Hyoun. July 2019. "The death of big data and the emergence of the multi-cloud era," KD Nuggets, www.kdnuggets.com/2019/07/death-big-data-multi-clo ud-era.html.

Reinsel, David, Gantz, John, and Rydning, John. November 2018. "Data age 2025: The digitization of the world," IDC Whitepaper Report, www.seagate.com/file s/www-content/our-story/trends/files/idc-seagate-dataage-whitepaper.pdf.

Rosenbush, Steven. November 16, 2019. "New Stanford Hospital takes holistic approach to technology," *The Wall Street Journal CIO Journal*, www.wsj.com/art icles/new-stanford-hospital-takes-holistic-approach-to-technology-11573905600.

Singh, Gagandeep. August 2018. "A review of near-memory computing architec-tures: Opportunities and challenges," IEEE, Conference Proceedings: 2018 21st Euromicro Conference on Digital System Design.

Singh, G., Chelini, L., Corda, S., Awan, A. J., Stuijk, S., Jordans, R., ... Boonstra, A.-J. 2019. "Near-memory computing: past, present, and future," *Microprocessors and Microsystems,* 71 [102868], https://doi.org/10.1016/j.micpro.2019.102868.

Sivalingam, James. July 2019. "What does the death of Hadoop mean for big data?," TechWire Asia, https://techwireasia.com/2019/07/what-does-the-death-of-hado op-mean-for-big-data/.

Spacey, John. January 2018. "12 examples of event data," Simplicable, https://simpli-cable.com/new/event-data.

Woodie, Alex. August 2015. "Why Gartner dropped big data off the hype curve," Datanami, www.datanami.com/2015/08/26/why-gartner-dropped-big-data-off -the-hype-curve/.

Woods, Dan. November 2011. "Explaining Hadoop to your CEO," *Forbes*, www.f orbes.com/sites/danwoods/2011/11/03/explaining-hadoop-to-your-ceo/?utm _source=datafloq&utm_medium=ref&utm_campaign=datafloq#1b76c0c16053.

For the Avid Learner

1 See Spark Resources such as http://spark.apache.org/ (Under the Library tab – SQL and Data Frames, Spark Streaming, MLib and GraphX among other content).

2 A brief discussion of structured, unstructured and semi-structured data with examples in an October 2019 article by Bernard Marr: "What's the difference between structured, semi-structured and unstructured data?" at https://ww w.forbes.com/sites/bernardmarr/2019/10/18/whats-the-difference-between-stru ctured-semi-structured-and-unstructured-data/#55ade9bb2b4d.

3 Tech Republic has a nice primer with an executive summary covering questions like: What is Hadoop? Why does Hadoop matter? Who does Hadoop affect? and more. See " Apache Hadoop: A cheat sheet" at https://www.tec hrepublic.com/article/apache-hadoop-the-smart-persons-guide/.

4 Curated Data is a very hot topic. Here is an introductory resource: Data Curation 101: The What, Why, and How by Dataversity (November 2017, https ://www.dataversity.net/data-curation-101/).

5 Huskin, Edward In-Memory Computing and the Future of Machine Learning. August 30, 2019. The Data Warehousing Institute (TWDI), https://tdwi.org/Art icles/2019/08/30/ARCH-ALL-In-Memory-Computing-and-Future-of-Machine-Le arning.aspx?Page=1

Chapter 10

Statistics, Causation, and Prescriptive Analytics

Keywords: Frequentist, Classical Statistics, Bayesian Statistics, Inference, Significance Testing, Non-parametric, Criminal Trial, Structural Causal Models

Preamble

In the last chapter, we covered big data to little data. We now move to a commonly misunderstood subject, statistics. We will cover various forms and put statistics in context with analytics, data science, machine learning, and AI. A data scientist should be well versed in statistics, as we will see that statistics is the foundation for virtually all forms of analytics. We then follow with bridges between predictive analytics and prescriptive analytics, and one of these bridges is statistics.

This chapter will be a bit eclectic since statistics is so broad and we want to tie statistics to the subjects we presented. Therefore, we thought we would provide a brief layout of this chapter, which has these five main pillars:

- Some Statistical Foundations (related to analytics, what you should know)
- Predictive Analytics vs Prescriptive Analytics – The Missing Link Is Causation
- Assuming or Establishing Causation
- Ladder of Causation
- Predicting an Increasing New Trend – Structural Causal Models and Causal Inference

Some Statistical Foundations

Introduction

The subject of statistics throws many people off. Some may even confuse statistics with sadistics. However, at its core, statistics is very simple. **Statistics are characteristics** (average, minimum, maximum, etc.) **of samples**. **Parameters are characteristics** (average, minimum, maximum, etc.) **of populations** and populations are **NOT** just current or historical. Processes can produce population observations that can project into the future (we spoke in depth about processes in Chapter 3, see the sections "Processes Are Everywhere" and "Processes Drive Data"). **Samples are subsets of populations**. Populations are defined as the collection of objects under study (patients, widgets, voters, etc.). We want to learn/describe populations or make decisions/judgments about a population/process and we do this by estimating parameters with statistics via a sample. **That's it! That is statistics.**

Therefore the whole idea of creating training, testing and validation sets for machine learning and AI involves sampling, and we calculate statistics from these samples – **therefore you cannot do machine learning or AI without the concepts of sampling and statistics**. This is using statistics at a very primary level.

The following figure (Figure 10.1) illustrates an example of simple random sampling (SRS). The goal of SRS is to derive a representative subset

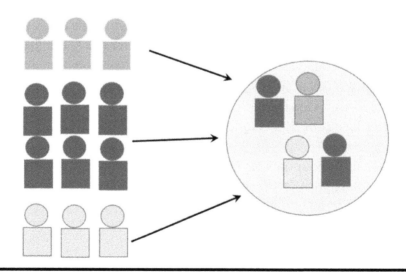

Figure 10.1 Illustration of SRS (Simple Random Sampling).

of a population. The population is on the left and every element of the population has an equal chance of being drawn into the sample. If done correctly the elements of interest in the sample will be a mirror of the population, but just a smaller number. There are 12 elements in the population, 4 in the sample. This illustrates that virtually all analytics uses statistics.

Let us look at the statistical subjects we want you to know at a high level, and then we will jump in:

1) Two Major Divisions of Statistics – Descriptive Statistics and Inferential Statistics
2) What Made Statistics Famous?
3) Two Major Paradigms of Statistics
4) Dividing It Up – Assumption Heavy and Assumption Light Statistics
5) Four Domains in Statistics to Mention
   a. Statistical Prediction and Estimation
   b. Design of Experiments (DoE)
   c. Statistical Process Control (SPC)
   d. Time Series(TS)
6) An Ever-Important Reminder
7) Statistics Summary
8) Comparison of Data-Driven Paradigms Thus Far

Two Major Divisions of Statistics – Descriptive Statistics and Inferential Statistics

Descriptive Statistics is a branch of statistics concerned with describing characteristics of the population under study. Thus, descriptive statistics supports and is part of analytics. These characteristics / descriptive statistics are retrospective in nature. Most people are familiar with averages, minimums, maximums, etc., which people refer to as "statistics." However, these are not the only ones. There are thousands of various statistics that can be calculated. Business intelligence (BI) is primarily focused on description and retrospection – therefore **descriptive statistics is at the heart of BI**. Remember, a statistic is **ANY** characteristic of a sample – they may be useful or un-useful. Good statistics are useful. **No assumptions have to be made using descriptive statistics**. When the data scientist applies machine learning and AI, which uses algorithms in training samples to build models, they are using descriptive statistics.

Inferential Statistics is a type of statistics that focuses on drawing conclusions about the population, based on sample analysis. This conclusion about the population may extend beyond the data currently available, meaning processes drive (future) data such that the entire population is not currently available to sample. *Inferential statistics typically requires assumptions.* For example, we assume the parent population from which we are drawing a sample has a "bell shape" (a distribution, a model). This has benefits and drawbacks as we will we see. However, one benefit typically cited for machine learning and AI is that these methods are "model free" or "distribution free," meaning we do not need to assume something like the "bell shape" just mentioned. This frees the data scientist from worrying about testing assumptions or making an incorrect assumption. Quick note: statistics also come in "model free" forms, they just are not as well known to the general public (we will get to that later in this chapter in the section on "Non-parametric distribution free statistics (assumption light)").

What Made Statistics Famous?

There are several things that made statistics famous; we share two of the most well-known and describe them briefly.

- Criminal Trials and Hypothesis Testing
- The Scientific Method

Criminal Trials and Hypothesis Testing

Statistical hypothesis testing (a form of statistical inference) is intuitive. **Criminal jury trials and statistical hypothesis testing** have a lot in common. Here is an analogy – the prosecution (a researcher) based on preliminary observation and evidence (observation or exploratory data analysis) believes a defendant (process) is guilty (a causal effect, A causes B). The court will assume the defendant is innocent (A does not cause B). They present accumulated evidence (data from a representative sample) to the jury (hypothesis test). The jury (hypothesis test) decides if there is enough evidence (sufficient statistical evidence) to reject the presumption of innocence (A does not cause B). If there is enough evidence, the jury rejects the assumption of innocence and concludes that the defendant is guilty (A causes B).

There are many references to this relationship; we provide a link to a discussion with a 2×2 decision table in the "Resources for the Avid Learner" section. Also see the references (Liu and Stone, 2006; Davis and Mukamal, 2006; Devine, 2012).

NOTE: You may have heard of "**statistically significant**." Statistical significance equates to the evidence needed to find someone guilty in the court trial. A hypothesis test is a method of statistical inference.

The other issue where society sends innocent people to prison needs to be considered; this is analogous to the researcher thinking that A causes B when in fact it does not. This is a "false discovery rate" and there is no way around it. The more you want to send more guilty people to jail, the less evidence you require to convict and the more often you will send someone innocent to jail. The converse is also true, of course. Statisticians control this type of error with the "level of significance." For criminal cases, and medical life-and-death issues, we need carefully consider the "level of significance."

The reason there is no way around this "false discovery rate" is that "you can't prove a negative." An interesting read on this is the "**Black Swan Problem**" (see "Resources for the Avid Learner" section for a reference). However, the short story goes that for a long time it was believed that black swans did not exist. Only white swans had ever been seen according to historical records. Seeing only white swans seemed to prove that only white swans existed. Until of course one day, someone saw black swans in South Central Australia, thus, disproving that only white swans existed. (And your second author, Gary, has been to the preserve in South Central Australia and seen these black swans with his own eyes, so YES it is TRUE; and in fact now he even has friends in the United States who raise these Black Swans!!!).

NOTE: Statistics is about quantifying uncertainty. It is not about eliminating uncertainty. It is not about making decisions that are 100% accurate and 100% precise. That is impossible with any methodology.

The Scientific Method

The scientific method is taught early in school, often in U.S. elementary schools. A logical methodical process teaches at any age a practical way to look at the world, formulate ideas about the mechanism that causes results and ways to test these ideas. The scientific method is about observations, formulating intelligent hypotheses. Nevertheless, how can you confirm /

deny that your thoughts are accurate? You can use statistics to help. If we want to be very precise about this, we can use the following set of statistical and scientific research steps:

1) Ask a question.
2) Do background research.
3) Construct a hypothesis (a hypothesis is an educated assumption – based on research and observation).
4) Construct a statistical experimental design. This does not have to be elaborate. However, it needs to be done prior to the experiment. It should include how you are going to sample (like the number of runs, how you are going to vary factors). Written hypotheses and a significance level for testing.
5) Run your experiment as stated in #4.
6) Analyze the results and determine the hypothesis outcome.
7) You can use the results as feedback into #2 above.
8) Communicate results whether they confirm or deny your original hypothesis.

NOTE: Communicating results is important. There has been an asymmetric reward for publishing based on "success." We hope the tide is turning and scientific journals will publish and reward research that publishes statistically significant and non-significant results. Both contribute to scientific understanding.

TORTURE THE DATA LONG ENOUGH AND THEY WILL ADMIT TO ANYTHING!

There is a saying among statisticians: "Torture the data long enough and they will admit to anything!" We covered this when we talked about data dredging in Chapter 6. Since we are in the statistics chapter and we have introduced statistical inference, we will go a bit deeper into what we mean by this. Suppose I am working on my Ph.D. in social sciences (criminology) and I have a very large set of data. Suppose I want to find the major factors of recidivism. I can perform hundreds of hypothesis tests with different factors. If I find one that is significant it will provide the support I need for my thesis/dissertation. As stated, I control the false discovery rate. Uninformed students or students that need to finish their research very rapidly may misapply this rate by not adjusting it for the hundreds of times they are testing. This is torturing the data. If you sift through enough data without applying the appropriate correction for the false discovery rate, you will declare something significant when in fact it is just by chance alone.

STATISTICAL SIGNIFICANCE VS PRACTICAL SIGNIFICANCE

Statistically significant means that there is a mathematical difference in the outcome. It does not imply that the outcome is useful. For example, it is possible to show that a drug is effective in reducing blood pressure, but if it only drops it by 0.05%, the treatment may not be practically significant for the cost of the drug.

Two Major Paradigms of Statistics

"The subject of probability theory is the foundation upon which all of statistics is built, providing a means for modeling populations, experiments or almost anything else that could be considered a random phenomenon" (Casella and Berger, 2001). Next, we briefly introduce two paradigms, both deeply rooted in probability theory.

Bayesian Statistics

Bayesian statistics was formulated upon the Bayes theorem, published in 1763 authored by Reverend Thomas Bayes, who died prior to it being published (he lived 1701 to 1761). It is one of the most important practical mathematical results ever published and can be represented for a specific case with a simple formula that can be taught to a high school mathematics class. Bayes's solution to a problem of inverse probability was presented in "An Essay towards Solving a Problem in the Doctrine of Chances," which was read to the Royal Society in 1763 after Reverend Bayes's death.

One great thing about Bayesian results is that when doing inferential statistics the results are expressed as true probabilities, and in fact, they are true probabilities. Contrast this to classical statistics (presented in a moment), where we speak in terms of confidence and conditional results of unrealized sample results. Bayesian statistics also takes into account prior knowledge of a researcher or practitioner. Bayesians, and many other people, like this because you are not throwing away any information. Imagine a physicist who has been experimenting in a lab for 30 years. You would think they have some knowledge of the underlying process that should be part of an experiment. Bayesians **may** combine this knowledge with the data from actual experiments to formulate results. If they use this prior information, it is explicitly stated and is represented as a "prior distribution" (just like the statistical distributions we talked about before). Therefore, they are not hiding anything and all assumptions and necessary criteria on how the experiment is to be conducted and analyzed are expressed before any data from the experiment is collected. Classical / frequentist statisticians do not like the idea of subjective prior information.

There are literally thousands of Bayesian methods that have been developed over the last two hundred years. They are very powerful. One thing that kept them from becoming more widely used years ago is that, unlike "closed-form" methods, you have to numerically approximate results, so it requires a great deal of memory and processing power. However, this is not the primary limitation. Knowledge is.

Bayesian methods got a big bump in usage in the late 1990s and early 2000s when statisticians like Andrew Gelman at Columbia University popularized them, particularly in open source coding libraries (Gelman, 2010). They then fell out of vogue for about 10 years and now are back on the rise. With knowledge comes power.

Classical or Frequentist Statistics

While Bayesian methods have been around for hundreds of years, they were not used largely due to the computational complexity until recent years. Therefore, the term "classical statistics" is based on a repeated sampling paradigm. So, when using "classical statistics" we talk in terms of "frequentist methods." So, while confusing, you may generalize these three terms – classical statistics, frequentist statistics, repeated sampling paradigm – as generally the same. Let us take up the motivation for this idea of a repeated sampling paradigm with an example.

Imagine we want to estimate the outcome of a new school referendum. All that is needed for this to pass in a balloted vote is a simple majority. There are about 100,000 voters. How could a statistician approach this problem? They would take a representative sample of likely voters, as it would be impossible to interview all possible voters. What do we mean by a representative sample? We would want to be sure that our sample matched the population, not biasing for ANY factor (age, where they lived, income, ethnicity, religious preference, children in the home, etc.). See SRS at the beginning of this chapter.

Suppose we get a representative sample of 1,040 voters. In our sample, the proportion of people saying they will vote "yes" is 52.0%. Should we conclude that the proposition will pass? The statistician says we should not because of something called sampling error. She asks us, is ours the only representative sample that could have been taken from the population? No. How many? A very large number! Would these theoretical samples (notice repeated samples, i.e., repeated sampling paradigm) all generate a proportion of 52%? No. If the population had a proportion of 50%, what would be the range of our sample proportions? With some theory already developed (via calculus), the statistician could plug numbers into a formula and tell us that if the true population proportion is 50% then you would expect representative samples (of size 1,040) to generate proportions from 46% to 54%, 99 out of 100 times (frequentist). Therefore, 52% is within the margin of error, therefore not statistically significant. Without being entirely precise we would need our sample proportion to be about 54% or greater to be extremely confident the referendum will pass. Note: the problem with surveys is *not* the statistical theory, as the math the solid. The real problem is the difficulty in getting a truly representative sample, especially about a future event.

Dividing It Up – Assumption Heavy and Assumption Light Statistics

We spoke previously about the fact that BI, machine learning and AI all use the statistical paradigm, i.e., they use samples. However, we understand when people compare "statistics" to machine learning and AI they are generally speaking about a very specific subset of statistics. This subset is **parametric statistics and we will call these assumption heavy statistics**. We will elaborate on this extensively in this chapter since it is a very important and very often misunderstood concept. One of the advantages of machine learning vs parametric statistics is that there are far fewer assumptions required with machine learning. This **may** be an advantage. It certainly simplifies things.

Here we point out some statistics that do *not* require assumptions (or have minimal assumptions) in the traditional sense:

1) When using the sampling / statistical methods for machine learning (noted above)
2) Descriptive statistics (as stated previously, these require no assumptions)
3) Distribution free statistics / non-parametric statistics (see following section)

On the opposite side of these minimal assumption-based statistics, we have parametric statistics that require an understanding or assumptions of the shapes or types of the data from the population we are sampling. If we are correct in these assumptions, parametric statistics will often outperform machine learning and AI methods (see gray box on "Parametric Statistics and Where they may Outperform Machine Learning Paradigms"). When these assumptions are not correct, our results can underperform machine learning and AI methods. In addition, if we are far off in our assumptions the results can be very poor. One thing for sure, having to add assumptions adds work for the data scientist. However, it is also a misnomer that machine learning requires no assumptions. Every analytics technique requires certain assumptions; it is only the depth and complexity of assumptions that change.

PARAMETRIC STATISTICS AND WHERE THEY MAY OUTPERFORM MACHINE LEARNING PARADIGMS

Parametric statistics is a branch of statistics that assumes sample data come from a population where the population can be adequately modeled by a family of statistical distributions. A family of statistical distributions is just a set of functional (mathematical) forms with a set of constants or parameters – thus "parametric." If you have heard of the "Bell Curve" you have heard of a statistical distribution, a functional form. Statisticians have developed many of these distributions and the mathematics that goes along with them to solve a wide range of problems. If I can assume a functional form and those assumptions hold, then algorithms using statistical distributions are often more powerful than distribution free methods like classification and regression trees and other methods we covered in Chapter 6.

How can parametric statistics outperform machine learning?
The estimators in many statistical methods are determined via mathematical application, typically calculus (e.g., first and second derivative tests). This results in the closed-form solution we previously discussed. This area of statistics is "mathematical statistics." When an optimum is found using these methods, it means there is no better estimate, period. However, this optimum requires certain conditions; for example the data was drawn from a family of "Bell Curves."

Non-parametric statistical learning, machine learning and AI methods are "model free" and have no closed-form solution for an optimum. Instead, a computer algorithm is used to search for an optimum (see Chapter 6, "AI models may think locally (greedy)"). NOTE: Not all machine learning methods are non-parametric! We use this computer algorithm to cycle through a set of operations and search for this optimum within a specified search space. The downside is that the algorithm may get stuck and not finish, or it may stop in a local optimum, meaning there is a better result, a global optimum that exists, but it could not find it.

Supposing that the assumptions of the parametric statistical method holds, it may outperform a machine learning method.

Non-Parametric and Distribution Free Statistics (Assumption Light)

Non-parametric statistics do not include assumptions of parametrized families of probability distributions (like the "Bell Curve" family mentioned). For simplicity, let us consider distribution free statistics, sometimes called "order statistics" or "rank statistics." This type of statistics requires no assumption of the functional or statistical distribution of the population; thus they are non-parametric. This branch of statistics mimics parametric statistics in many ways. However, after drawing the sample, the values of the sample are sorted low to high. Non-parametric statistical inference can be performed with these ranked samples. The median is an often-reported statistic and it is the middle value in an ordered or ranked list of values. An example of rank order inference is trying to estimate the population median.

This form of statistics is very robust and there are many forms of it including Bayesian forms. One example, in addition to all the forms of regression mentioned in Chapter 6, we can add "median," "percentile" or "quantile" regression that overcomes some of the shortfalls of standard forms of regression. Quantile regression is part of a broader class of regression called "robust regression." The advantage of robust methods is that we do not have to make many assumptions. On the downside, they take longer to compute and they may not be as powerful as parametric methods.

Note: unlike closed-form parametric statistical methods, we use recursive algorithms to find solutions to these robust methods.

ANOTHER TERM – STATISTICAL LEARNING!

A very good reference for the intersection of Statistics and Machine Learning was written by three Stanford authors (Drs. Hastie, Tibshirani, and Friedman; see Hastie, 2017 – second edition). It is a landmark book titled *The Elements of Statistical Learning: Data Mining, Inference, and Prediction*; in the preface you will read:

> With the advent of computers and the information age, statistical problems have exploded both in size and complexity... Vast amounts of data are being generated in many fields, and the statistician's job is to make sense of it all: to extract important patterns and trends, and understand "what the data says." We call this *learning from data*. The challenges in learning from data have led to a revolution in the statistical sciences. Since computation plays such a key role, it is not surprising that much of this new development has been done by researchers in other fields such as computer science and engineering... This book is our attempt to bring together many of the important new ideas in learning, and explain them in a statistical framework.

We like this quote: it illustrates the marriage of statistics and data mining (machine learning) and AI. The book is a great reference for machine learning methods for practitioners and developers.

Four Domains in Statistics to Mention

Statistics in Predictive Analytics

It is useful to note that statistics is an integral part of all predictive analytics. From the simple idea of sampling to the complete end-to-end model development including the predictive analytic algorithm itself, statistics will be involved somewhere. However, you will hear about machine learning and AI vs statistics to build predictive models. What this means is something more specific; it typically means a choice between using a parametric statistical model development method that carries with it more assumptions and using a "model free" machine learning or AI model development method. From a practical standpoint, it is often preferred to go with a "model free" machine learning or AI algorithm. Why? Because it doesn't carry the burdens of the assumptions. And, if we use the statistical alternative and it turns the assumptions are wrong I can end up with a bad predictive model.

NOTE: As we have said all predictive analytics has assumptions. We use the term "parametric statistical model" above to contrast it to "model free" statistical methods such as quantile regression mentioned previously.

Design of Experiments (DoE)

The gold standard for proving whether one factor causes another is a randomized controlled trial (RCT). RCT requires a design of treatments (interventions) and responses (results). Statistical DoE (see Kirk, 2012) is the hallmark to make sure the statistical design supports the intents and hypotheses of the study (experiments). The importance of establishing causation means that you know more than the fact that two things are merely associated. One causing the other means you may be able to intervene in the system and alter inputs that dictate the output. Without an RCT, it is difficult to "prove" causality. We will look at alternatives in this chapter as well as discuss a Bayesian network as an implementation of a causal model.

BMJ (a global healthcare knowledge provider affiliated with 8,000 medical organizations worldwide) presented a nice paper on the importance of controls in experiments (Wartolowska et al., 2014).

Statistical Process Control (SPC)

As we said in Chapter 3, all data is driven by processes. Everything we observe and tabulate is generated from a process. SPC is a very popular statistical method used in manufacturing, healthcare and business processes. The manufacturing case is the most intuitive for understanding and was the original intent for SPC (Muelaner, 2019). In a simple case, you have a machine producing a part. You need this part manufactured within specification limits (measurements the part was designed for and will be sold against such requirements). Suppose we have upper and lower design limits for diameter. Machines naturally produce parts that will vary even when a machine is running as intended. You also have machine drift, meaning that the machine will produce parts that grow a little larger, then a little larger still, so that if an intervention is not taken and the machine recalibrated, the parts it produces will not be within the specified limits and the parts are scrapped.

SPC allows you to determine when that machine is producing as it should, or whether an intervention is needed before it starts producing scrap. You might think an expert operator could do this without SPC, but humans cannot determine the difference between normal variation and special variation (Hunter, 2014). SPC saves companies huge scrap costs. And SPC is not limited to manufacturing; it is very useful in service industries (Zolkepley, Djauhari and Salleh, 2018).

There are thousands of statistical procedures. **Why are we highlighting SPC?** The reason we are specifically calling out SPC here is its power, long history, and wide use; it does not have a surrogate in the other data-driven techniques we are describing. In other words, you cannot achieve the goals of determining process control in machine learning, AI or an optimization technique. It supports our continuing message that you need knowledge of many varied techniques and methods to be ready to handle any sort of data-driven problem you might face.

Time Series

Time series is a widely used technique in economics; in fact, it might be the most widely used statistical method that the U.S. government uses for forecasting economic data. De-trending, seasonal adjustments and forecasts are time series methods used by federal and state governments. Economists and econometricians are big users of the time series. Finance professionals in banking, brokerage and investment corporations also use it in the capital markets (stocks and bonds) analysis and trading.

We highlight time series for similar reasons that we mentioned SPC: for its power, long history, wide use, and the fact that it does not have a (good / transparent) surrogate in the other data-driven techniques we are describing. Time series is a good tool for any analytics professional to have in their repertoire.

An Ever-Important Reminder

In many chapters, we have compared methods providing their strengths and weaknesses. It is time to repeat something we said earlier in the book. When someone asks you what is the best machine learning method for classification? Or, says "Random Forests are better than k-nearest neighbors." Respond by saying: "according to what criteria?" We get involved in this trap of jumping to offer an opinion or suggestion by assuming we know what the criteria are. It is human nature. It is likely because we are all busy and assumptions save time, but it is important to know what the constraints and goals are before making recommendations. A good idea is to pause and reflect now and then.

That is one of the main motivations of this book. Remember the "No Free Lunch Theorem" in Chapter 3. No paradigm, methodology or technique is universally optimal to solve all problems. If it was, game over; go home. That is why we think that the more knowledge of the tools, techniques, and interdependency of these domains (computer science, operations research, statistics, etc.), the better equipped anyone is for a career in analytics. And we mean analytics from the C-suite to the department manager to the production engineer or physician.

So, if someone says deep learning will solve the entire world's problems, or everything can be formatted as a linear program (more on that in Chapter 11), then just smile. They have just indicated they likely have a limited tool set. Moreover, they definitely have a limited way of looking at solutions to problems.

WHEN STATISTICS FAIL

Statistical inference for very large samples fails. Why? One of the components of determining a significant difference is the standard error of the estimate. The standard error is a function of the sample size. As the sample size increases, the standard error decreases. This makes sense: the larger sample size implies more information thus less error. However, for very large samples this will lead to calling everything statistically significant.

A POTENTIAL ISSUE WITH ANY DATA-DRIVEN APPROACH – SAMPLING BIAS

One of the biggest problems in any analytics method is sampling bias. We mentioned bias in the section "Classical or Frequentist Statistics" in talking about our new school referendum poll. Statistics get a bad rap about missing actuals in elections and polling. There are several reasons for this, but this is primarily due to sampling bias and not mathematics.

Statistics Summary

What is the basis for statistics? Using a sample to describe, understand or make an inference. That is 99% of it. Statistics is part of the analytics eco-system and a part of the machine learning and the AI process. As we have been saying, these technologies work together and therefore you should have some basic knowledge of all of them.

However, there are some drawbacks; let us discuss these drawbacks now. Statistics *may* involve:

1) Assumptions of functional forms for the populations, relationships of the observations from populations and more
2) Misunderstanding and misapplication of statistical methods

The first point involves the applications of statistics; the practitioner carries extra responsibilities with these assumptions. The second is not the fault of statistics, but the practitioner. If a cook cuts themselves dicing onions with a knife, the problem is not the knife, but the misapplication of the knife.

Additional tools are useful. Machine learning avoids many of the issues of statistical assumptions and maybe a preferred method for many problems (use a food processor instead of a knife). Knowledge is power and it does befit the data scientist to understand the power and limitations of statistical theory and methods.

Advantages of Statistics vs BI, Machine Learning and AI

1) Statistics work with small samples. Data scientists may work with data in small samples where many machine learning algorithms will fail. AI

algorithms typically require even more data when compared to other machine learning algorithms.

2) Statistics work with a univariate series (a single variable). Time series forecasts can be made using the historical series. Statistical Process Control uses the past behavior of a series to determine whether a process is acting as expected (in control) vs not as expected (out of control).

3) Career variety and interests. Data scientists and others that add statistical methods to their tool set face new problems and solutions every day, thus there is more variety. Machine learning modelers that use the same algorithms, apply the same process over and over – data prep, model, compare models, deploy – may make significant mistakes that would not have been made if they had knowledge of all the tools.

Disadvantages of Statistics vs BI, Machine Learning and AI

1) Statistical hypothesis (significance) testing falls apart for very large samples. You will always reject the null hypothesis concluding a statistically significant result when there may not be any practical significance. This is because as the sample sizes get very large (like millions of observations) the standard error gets very small and you will reject even minute differences.

2) More assumptions are required for any problems of inference, except in distribution free statistics / non-parametric statistics.

POLLS AND STATISTICS – APPLICATION PROBLEM, NOT A METHODOLOGY PROBLEM

Many things are misunderstood about statistics; as the saying goes – Lies, Damned Lies and Statistics.

Statistics is rooted in mathematics. The theory is solid. The methodology is built on this theory. You have to mathematically prove statistical theorems. However, there is a **lot** of room for misapplication and assumptions that invalidate the practice. A perfect example is polling. The actual mathematics is solid and unlike what most people think, you can estimate a binary (yes/no) outcome within a margin of error of ±3% from just 1,067 respondents (if these 1,067 respondents represent a "truly random sample").

However, the practice of sampling must be followed carefully and the **results are only valid at the time of the poll** – not 3 weeks into the future. These are where the application of statistics fails. Here are the biggest failures in polls:

1) People lie. Sorry, to be so blunt, but it is true. There are a number of reasons this happens. It could be intentional or by mistake/accident. It could be to avoid embarrassment when being asked by a pollster.
2) Time lapses between polling and action. People change their minds, they may answer a poll one way and by the time of the vote, they go in a different direction.
3) The poll sample is not taken correctly. This is an example of sampling bias. Sampling bias exists when your sampling is not representative of the population under study. See Shirani-Mehr et al., 2018.
4) Misunderstanding. Questions on questionnaires can be leading, non-objective.

Comparison of Data-Driven Paradigms Thus Far

Keeping in mind the last section, where we want to be sure we define what is the best analytics to use, or simply state the assumptions, we can look at a comparison of the data-driven methods, keeping in mind that there are always trade-offs. Please see the individual chapters for detailed strengths and weaknesses of various analytic methods. The following provides quick elevator pitches on the major categories we have presented.

Business Intelligence (BI)

BI is a form of **descriptive analytics**. BI should not be an end solution, but as an adjunct to more powerful **predictive and advanced analytics** (unless the organization is just getting started or has a very limited budget). Note, when these methods are employed and become part of the culture, the return on investment is positive so you can scale quickly. *Operational BI* is embedded within the fabric of the organization and provides a "single version of the truth" since the dashboards were approved by leadership. *Project-based Visual BI* is great for discovering relationships at the beginning of a project before predictive analytics is started and at the end when the team is presenting the project story with dashboards. (See Chapter 5 for details.)

Machine Learning and Data Mining

Machine learning and data mining have separate histories. They make separate titles of books. However, from a practitioner's standpoint, there are no major differences between machine learning and data mining (refer to Chapter 6). Both are part of **advanced analytics.** The power to predict an outcome provides a significant return on investment and the power to prescribe a course of action to achieve the desired outcome provides the greatest value of all (excluding optimization). (See Chapter 4 for details.)

Artificial Intelligence (AI)

AI is all the rage these days even though digital AI has been around for almost 70 years. AI is also a form of **advanced analytics** and can provide predictive and prescriptive insights (**prescriptive analytics**). AI can be extremely powerful and available to savvy business users, or what are called citizen data scientists. The only problem is that you do not always know how AI is coming up with its predictions and that is unacceptable in certain business domains and government agencies.

Statistics

Statistics has been around a long time and can provide **descriptive and advanced analytics**. Statistics are embedded in BI, machine learning and AI. There is a significant overlap of statistical learning and machine learning (like Bayesian networks). For some statistics, you have to make certain assumptions, which is an added burden, and if your assumptions are wrong, your models may not be very good. Statistics can help with determining causality, which is needed to prescribe a course of action.

We hope you noticed the common thread: **It's All Analytics!**

ANECDOTE AND CONFIRMATION BIAS

Statistics and analytics work with samples to model populations. Anecdote describes individuals.

We often disregard statistics because they do not substantiate our present thought and often we have experiences, little stories or anecdotes that are not upheld by some statistic. That is often because the statistic is not wrong, but because we love story and anecdote. You should not try and apply a statistic to an individual. Kobe Bryant was 6'6", certainly taller than the average U.S. male, but not an extreme outlier. **Don't force an average on an individual and do not think an individual is average.**

Individuals are unique. Statistics are generalities.

People often look for news or material that supports their prior beliefs. This is confirmation bias. The definition of confirmation bias "is the tendency to interpret new evidence as confirmation of one's existing beliefs or theories" (12/30/19, Bing, Powered by Oxford Dictionary). It is important to note that we are all biased by our experiences and opinions. Scott's major professor (a true Bayesian) had a saying that "the only objective people were the ones that knew they were subjective."

Predictive Analytics vs Prescriptive Analytics – The Missing Link Is Causation

In Chapter 4, we covered the various types of analytics and showed a figure that illustrates the common categories. The analytics community uses this diagram to illustrate the increasing value from moving from one type of analytics to another form (see Figure 10.2). The gold standards are prescriptive analytics and process optimization.

In **predictive analytics**, we want to predict an outcome (disease, purchase, success) for a new observation based on characteristics of this new observation. For disease classification (disease present / disease not present), we use historical data to build and validate our predictive model. We can then use data on a new patient to determine the probability (score) that this new patient has the disease. These models are extremely useful, as oftentimes all you need is to predict an outcome, as you have no practical way of controlling the inputs to the process or systems that produce this outcome.

What if we can control the inputs? What if we can influence the outcome by manipulating the inputs? This is **prescriptive analytics**. Further, it can lead to the top of the mountain, which is **process optimization** (a little about that in the next chapter).

Suppose we want to determine the likelihood a given high school student will go to college upon graduation. It is simple enough to use historical data

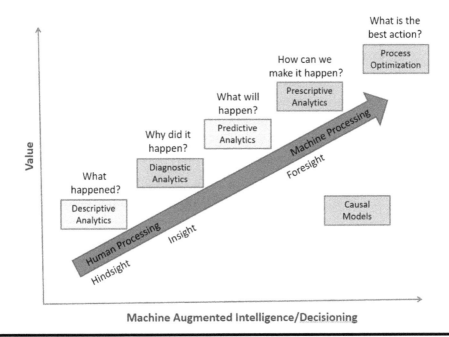

Figure 10.2   A visual reference of a generally accepted classification scheme for analytics.

and build a predictive model to determine the probability that a new student will go to college based on these factors. Suppose I do this and the model works great (high predictive accuracy and reproducibility).

What is the next logical step? I want to increase the number of high school graduates that go to college. Can I use my predictive model to prescribe a method to increase this rate? The simple answer is not without more consideration. To turn a predictive model into a prescriptive model we need to:

1) Assume or establish causation
2) Be able to manipulate the important variables
3) Not perturb the system

Some professionals build predictive models, look at the primary factors that determine the outcome (the highest associated predictors to the outcome) and say we can manipulate these inputs to get the desired output. **No**. The difference between predictive analytics and prescriptive analytics is **causation**.

Note the shade difference in the boxes in Figure 10.2. **Descriptive analytics** requires no relationship between any variables. **Predictive analytics** requires a correlation between the inputs and the outcomes. **Diagnostic** and **prescriptive analytics**, as well as process optimization, require causation between the inputs and the outcome.

You can build a good predictive model without causation. You just need correlation/association. We have addressed this in several sections. It is amazing that professionals that know correlation does not mean causation will still think it is okay to just "turn" a predictive model into a prescriptive model. You can do it of course, but you should at least be careful and know the assumptions you are making. If you simply take a predictive model and use it as a prescriptive model, there are two things that can happen. One has to do with correlation vs causation. The second has to do with the limitations of systems.

1) You could be wrong in assuming that your factors are causative. Thus, manipulation of the inputs will not provide the results you are expecting.
2) You may perturb the system. If the system has a causal relationship and you manipulate variables, you will affect the system itself. This can also happen whether you manipulate variables or not, as systems change over time. However, you should take care in your manipulation and not try and "shock" the system with the manipulation of your inputs.

MODEL DECLARATION AND HUMOR

Scott likes the show *The Office*, and the whole issue of declaring a predictive model as a prescriptive model reminds him of an episode. Michael Scott is underwater financially, and Oscar is helping him with the situation. Oscar tells him that he feels Michael should declare bankruptcy. Michael is distraught, but later in the show comes into the bullpen of the office, climbs on desk and shouts, "I declare bankruptcy!" Sometimes, you need just a little more.

Assuming or Establishing Causation

For the purposes of "turning" predictive models into prescriptive models we must do one of the two:

1) Assume causation
2) Determine causation

In certain applications, it is acceptable to assume causation. If you have good research or reason to assume causation, you can do that; just be aware there is a significant downside if you are wrong. In the areas of physics and chemistry where relationships are well behaved, it is easier to assume causation. Many of these relationships are rooted in deep scientific inquiry and are well documented. These are typically determined by the scientific method and statistics, which we previously discussed. Alternatively, things like vehicle traffic optimization are causal, as we know the route taken has a causal effect on the time it takes to get to the destination.

In other areas, such as the biological and behavioral sciences, the relationships are more unclear. They could be causal or just correlated. Biological systems are messy in that there are tens of thousands or even millions of factors involved. How many times have you heard medical science and the FDA (Food and Drug Administration) reverse itself **even with published peer review research**? Behavioral mechanisms often lack effective measurement systems and we often measure downstream activity. Rather than assume causation, it is often preferred to establish causation.

Causality at a minimum requires three elements:

1) Correlation (covariation) of cause and effect.
2) Time order (temporal precedence). The cause happens before the effect.
3) Elimination of extraneous causes.

Determining causation scientifically requires manipulation of treatments or some intervention based upon some experimental design. This design has to include some time (temporal) component so that the practitioner can see the "before" and the "after" effect. Again, the gold standard to determine causation is the RCT described under the "Design of Experiments (DoE)" section above.

THREE COUNTER-EXAMPLES WHERE GOOD PREDICTIVE MODELS DO NOT MAKE PRESCRIPTIVE MODELS

- ▪ Time (temporal) relevance
- ▪ Spurious correlation or confounding variable
- ▪ Mediation problems

Time Dependency – Suppose I tell you I have a great predictive model for predicting rain and my model is almost 100% accurate! The model has been cross-validated with precision. I have used all of the most relevant techniques and my methodology is sound. Then you ask me what the strongest predictor in my model is and I say the presence of mud! This model is very predictive! Can it be used as a prescriptive model? No. Why? **For a prescriptive model, you need causality**. For X to cause Y, then X must precede Y (temporal precedence). In simple words, the "presence of mud" can ONLY come about AFTER the rain has occurred – thus MUD is a result of rain, not a cause or predictor of rain!!!

Suppose that X causes Z (X → Z) and X causes Y (X → Y). Can you conclude that Y causes Z? No. We have heard that salt causes heart problems. Is that true? What seems to be established is that salt is associated with hypertension (high blood pressure) and hypertension is associated with heart and vascular problems. However, there is not a lot of evidence that salt causes heart and vascular problems. There is a nice article by Harvard, "Heart Failure and Salt: The Great Debate" (Harvard Health Publishing, December 2018) that states there is no conclusive evidence that you can say that salt causes heart disease.

Suppose you have X → Y → Z (X causes Y and in turn Y causes Z). Y, in this case, is the mediator. The mediator may have a minor effect or a major effect. In other words, is X the primary causer of Z or only when Y is present do you see a strong causal relationship? Traditional predictive models will not tease out the strength of these relationships. That is where mediation statistics can provide the answers and help with prescription (Columbia Public Health, Causal Mediation).

Ladder of Causation

Let us briefly comment on Judea Pearl's "Ladder of Causation"; this can be found in Pearl's latest book, *The Book of Why: The New Science of Cause and Effect* (Pearl and Mackenzie, 2018). It describes causation as a continuum and not a yes/no proposition. To discuss three levels in simple terms we like, we refer to examples in a blog by Michiel Stock (https://michielstock.github.io/causality).

Prediction is what we have been discussing. An example of this "What is the expected lifespan of somebody who is vegetarian and does not smoke?" This is what we want from predictive models.

Intervention is being able to guess what the effect will be if one performs an action. This is what we want from prescriptive models. Example: How would my expected lifespan change if I become a vegetarian? NOTE: Our intervention changes the system. If our intervention changes the system too much, we may warp the system and not get the results we want in the future with our current prescriptive model.

Counterfactuals (imagining) are being able to reason about a hypothetical situation. What are the things that could happen? Imagining in intellectual activities, such as performing thought experiments, making up a story or inventing a new cooking recipe. Example: Would my grandfather still be alive if he did not smoke?

Predicting an Increasing Trend – Structural Causal Models and Causal Inference

Although it is not new, we believe the work by Judea Pearl and similar researchers in causal models will be adopted more and more over the next few years. It is extremely powerful and promising. It incorporates the Bayesian paradigm, which we mentioned near the beginning of the chapter (we also believe general Bayesian methods are poised for a new resurgence). It can answer questions that many other methods cannot, such as the examples in the preceding section, "Ladder of Causation," and in the following gray box, "What Is Causal Inference?"

How these models are constructed is beyond the scope of this book. Let us just note a few highlights and provide a few references.

■ **Data are dumb.** There are articles that have proposed "big data" (massively abundant data) will be the death of the scientific method and even the death of the need for models! Do they know the definition of a model? We think these are typically written by the uninitiated or Hypers! For example, in "The End of Theory: The Data Deluge Makes the Scientific Method Obsolete" (Anderson, 2008), Judea Pearl states, "We live in an era that presumes Big Data to be the solution to all our problems... but I hope with this book to convince you that data are profoundly dumb" (referring to his *The Book of Why*; see Pearl and Mackenzie, 2018). Furthermore, "You will never get causal information out without beginning by putting causal hypotheses in," which means you will never get knowledge by throwing a bunch of data in an algorithm and hoping for the best (Maudlin, September 2019).

- **We need education to start the revolution**. We need education at all levels, but we need to start by replacing much that is taught currently as statistics in undergraduate and graduate programs. Classical statistics is taught the same way it has been taught for decades. There is some value in this, but if students are going to be taught one course, Bayesian and causal modeling are much more productive – i.e., practical for the needs of society. To this end, Judea Pearl has donated the Turing Prize money to the American Statistical Association to establish an annual prize for a person or team that contributes substantially toward introducing causal inference in education.
- **Data may help us predict what will happen, but even today's most sophisticated machine learning can't tell us why.** That is the crux of the last two sections of this chapter. You need to know why something is happening before you can prescribe (prescriptive analytics) the actions to take to achieve the desired results.
- **Use of graphical methods** (combinations of equations and graphs) and graph data will continue to explode. Causal models are often built on directed acyclic graphs (DAGs, see Chapter 6). The data in graph databases will be greatly increasing as well as the practical application of these methods. For a basic introduction to DAGs applied to pediatric medicine and research, see Williams, Bach, and Matthiesen et al. (2018).

WHAT IS CAUSAL INFERENCE?

In his own words in an interview with Ron Wasserstein (Amstat News (2012) Judea Pearl defines Causal inference as

Causal inference is a methodology for answering causal research questions from a combination of data and theoretical assumptions about how the data are generated. Typical causal questions are the following: What is the expected effect of a given treatment (e.g., drug) on a given outcome (e.g., recovery)? Can data prove an employer guilty of hiring discrimination? Would a given patient be alive if he had not taken the drug, knowing that he, in fact, did take the drug and died? The distinct feature of these sorts of questions is that they cannot be answered from (nonexperimental) frequency data alone, regardless of how many samples are taken; nor can they be expressed in the standard language of statistics, for they cannot be defined in terms of joint densities of observed variables. (Skeptics are invited to write down a mathematical expression for the sentence, "The rooster crow does not cause the sun to rise.")

Summary

Some authors and practitioners have said that machine learning and AI will replace statistics: that now, with extremely powerful computers and unlimited data storage, we don't need statistics anymore. They either didn't know or have forgotten that machine learning uses statistics extensively – all the time – without fail. Remember our definition of statistics – characteristics of a sample – a training set, a test set, a validation set – all subsets of a population. In addition, there are thousands of statistics generated in the machine learning process. Any prediction is about a future observation and that observation is generated from a process. This gets some people because they think of populations as static and historical. Therefore, in any predictive analytics we are using past data, a population subset, ergo a sample to predict future values (part of a population). Thus, predictive analytics is predicated on statistics!

Postscript

This has been a lengthy and important chapter. Statistics, prescriptive analytics, and causal modeling are three very important subjects for all informed analytics professionals and data scientists. It will be very exciting to see how these subjects advance over the next few years.

In the next chapter, we provide some final insights on data-driven methodologies and academic disciplines as endnotes for future considerations. These are deeply applicable to analytics.

References

Amstat News. November 1, 2020. (ASA Executive Director Ron Wasserstein interviews Judea Pearl) - Turing Award Winner, Longtime ASA Member Talks Causal Inference. *Amstat News*, https://magazine.amstat.org/blog/2012/11/01/pearl/

Anderson, Chris. June 23, 2008. "The end of theory: The data deluge makes the scientific method obsolete," *Wired Magazine*, www.wired.com/2008/06/pb-theory/.

Casella, George and Berger, Roger L. June 18, 2001. *Statistical Inference* (2nd ed.). Cengage Learning.

Columbia Public Health, Causal Mediation. www.mailman.columbia.edu/research/population-health-methods/causal-mediation.

David, R.B. and Mukamal, K.J. 2006. "Hypothesis testing," *Circulation*, 114: 1078–82, www.ahajournals.org/doi/10.1161/CIRCULATIONAHA.105.586461.

Devine, D.J. 2012. *Jury decision making: The state of the science.* New York University Press.

Gelman, A. 2010. "Bayesian statistics, now and then," *Statistical Science*, 25 (2): 162–65. DOI: 10.1214/10-STS308B Main article DOI: 10.1214/09-STS308 © Institute of Mathematical Statistics.

Harvard Health Publishing. December 18, 2018. "Heart failure and salt: The great debate," www.health.harvard.edu/blog/heart-failure-and-salt-the-great-debate-2018121815563.

Hastie, Trevor, Tibshirani, Robert, and Jerome, Friedman. April 2017. *The Elements of Statistical Learning: Data Mining, Inference, and Prediction* (2nd ed.). Springer Series in Statistics. Springer-Verlag New York.

Hunter, J. March 10, 2014. "Lessons from the red bead experiment with Dr. Deming," *The W. Edwards Deming Institute Blog*, https://blog.deming.org/2014/03/lessons-from-the-red-bead-experiment-with-dr-deming/.

Kirk, Roger E. June 13, 2012. *Experimental Design: Procedures for the Behavioral Sciences* (4th ed.). SAGE Publications.

Liu, T. and Stone, C.C. January 23, 2006. "Law and statistical disorder: Statistical hypothesis test procedures and the criminal trial analogy," www.cs.bsu.edu/homepages/tliu/research/papers/bsuecwp200601r1liu.pdf.

Maudlin, Tim. September 2019. "The why of the world," *Boston Review*, https://bostonreview.net/science-nature/tim-maudlin-why-world.

Muelaner, J. October 2019. "An introduction to statistical process control (SPC)," https://new.engineering.com/story/an-introduction-to-statistical-process-control-spc.

Pearl, Judea and Mackenzie, Dana. May 15, 2018. *The Book of Why: The New Science of Cause and Effect.* Basic Books.

Shirani-Mehr, Houshmand, Rothschild, David, Goel, Sharad, and Gelman, Andrew. February 2018. "Disentangling bias and variance in election polls," *Journal of the American Statistical Association*, 113: 1–23. 10.1080/01621459.2018.1448823.

Statistical Hypothesis Testing. Accessed December 8, 2019, https://en.wikipedia.org/wiki/Statistical_hypothesis_testing.

Wartolowska, Karolina, Judge, Andrew, Hopewell, Sally, Collins, Gary S., Dean, Benjamin J, F., Brindley, David, Savulescu, Julian, Beard, David J., Andrew, J. Carr, and Romabch, Ines. May 2014. "Use of placebo controls in the evaluation of surgery: Systematic review," *BMJ, British Medical Journal*, Vol 348: g3253.

Williams, T.C., Bach, C.C., Matthiesen, N.B., et al. 2018. "Directed acyclic graphs: A tool for causal studies in paediatrics," *Pediatric Research*, 84: 487–93. doi: 10.1038/s41390-018-0071-3.

Zolkepley, Z., Djauhari, M.A., and R.M. Salleh. June 2018. "SPC in service industry: Case in teaching and learning process variability monitoring," https://aip.scitation.org/doi/10.1063/1.5041700 (Originally published: AIP Conference Proceedings 1974, 040026).

Resources for the Avid Learner

1 An interesting and highly cited book, *The Black Swan: Second Edition: The Impact of the Highly Improbable* (with a new section: "On Robustness and Fragility") by Nassim Nicholas Taleb (May 11, 2010) defines a "black swan" as an event that cannot be predicted by most data-driven methods. It is deemed improbable yet causes massive consequences.

2 *Bayesian Statistics and Decision Theory* – D.V Lindley is a foundational leader and research pioneer. This book is one of the most widely used books for professionals wanting to know more about Bayesian inference, value of information, decision trees and interesting tidbits like Simpson's Paradox. It is presented at an elementary level with some elementary mathematics.

3 *Making Decisions*, 2nd ed., Wiley Publishing is another great book by D.V. Lindley

4 There are several resources on Dr. Judea Pearl's research on the Internet. Many are based upon the book, *The Book of Why: The New Science of Cause and Effect* (May 15, 2018), by Judea Pearl and Dana Mackenzie, Basic Books, 1st edition. Also see an interview with the American Statistical Association President, "Turing Award Winner, Longtime ASA Member Talks Causal Inference," https://magazine.amstat.org/blog/2012/11/01/pearl/.

5 Stanford provides a good amount of information on causal models. An example in medicine, epidemiology and informatics is the colloquium, "Is prediction enough?" with recordings, bios and more: https://med.stanford.edu/epidemiology/causal_inference_colloquium.html. Another example, https://plato.stanford.edu/entries/causal-models/#Intr, is mathematical but may be useful to some readers.

6 There is a nice 2×2 decision table for court trials and the null and alternative hypothesis at https://en.wikipedia.org/wiki/Statistical_hypothesis_testing.

Chapter 11

Other Disciplines to Dive in Deeper: Computer Science, Management/Decision Science, Operations Research, Engineering (and More)

Keywords: Computer Science, Management Science, Decision Science, Operations Research, Engineering, Econometrics, Finance, Simulation

Preamble

We have covered many disciplines in this book. By now, you certainly understand that these are not freestanding disciplines, but methodologies built over many years with a lot of cross-pollination by very intelligent and dedicated professionals. If we wrote everything we would like to say, this book would be far too long. So, we thought we would include some end notes and some areas for future considerations that are deeply applicable to analytics.

Introduction

From an academic departmental view, many disciplines feed into analytics. They have their own version or application of analytics that are specific to professionals or academics in that field. There is origination of ideas, there is borrowing of ideas and there are movements of great thinkers across disciplines.

Today, analytics is so prevalent that we cannot think of an area that does not include some sort of analytics. Music, for example, would seem an area independent of analytics. But music actually offers a great opportunity for research with machine learning. History and literature are huge areas for text analytics.

We have covered many areas of study, but we want to be sure to mention some areas that are particularly ripe with their own contributions and offer specific analytic tools that we have not covered.

Computer Science

Computer science is such a large field that has its fingerprints all over analytics. We have touched on some form of it in every chapter and deeply in some; for example, see the extensive discussion of data engineering in Chapter 8. Data engineers and many analytics professionals come from computer science programs or experiential backgrounds. In this section, we just want to point out one important area of contribution that you should consider exploring more deeply.

Many academic computer science departments have dedicated divisions (or labs) in cognitive systems or AI. We spoke in the last chapter about Judea Pearl, who is a professor in the Cognitive Systems Lab of the Computer Science Department at UCLA. He also won the Turing Award from the Association for Computing Machinery. If you are a movie fan, see *The Imitation Game* (2014), which portrays the genius of Alan Turing. Dr. Pearl represents a cross-section between data science, AI and statistics. He has a Ph.D. in electrical engineering, teaches in a computer science department and was awarded a Fellowship of the American Statistical Association in 2019.

We mentioned connections of AI to computer science in Chapter 7. When expanding your data science and AI horizons, keep computer science in mind. We list a few options in the "For the Avid Learner" section at the end of this chapter.

A STATISTICIAN OR A COMPUTER SCIENTIST?

Judea Pearl was asked a question in an interview with the president of the American Statistical Association, Ron Wasserstein (see Pearl, J. as interviewed by Wasserstein, R., *Amstat News* (2012)). "Do you consider yourself a statistician or a computer scientist, or is that a distinction you even make when you think of yourself and your work?"

To which he replied,

There is a lot in common to statisticians and computer scientists, especially those working on machine learning and inference under uncertainty. Both are attempting to make sense of data, and both are going about it in a systematic way. The distinction comes in two dimensions: first, what it means to "make sense of data" and, second, what language we use in our mathematics.

There is a great opportunity for academic and professional camps to work together and learn from each other.

Management Science

The origins of management science are rooted in operations research, which we will cover in a moment. Both are covered by a large professional organization, INFORMS (The Institute for Operations Research and the Management Sciences), which is "dedicated to and promoting best practices and advances in operations research, management science, and analytics to improve operational processes, decision-making, and outcomes." INFORMS has a very active community of researchers and practitioners.

According to INFORMS, topics covered in *Management Science* (journal) include:

Business Strategy
Decision Analysis
Entrepreneurship
Operations
Optimization and Modeling
Product Development
Simulation
Social Networks
Stochastic Models
Supply Chain Management

Academic programs normally merge operations research and management science together into one program (e.g. Berkeley College of Engineering). However, there are differences and you will see books dedicated to management science; for example, see Winston and Albright (2018), which is a great survey book of the subject.

Decision Science

Decision science is a broad and varied field. From our research, there is a bit of a divide with some camps calling it more behavioral, social and public policy oriented, and others calling it more business focused. Decision science is strongly aligned with analytics.

From a view of academic programs (such as University of Pennsylvania and Harvard), decision science has strong roots and alliances in social and public policy and public health.

On the business side, in an article in *INFORMS Analytics Magazine* (see Rajaram, 2018), Dhiraj Rajaram defines decision science as an overarching discipline above data science and that while data science problems are normally clearly defined, decision science problems are not:

> Decision science is the interdisciplinary application of business, math, technology, design thinking, and behavioral sciences to enable better decisions. Decision science enables addressing **business problems that are ill defined** and shifting and where the factors affecting the problem are not completely understood. It facilitates the design thinking paradigm: Taking business problems that start off as a hunch or as mysteries to becoming heuristic, rules, and judgment based, to becoming algorithm as one starts to see patterns, to becoming codified and tool-ified in parts before being operationalized in systems. Further it enables the on-going creation, translation, and consumption of data-driven insights to help organizations make better decisions. **Decision science integrates and builds on data sciences by adding the aspects of business context, design thinking, and behavioral sciences**.

There are schools, such as Notre Dame, whose programs are more business oriented. One thing in common among the camps is that decision science includes the way we think, along with the way judgments and decisions are made. This is an extension outside of traditional data science.

Operations Research

Operations research is the application of scientific and mathematical methods to the study and analysis of problems involving complex systems. We mentioned that operations research is akin (the father) to management science. Modern operations research got started in the world wars by British and U.S. forces. It was developed primarily in the areas of logistics (moving troops and supplies), communications, optimizing weapon effectiveness and efficient use of Allied forces and supplies. In WWII, Britain had close to 1,000 women and men engaged in operations research. In the United States, George Dantzig, who is considered the father of linear programming, helped with U.S. logistics. Dantzig had a huge impact on the field and developed the Simplex Algorithm, which efficiently solved complex linear programming problems. Dantzig was the first to express the criterion for selecting a good or best plan as an explicit mathematical function, a function that we now call the "objective function."

In a nutshell, operations research is focused on mathematical optimization by using a broad array of modeling paradigms and algorithms. Its contribution to data science is rich and important. Route optimization (which includes programming your car's GPS) uses operations research methods, social analytics uses operations research network models, and pricing science uses operations research constraint optimization.

NOTE: these optimization techniques are not informal – they are mathematical. This means that they don't loosely fulfill a heuristic like "I want to optimize my customer outreach." Instead, they optimize a quantitative objective function such as "what is the price that maximizes margin given a set of mathematical constraints such as production volume limits, geographical constraints, cross-product cannibalism maximums?" These formulas are configured into an optimization engine that performs thousands and thousands of calculations and provides a solution for the price that maximizes the objective. The positive is that you find "the right price" the drawback is that you have to rigorously define and formulate the problem.

The study of operations research is very useful for any analytics professional as it provides a rich area for finding solutions to a broad set of problems.

Engineering

Engineering is an extremely wide-ranging field. It is deeply grounded in mathematics and analytics. At the same time, it develops *new applications* of analytics all the time. Let us point out that computer engineering, software engineering, and electrical engineering are closely related to computer science, which we have briefly touched upon. All are quantitative in nature and intertwined with the methods of this book. Industrial engineering (IE) is similar to operations research in that IE employs methods of linear programming, constraint optimization, and other optimization techniques. It is useful for data scientists and analytics professionals to explore these methods further.

Finance and Econometrics

Finance and economics are big producers and users of analytic methods. The development of such models as asset pricing (like capital asset pricing models, CAPM) and bond duration (Macaulay and modified duration) are financial models that make sophisticated practices more accessible to practitioners in finance. Econometricians use calculus and mathematics to develop close-formed solutions such as the demand function (differential calculus). They also use the advanced statistical and machine learning algorithms we discussed in Chapters 6 and 10 to model markets and economies.

Simulation, Sensitivity and Scenario Analysis

While not an academic domain, we did want to mention some techniques used across a broad spectrum of analytics. We mentioned simulation in Chapter 9 as part of the synthetic data topic. This data is generated by a computer from a conceptual (mental) model. The model is based on our subjective knowledge of a process or phenomenon. We can generate data via computer code to formulate and augment our intelligence. No formal data is required.

Here are some quick applications of simulation:

Sensitivity Analysis

While some models, like AI, are a black box and we cannot trace the exact method that algorithm is using to generate an output (score), we can determine which are the most important contributors to that outcome using sensitivity analysis. Simplistically, we take the model code and perturb the inputs (thousands of times) while examining the effect on the outcome via a simulation. The inputs that contribute the most variability in the outcome are the ones most important to the model.

Scenario Analysis

Scenario analysis uses simulation to analyze potential future events by considering alternative possible outcomes. It is very popular in financial, economic and political domains. Once a conceptual model is formulated, a researcher can input potential future events and see how the impact affects the system.

Systems Thinking

A very powerful and often underused method of simulation applies to "systems thinking." It applies to biological systems, education, chemistry, physics, medicine, social and behavioral sciences, government, business and more. Systems are sets of interrelated processes and the world is full of processes. These systems and processes can be modeled with software. A programmer can write the code for this software, or commercial systems are available. A researcher models the system of interest and simulates it. The researcher then gains insight from the system such as unknown relationships, feedback and reinforcement mechanisms. These solutions are very useful in nonlinear analytics.

Postscript

The opportunities for application and use of analytics goes on and on. We find analytics used everywhere and its development and use will continue to impact our lives.

The next chapter is very brief as we look forward to our next engagement.

References

Pearl, J. as interviewed by Wasserstein, R. November 2012. Turing Award Winner, Longtime ASA Member Talks Causal Inference, *Amstat News*, https://magazin e.amstat.org/blog/2012/11/01/pearl/.

Rajaram, D. 2018. "Why some data scientists should really be called decision scientists," *INFORMS Analytics Magazine*, http://analytics-magazine.org/executive-edge-why-some-data-scientists-should-really-be-called-decision-scientists/.

The Imitation Game. 2014. Director: Morten Tyldum (Graham Moore, Andrew Hodges (book authors)).

Winston, Wayne L. and Albright, S. Christian. January 1, 2018. *Practical Management Science* (6th ed.). Cengage Learning.

Resources for the Avid Learner

1 There are several resources on Dr. Judea Pearl's research on the Internet. Many are based upon *The Book of Why: The New Science of Cause and Effect* (May 15, 2018) by Judea Pearl and Dana Mackenzie, Basic Books, 1st edition.

2 The Association for Computing Machinery (ACM) has been a huge contributor to educational opportunities in analytics and machine learning since the early days of KDD. Check out their conferences and educational programs – www.acm.org/. It is the world's largest scientific and educational computing society with nearly 100,000 student and professional members as of 2019. Its headquarters are in New York City.

3 Dantzig's book *Linear Programming and Extensions* (Princeton Landmarks in Mathematics and Physics) is a classic. It is meant to be a textbook and it was written years ago. There are more readable books on the subject, but if you want to feel and read a classic you might check it out at a local library (Scott's had his copy 30 years).

4 If you would like to know more about systems thinking (theory) you might want to check out "The Systems Thinker," which speaks to philosophy as well as tools; see https://thesystemsthinker.com/systems-thinking-what-why-when-where-and-how/.

5 You can jump from this page to many related topics including "Scenario Planning," "Public Policy," "Government," "Healthcare" and "Business."

6 INFORMS 2020 ANNUAL meeting which took place on November 8, 2020 in Maryland, http://meetings2.informs.org/wordpress/nationalharbor2020/.

7 The Institute for Operations Research and the Management Sciences, https://www.informs.org/.

Chapter 12

Looking Ahead

Farewell, Until Next Time

Scott and Gary (the authors) have enjoyed and been rewarded by many years of learning and applying the art of data-driven solutions. The problems are so varied and the techniques to apply to these problems are so rich and interesting that there is always something to be learned, something to be nuanced in a way to fit the problem at hand. It makes for a career of lifelong learning and no time to waste. It is always interesting and rewarding if approached in an appropriate way. That is the reason for this book.

We feel one should not go forward blindly with a hammer searching for a nail. The task at hand is likely different from the one encountered yesterday and requires a different set of tools or a twist of the application previously employed. Moreover, whether the technique you apply to your problem is a deep learning AI solution, a statistical technique, a visual dashboard, a mathematical linear program, a computer simulation or even a heuristic one, **It's All Analytics!**

We have more we want to say. Therefore, in our next book we will discuss a very important subject – what should your analytics *architecture* be for your enterprise? Obviously, there is a range of options and recommendations, but there are some key components and considerations we will be covering. And, there are three major architectures that need to be considered to support your analytics:

- The Organizational Structure and Design
- The Data Architecture
- The Analytics / Data Science Architecture

We hope to see you again soon. We wish you success in your data-driven adventures!

Index